Public Management and Administrative Reform in Western Europe

Public Management and Administrative Reform in Western Europe

Edited by

Walter J.M. Kickert

Professor of Public Management, Erasmus University Rotterdam

Edward Elgar
Cheltenham, UK • Northampton, MA, USA

Published by
Edward Elgar Publishing Limited
8 Lansdown Place
Cheltenham
Glos GL50 2HU
UK

Edward Elgar Publishing, Inc.
6 Market Street
Northampton
Massachusetts 01060
USA

A catalogue record for this book
is available from the British Library

Library of Congress Cataloguing-in-Publication Data

Public management and administrative reform in Western Europe / edited
  by Walter J.M. Kickert.
    Papers from the 1995 annual conference of the European Group of
  Public Administration.
    Includes bibliographical references and index.
    1. Administrative agencies—Europe—Management—Congresses.
  2. Executive departments—Europe—Management—Congresses.
  3. Europe. Western—Politics and government—Congresses. 4. Public
  administration—Europe, Western—Congresses. I. Kickert, Walter J.
  M. (Walter Julius Michael) II. European Group of Public
  Administration.
  JN94.A58P83   1997
  351'.00094—DC20   96–35155
                                                                CIP

ISBN 1 85898 553 6

Typeset by Manton Typesetters, 5–7 Eastfield Road, Louth, Lincolnshire, UK.
Printed and bound in Great Britain by MPG Books Ltd, Bodmin, Cornwall

Contents

Part Three: Management, Rechtsstaat and Democracy

Part Four: Epilogue

List of Figures

List of Tables

List of Contributors

Carlos Alba is Professor in Political Science at the Universitat Autonoma in Madrid. He got his Ph.D. at the University of Granada and his M.A. and M. of Ph. in Political Science at Yale University. Main fields of research are: political socialisation and political elites, bureaucratic organisations, higher civil servants and the political processes. He is President of the Spanish Political Science Association and author, among others, of *The organisation of authoritarian leadership: Franco Spain, Presidents and Prime-Ministers* (R. Rose and E. Suleiman, eds); *Bürokratie und Politik. Hohe Beamte in Franco-Regime (1938-1975)* (with P. Waldman *et al.*); *Sozialer Wandel und Herrschaft in Spanien Francos* (with F. Schöningh); *Administracion y Politica*, in Libro Homenaje al Prof. Francisco Murillo Ferrol Politica y Sociedad. He is editor and contributor of a book on Spanish local government, *Perspectiva sobre el gobierno local: Un analisis politico* (in print).

Werner Jann studied Political Science, Mathematics and Economics in Berlin and Edinburgh, Dipl.Pol. (Berlin 1976), Dr.rer.publ. (Speyer 1982). He was Research Fellow and Assistant Professor at the Post-Graduate School of Administrative Sciences in Speyer. He was Congressional Fellow in Washington DC and Research Fellow at the University of California, Berkeley. He was a civil servant and leader of the *Denkfabrik Schleswig-Holstein* in the Prime Minister's Office in Kiel. Since 1993 he has been Professor at the Chair for Political Science, Administration and Organisation at Potsdam University. He is a member of several government commissions concerning the modernisation of the public sector. He publishes in the field of comparative public policy and administration, parliaments and modernisation of the public sector.

Walter Kickert graduated in Experimental Physics and wrote his dissertation in Organisation Science. He is now Professor of Public Management at the Erasmus University Rotterdam and chair of the department of Public Administration. Previously he also was programme director at the Netherlands School of Government and director of the International PA Programme of the Rotterdam-Leiden departments of Public Administration. Formerly Councillor at the Ministry of Education and Sciences, his present academic interest lies in the field of public governance, management and organisation and (international comparative) administrative reform. He has acted as consultant to several ministries and other public organisations, lately the Ministry of Agriculture, Nature and Fishery. He has published on government planning, governance and management, most recently a book on *Changes in Management and Organisation of (Dutch) Central Administration* and on *Public Policy and Administration Sciences in the Netherlands.*

Klaus König is Professor of Administrative Science, Government and Public Law at the Post-Graduate School of Administrative Sciences at Speyer in Germany. He studied Law, Economics and Political Science, in 1961 he became Dr.Jur., in 1962 Dr.rer.Pol and in 1965 Ass.Jur. In 1970 he obtained his *Habilitation* for Public Law and Administrative Science and in 1971 professor and judge. From 1974 until 1976 he was the President of the Speyer Post-Graduate School. From 1982 until 1987 he was Director-General of the Federal Chancellor. He is a member of the German and foreign scientific PA societies. He is Vice-President of the International Institute of Administrative Sciences, editor and co-editor of scientific journals, including the *Verwaltungsarchiv* and the *International Review of Administrative Sciences.* His fields of interests and publications are: government and public administration in general, planning and legislation, public functions, organisation of government and administration, civil service and international administrative cooperation.

Linda deLeon is an Associate Professor at the Graduate School of Public Affairs at the University of Colorado at Denver, where she directs the Master of Public Administration program. Prior to joining the GSPA faculty, she was Director of Human Resources and Administration for an insurance-brokerage firm. Her research interests include issues involving women in public employment, public sector professional and organisation theory.

Rudolf Maes is Professor of Public Administration and Public Law at the Catholic University of Leuven (Belgium) at the Department of Political Sciences (Section of Public Administration and Public Management). His research interests lie in the fields of comparative local government and public management and changes in the legal and political system. Recent publications are on intermunicipal cooperation, subnational authorities in the European integration process and a new profile for the Belgian provinces.

B. Guy Peters is Maurice Falk Professor of American Government of the Department of Political Science at the University of Pittsburgh. He is also currently a Senior Fellow at the Canadian Centre for Management Development. Among his publications are *The politics of bureaucracy, European politics reconsidered* and *Advising West European governments* (with Anthony Barker).

Christoph Reichard is Professor for Public Management at the Polytechnic for Technology and Economics in Berlin. After studying business administration at the Free University of Berlin he got his Ph.D. in Economics and Public Administration at the University of Freiburg. For 20 years now he has been Professor of Public Management at the Berlin School for Public Administration. His main research fields are: (new) public management, public personnel, institution building in developing countries. Actual research activities: comparative studies on international trends in new public management, follow-up and evaluation of on-going administrative reforms in different local governments in Germany, contracting-out and public-private partnership in the public sector, administrative culture in the new German *Länder*, development and implementation of a new study programme (Public Management). He has written about 100 publications, among them several books about public management (in German).

R.A.W. Rhodes is Professor of Politics (Research) at the University of Newcastle-upon-Tyne. Between 1989 and 1995, he was Professor of Politics and Head of Department at the University of York. Between 1987 and 1989 he was Reader in Government and Chair of Department at the University of Essex.

He is the author of 15 books, including: *Public Administration and Policy Analysis*; *Control and Power in Central-Local Relations*, *The National World of Local Government*, *Beyond Westminster and Whitehall* and (with David Marsh, eds) *Policy Networks in British Government*. He has also published more than 60 chapters in books and articles in such major journals as *Political Studies*, *British Journal of Political Science*, *Public Administration*, *Parliamentary Affairs* and *West European Politics*. Recent publications include: (with Patrick Dunleavy, eds) *Prime Minister, Cabinet and Core Executive* (with P. Weller and H. Bakvis, eds) *The Hollow Crown* and *Understanding Governance*. He has been editor of *Public Administration* since 1986.

Currently, he is Director of the Economic and Social Research Council's Whitehall research programme, chair of the ESRC's research programme on local governance, chair of the Public Administration Committee of the Joint University Council for Social and Public Administration and chair of the Political Studies Association of the United Kingdom's Specialist Group in Public Administration.

Luc Rouban is Researcher at the National Centre of Scientific Research at the Fondation Nationale des Sciences Politiques, *Centre de Recherches Administratives* in Paris. His research interests are: public administration, civil service and State theory in a comparative perspective. His most recent publications include: *Le pouvoir anonyme, les mutations de l'Etat à la française*; *La fonction publique*; *De la Cinquième République à l'Europe* (co-edited with François d'Arcy). He has also published many articles about public administration and State reform in major scientific reviews.

Kuno Schedler was born in St. Gallen, Switzerland. After studies in Business Administration and Banking at the University of St. Gallen (master degree) he worked for *UBS* Zürich and was later a partner in a small company in the Executive Search Business. He received his doctorate in Economics at St. Gallen in autumn 1993. From 1994 to 1996 he was a lecturer in Public Management at the University of St. Gallen and Manager of the Public Management Department at the Institute of Public Finance and Fiscal Law in St. Gallen. Since 1995 he has been Vice President of the Institute. In 1996, he was appointed Professor of Public Management at the University of St. Gallen and director of the Institute.

Franz Strehl has been Rector at the Johannes Kepler University of Linz in Austria since 1995. From 1988 to 1995 he was Professor at the University of Innsbruck in the Department of Public Sector Management. From 1976 to 1988 he was Assistant Professor at the Johannes Kepler University of Linz. He conducted research and consulting projects on national federal and on state and community level on concepts of organisational efficiency and effectiveness and their implementation. He is president and project manager of working groups on Public Sector Management of the International Institute of Administrative Sciences in Brussels. He teaches general business management and public sector management at the University of Innsbruck and the University of Linz.

Frans O.M. Verhaak studied Public Administration at the University of Leiden. At the moment he is a research assistant at the Erasmus University Rotterdam, preparing his dissertation on autonomical reform in Dutch administration. He is author of papers and articles on autonomisation. He is co-editor of *Core departments at a distance? A comparative investigation of departmental change processes in Dutch central government.*

Vincent Wright is Fellow of Nuffield College in Oxford. His previous post was at the London School of Economics. He has also taught at the European University Institute in Florence and in several other European and American universities. He is the joint editor of *West European Politics* since its creation in 1977. He has written books on French government and politics, most notably on the French prefects and on the *Conseil d'État* and has edited or co-edited several volumes on government and administration in Western Europe. He is currently joint director of a major comparative project on core-executive policy coordination in Western Europe.

Preface

Jacques Ziller
President of EGPA

The European Group of Public Administration (EGPA), a 'regional group' of the Brussels based worldwide public administration network, the International Institute of Administrative Sciences (IIAS), has been acting for more than thirty years as the representative organisation of European professionals and scholars involved in the field of public administration. As such, EGPA has been organising yearly conferences with the help of universities, public administration institutes, schools and other institutions which specialise in the development of public administration as a science. The results of EGPA permanent working groups have been regularly published under book form or in European and international journals of public administration or political science, especially in the *International Review of Administrative Sciences*, but a big part of the papers produced for these yearly conferences has only been kept available as grey literature at the library of IIAS.

The first EGPA Yearbook, edited by Walter Kickert from the Rotterdam Erasmus University where the 1995 annual conference of EGPA was hosted and remarkably organised by him, is a first attempt to enable a larger public to get acquainted with the production on EGPA meetings. The current theme of the Rotterdam conference fits such an enterprise particularly well.

I want to express my thanks to the editor for his very active and effective work and my hope that many readers of this Yearbook will get in touch with EGPA in order to support its efforts for a continuous interchange in the field of European public administration.

Part One

**Introduction: Public Management
and Administrative Reform**

CHAPTER ONE

Introduction

Walter Kickert
Erasmus University Rotterdam

This volume is the follow-up to the 1995 EGPA conference on *Public Management and Administrative Modernisation* which was held at the Erasmus University Rotterdam in September 1995. More than 150 scholars from all over Europe and the United States attended the conference which consisted of four working groups centred around the main conference theme – public management, administrative reforms, the legal perspective and the historical perspective – and a number of permanent EGPA study groups. Before presenting an overview of the contributions to this volume, let me first briefly introduce the notion of an EGPA yearbook.

At the 1994 EGPA conference in Bad Tatzmandorf in Austria the idea was suggested to start a kind of European journal of Public Administration. The EGPA steering committee, chaired at that time by Professor Hugo van Hassel, and Guy Braibant, then president of IIAS – the European Group of Public Administration (EGPA) is a group within the International Institute of Administrative Sciences (IIAS) – in principle favoured the idea but advised a modest beginning in the form of a yearly publication, a sort of EGPA yearbook. By beginning to publish a number of yearbooks we could find out whether the sales market is large enough, and above all, whether the supply of high quality articles is sufficient in order eventually to proceed to a next stage of some kind of European PA journal. It was agreed to use the 1995 EGPA conference as a first try-out.

A large number of participants of the 1995 conference actually presented a rich abundance of excellent papers in Rotterdam. In order not to delay the publication of a first 1995 EGPA yearbook – the unhappy fate of some yearbooks is that they come out many years afterwards – the successor-president of EGPA, Professor Jacques Ziller, agreed that I should go ahead and publish this yearbook *avant la lettre*. Preceding the actual configuration of a yearbook series – implying the choice of a clear concept of a yearbook, the formation of an editorial board and so on – Edward Elgar publishers agreed to publish the 1995 yearbook. In the meantime, we are still in the process of establishing a *real* yearbook series which will hopefully be realised at the end of this year.

Outline of the Volume

The rich and varied abundance of papers presented at the 1995 EGPA conference in Rotterdam made a restrictive selection of papers for the yearbook inevitable. Unfortunately Professor Victor Heyen of the University at Greifswald, who successfully led the working group on 'administrative reform from a historical perspective', could not receive the grateful and due respect for his many valued efforts in the form of a publication in this yearbook, for which I do offer my sincere apologies. Fortunately Professor Rudolf Maes of the Catholic University at Leuven, chairman of the working group on 'public management and changes to legal systems', was willing and able to deliver a contribution to the yearbook.

The theme of this yearbook is a combination of two main subjects of the 1995 conference, treated in the working group on 'administrative reforms and modernisation', chaired by Vincent Wright of Nuffield College at Oxford and Luc Rouban of the Centre de Recherches Administratives at Paris, and in the working group on 'American and European approaches of public management', chaired by myself. Both themes are separately introduced at the beginning of this volume.

Both themes are then combined by concentrating on management reforms in various countries of Western Europe. First a number of clear and successful examples of public management reforms are presented such as the trend of 'New Public Management', which dominates the reforms in the British civil service, the 'Neues Steuerungsmodell', which dominates the recent wave of local government reforms throughout Germany, and the new public management reforms in Austria and Switzerland.

The managerial reforms in Great Britain are relatively well-known to a wide English-reading audience. Most European and many American Public Administration scholars are acquainted with the British managerialist reform of 'next steps' agencies, the introduction of client-orientedness with the so-called Citizen's Charter, and the introduction of market competition with the concept of market testing in the government paper on *Competing for Quality*. The prominent British PA scholar professor Rod Rhodes of the University of Newcastle, editor of the British journal *Public Administration*, contributes a critical review of the reforms that have swept through Whitehall since 1979 when Margaret Thatcher took up office.

Less known is the widespread municipal reform trend in Germany which started in the early nineties with the adaptation of the so-called 'Tilburg model' – a medium sized town in the Netherlands – and resulted in the elaboration of the so-called *Neues Steuerungsmodell*. The international dissemination of knowledge about this relatively unknown but highly interesting and relevant development in Germany is surely worth two contributions. Professor Christoph Reichard of the

Fachhochschule in Berlin, who both nationally and internationally plays an active role in the reform debate, offers an overview of the local government reforms and the *Neues Steuerungsmodell*. Professor Werner Jann of the University of Potsdam subsequently offers an essayistic discussion of the model including the previous long history of institutional inertia of German administration.

Hardly known at all in the international Public Administration community is that Switzerland and Austria are also presently in the process of introducing and implementing widespread administrative reforms and are clearly adopting the model of New Public Management (NPM). Professor Franz Strehl, rector of the Kepler University at Linz, and Professor Kuno Schedler of the University of Sankt Gallen, two authoritative proponents of the NPM model who are both actively involved in the debate and the reform process itself in their respective countries, were specially invited to write a contribution to this volume on management reforms in Europe.

Although trend reports on developments of administrative reforms of the OECD repeatedly confirm that most developments point in the same direction of new public management, management reforms are, of course, not a success story in every European country.

Luc Rouban of the Centre de Recherches Administratives at Paris explicitly places the public management reforms in the French administration in the historical and socio-cultural context of the typical French model of administration, with its strong and particular institutional traditions. Public management cannot be detached from the political and socio-cultural context of the particular administration of France.

Dutch administrative reforms at the moment seem to be a clear example of public management. A closer look reveals that the managerial frame of reference has been preceded by various other ones. Although consensus and corporatist democracy still constitute main features of the Dutch state and by implication Dutch political decision making continues to possess a high degree of viscosity, the Dutch administration has nevertheless undergone relatively many serious reforms, both at local and national level. My colleague, Frans Verhaak of the Erasmus University Rotterdam, presents an overview of the shifting frames of reference behind the successive stages of reform in Dutch central administration during the eighties and nineties.

The administrative reforms in some countries are sometimes far from successful. In order to present some counter-evidence as well, Professor Carlos Alba of the Autonomous University Madrid was invited to contribute a paper. He reports on the disappointing results of successive attempts to reform the Spanish administration even though the fundamental political transformation process seemed to offer ample opportunities.

Besides critical empirical examples of failed managerial reforms, the trend of managerial reforms in various European administrations can also be criticised from a normative and theoretical point of view. Particularly from the legal perspective of the traditional continental European *Rechtsstaat* with its Weberian bureaucracy, as well as from the perspective of political democracy, serious questions can be asked about managerialism in the public sector. Professor Rudolf Maes of the Catholic University at Leuven approaches the subject of public management from the juridical *Rechtsstaat* perspective and raises fundamental questions about legality and legitimacy. His legal perspective is illustrated with the example of Belgian administration. Professor Klaus König of the Hochschule für Verwaltungswissenschaften at Speyer, vice-president of the IIAS and long-standing member of the EGPA steering committee, also raises serious questions regarding public managerialism from the viewpoint of the long and successful continental European tradition of *Rechtsstaat* and Weberian bureaucracy. Subsequently, our overseas colleague, Professor Linda deLeon of the University of Colorado at Denver, addresses the subject from the viewpoint of political democracy and especially discusses the problem of democratic accountability in managerial government.

The volume ends with an epilogue by Professor Guy Peters, a prominent North American scholar in comparative politics and administration and co-editor of the journal *Governance*. He concludes the overview of managerial reforms in Western Europe in this volume by contrasting the European developments with a North American perspective.

Although a collection of various papers by different authors from Europe and the United States to some extent inevitably suffers from a lack of coherence, this volume tries to offer a balanced overview of the managerial reform trend which is sweeping through Western Europe. It attempts to offer a balanced overview by presenting not only the well-known example of Great Britain, but also the less-known example of Germany and the hardly known examples of Austria and Switzerland. Moreover, the overview not only presents success stories but also nuanced stories from France and the Netherlands and the example of failed reforms in Spain. It also weighs the pros and cons by presenting serious criticisms and counter-arguments against the prevailing trend of public management. Balance in this volume is also sought by comparing the European reforms with the North American ones. Though the overview is neither exhaustively complete nor completely systematic, the intention is at least to be balanced.

Rotterdam, May 1996

CHAPTER TWO

The Paradoxes of Administrative Reform*

Vincent Wright
Nuffield College, Oxford

1. Introduction

The reform of the public administration has been placed on the policy agenda of almost every European government – whatever their political complexion – although the timing, the pace, the extent, the nature, the reasons and the impact vary greatly across European countries. Explaining the differences would in itself make a fascinating topic for a workshop of the European Group of Public Administration and several are touched upon in this book. But this is not the theme of this introductory chapter. Nor is it the intention to talk about the vast array of administrative reforms currently being pursued by European governments and which are intended to modify the size, the structure, the functions and functioning, the efficiency and even the culture of traditional public administrations: 'downsizing', 'resource-squeeze', 'cut-back management', 'effectiveness', 'efficiency' and 'economy' – the famous '3 Es', 'privatisation', 'outsourcing', 'marketisation', 'quasi-markets', 'surrogate markets', 'new public management', 'contractualisation', 'customerisation', 'automisation', 'agencification' – these are the buzz words that are currently infusing the vocabulary of public administration – as well as butchering that already much loved and much abused object, the English language.

The intention of this chapter is much narrower: it is to explore some of the general public policy lessons that may be derived from an analysis of the current reform programmes, for these programmes perfectly illustrate a whole range of major public policy phenomena or features. Of these, particularly the policy paradox will be dwelled upon, since it most spectacularly encapsulates some of the major characteristics of the reform programmes. However, before turning to the policy paradox, some of the other policy phenomena illustrated by current administrative reforms will briefly be mentioned, because they help, in some measure, to explain the paradoxes.

2.   Policy Phenomena

The first such public policy phenomenon is the *policy panacea*. For some countries, public administrative reform is seen as a universal remedy, a means of reducing the role of the state, of shifting the public-private boundary and of undermining some of the props of the semi-collectivist social democratic consensus allegedly so powerfully buttressed by bureau-expanding and budget-maximising bureaucrats. It is also tapping individual and organisational initiative, and is increasing consumer choice and for improving efficiency. Some current British rhetoric looks like the publicity for a particularly effective laxative guaranteed, according to the producer, to cleanse, to soothe and make you generally feel better!

The second policy feature is *policy fashion and policy diffusion*. Public sector reform is in fashion and no self-respecting government can afford to ignore it. How a fashion is established is one of the most intriguing questions of public policy. Part of the answer lies in *policy diffusion* brought about by the activities of international officials (whose zeal for administrative reform mysteriously stops short at the door of their own organisations), by meetings of public administrators, academics and the so-called policy entrepreneurs. Bodies like the European Group of Public Administration are arenas for the dissemination of ideas and, like the ambiguous hero in Graham Greene's *The Quiet American*, cause trouble without either knowing or wanting to.

My third policy phenomenon is *policy linkage*. Without doubt, public administrative reform is linked with a wider package designed at reshaping and reducing the state, reform of the public industrial sector, liberalisation, deregulation, privatisation, tax reform. This wider package harbours its own dynamic which generates new interests, strengthens some actors whilst weakening or marginalising others. The resultant reconfiguration of interests creates constituencies intent on further interlinked reform, which extends and consolidates their position: reforms, in other words, are not politically agnostic. They redistribute power both within the administration and between the administration and other groups.

Policy phenomenon number four: *policy slippage*. A gap between, on the one hand, ambitions and programmes, and on the other, the programmes and the outcomes or actual impact. There are numerous examples of wide-ranging ambitions being translated into timid programmes and of the impact of radical programmes being diluted by structural constraints or by the skill of strategically-placed sceptics, all too aware of the blessings of inertia.

On the other hand, we have policy phenomenon number five, which is *policy reversal*, to borrow the title of Christopher Hood's recent excellent book: a radical change of direction in existing policies. For a variety of reasons, traditional models of public policy making are profoundly conservative, since they emphasise incrementalism as the dominant mode and underline the tendency towards policy inertia, and the difficulties of policy termination. Yet recent evidence in some countries suggests that public policy specialists should pay more attention to processes of change provoked by exogenous shocks, new ideas, new coalitions, technology and even the exercise of political power. Administrative historians, looking back at the 1980s and early 1990s, may well identify the period as a significant watershed: a period when the pressures and opportunities for change were present.

The *policy dilemma* represents the sixth public policy phenomenon. There are many, one of which is inherent in the reform process. The central dilemma of the reformers may be stated simply: most public policy studies emphasise the fact that effective reforms must ideally attract the assent of the groups that are most affected (indeed, historically, the most effective reforms have come from within the administration itself). Yet, many of those directly affected by the reforms are either allergic or hostile to them, and this is not surprising since their jobs may well be at stake; only the most eccentric turkey looks forward to Christmas. Negotiation with a view to mobilising support invariably involves dilution, whilst lack of negotiation risks demoralising and demotivating those involved in implementation.

The seventh policy phenomenon, *policy contradiction*, is the pursuit of conflicting goals within a particular programme or between programmes. With respect to the current reform process they are too many to list and they are rooted in the multiple, different and sometimes conflicting reasons used to justify or to rationalise the reforms.

Finally, *policy perversity*, the unintended, unpredictable and sometimes unwelcome consequences of the reforms. Thus, the mania for evaluation, designed to reduce costs, has frequently had the unpalatable effect of identifying areas where efficiency demands an *increase* in spending.

3. Policy Paradoxes

Unreasonable ambitions, linkage, slippage, dilemmas, contradictions and perversions, all features of current public administrative reform, provide some of the clues to an understanding of the final and dominant feature, which is the policy paradox.

The first major policy paradox is that the most radical reform programmes appear to have been introduced in countries with the most efficient administrations, in other words, in those countries with the least need! Those countries with the greatest need, diplomacy forbids mentioning them here, have either few reform ambitions or totally inadequate reform programmes.

Paradox number two: many of the reforms are inspired by the theories or models of private management which are notoriously fickle indeed; they have the life span of the average heroine in a Puccini opera. Moreover, the record of private management in the country with the greatest propensity to emulate the private sector, the United Kingdom, is, to say the least, chequered. In Germany, on the other hand, where private management has an enviable record, there is little pressure on the public administration to imitate. In any case, it does seem time for specialists of public administration to turn a more critical eye on the weaknesses and problems of private-sector management, instead of limiting their analyses to the problems of the transplant of an idealised and misunderstood model.

The third paradox relates to the role of the top bureaucrats as one of the principal motors of reform. In much of the neo-liberal and public choice literature, which has provided so much intellectual ammunition for the political reformers, these bureaucrats are depicted as intrinsically inefficient, deriving job satisfaction from politicking, status, guaranteed pensions, and content to apply the rules. And, of course, they are intent on budget maximisation or bureau expansion. Or, according to another public choice school, they are embedded in the great 'distributional coalitions', those cosy and collusive networks guilty of expanding the state. Historically, this was always a caricature, even though there was some anecdotal empirical evidence in some countries to provide a semblance of truth to the portrayal. There is also considerable historical evidence that these bureaucrats were often the source of effective reform initiatives. More to the point, current evidence suggests that top bureaucrats are not all allergic to reform programmes, which, on the whole, impact most acutely on the lower ranks and which often open up more exciting opportunities of policy-oriented managerialism. Why spend your life mouthing 'Yes, Minister' when there is the siren call of autonomy?

The fourth paradox is that whilst many of the reforms are designed to cut costs, the end result of some of them may be quite the opposite. Take, for example, 'evaluation', a current craze which tends to ignore the manpower costs involved in the process. Evaluation may identify areas of waste. But it also tends to reveal disparities not only in performance but also in outcomes: some people are being relatively badly treated. These disparities were previously hidden. The result will be to create political pressures for such disparities to be ironed out. More profoundly, transforming citizens into clients or customers, with clearly defined rights fixed by targets may have the effect of improving quality. But it also creates anticipations and pressures for redress, often of a legal nature. We need no prophetic insights to forecast that expensive litigation will be one of the consequences of the present reform programme. Indeed, it is embedded in the very logic of the programme. Similarly, clarity or transparency, apparently desirable objects in themselves, may have undesirable hidden costs and not only organisational ones. A great deal of public policy is about rationing, about the distribution of scarce resources, about zero-sum games and opportunity costs. For rationing to work over any length of time it must either be ignored, obfuscated or it must be legitimatised. It is an intrinsically difficult exercise to undertake by a democratic society in peace-time and in periods of stagnation or recession. Yet, on the whole, rationing has been managed reasonably well by a combination of ignorance, obfuscation and legitimation.

However, some of the current reforms, driven by good intentions, seem designed to undermine those three essential props: ignorance is being replaced by defined rights and obfuscation by transparency. Even more significant is the *delegitimation* of the process: decisions about rationing are being removed from politicians and self-regulating professions like teachers and doctors and they are being transferred to managers and to entrepreneurs, who quite simply lack the essential legitimacy to spread the essential misery. We may expect, therefore, increased controversies and resort to the courts for redress, thus accentuating the trend towards litigation.

In short, the budgetary advantages of many of the current reforms are front-loaded, they are short-term.

The issue of clarity and transparency involves yet another paradox, paradox number five: namely, that transparency, translated into clear managerial goals or targets and combined with increasing managerial autonomy, is leading to greater obfuscation but not the kind of obfuscation which is desirable. It is obfuscation relating to *political accountability*. This is already difficult enough to establish. Yet it is so critical in a democratic polity. Managerialism is further blurring the lines of responsibility. It may be convenient for politicians to hide behind the smoke-screen of managerial discretion and autonomy, but this hardly adds to the democratic quality of decision making.

The penultimate paradox relates to *efficiency,* the 'Holy Grail' of administrative reformers. One can argue, with some justification, that one of the major achievements of the current reform programmes is to sensitise officials at all levels of the public administration to efficiency, however vaguely understood. And it seems highly desirable and perfectly legitimate to define the criteria for efficiency. However, it requires little sophistication to be aware that such an exercise is politically loaded, since efficiency in the delivery of public goods involves complex political and social externalities. We are not merely selling a disaggregated range of products like soap powder and potatoes. We are juggling with multiple, interlinked and often conflicting or nebulous requirements. More to the point, in terms of the efficiency paradox, the question is whether efficiency is likely to be maximised by systematically denigrating and openly despising the ethos and ethics of the public service and, by a whole swathe of measures, demoralising and demotivating those who uphold the principles of the public good. If citizens are turned into customers we will also slowly transform officials into producers, motivated by the logic and the rewards of the private market place. And in those circumstances, many hard-working and underpaid officials, previously driven by a commitment to the public good, will demand proper remuneration: if they receive it, costs will rise; if they do not: the most likely scenario, they will have little incentive to give their best. In that sense, the destruction of the public ethos is profoundly inefficient, even if the effects may take some time to emerge.

The final paradox is rooted in the reformers' ambition to reduce the role of the state. Yet, radical reform programmes designed to produce state retreat require a strong state to initiate and implement them; this is a familiar paradox and it may be seen in other radical reform programmes. Secondly, several of the reforms involve *increased* state activity, as anyone who has had the misfortune to be a British doctor or teacher or university professor will all too readily testify. Bodies which were previously largely self-governing have been assailed by evaluation exercises and performance indicators and targets and all the other time-consuming paraphernalia of an interventionist state. Incidentally, it is one of the delightful ironies of British political science that it has discovered the state as a subject of academic concern which was as the result of governments determined to diminish it ...

In short, the process of administrative modernisation has generated a set of paradoxes which confirm the old public policy dictum that today's solutions are merely tomorrow's problems.

4.   Conclusions

Fortunately, at least one of these paradoxes may be transient in nature, some are country-specific and some may be more apparent than real. Alternatively, they may be explained by policy slippage, or the unpredictable consequences of some of the reforms, although most of the unpredictable results were perfectly predictable.

Yet the major paradoxes, with their unpalatable medium-term and long-term implications, appear to be general and permanent in character and seem to be rooted in misunderstanding, in the policy contradictions which characterise the reforms and in the naivete of the reformers themselves. *Ignorance*, simulated or real, is most manifest about the needs of a democratic society with its messy trade-offs, with its constant need to balance inherent contradictions, with its requirements of equity and legitimacy. There is ignorance, too, about the true nature of public bureaucracies which rarely function according to the premises of *a priori* theorising.

The policy contradictions are too numerous to explore, but essentially, they stem from the conflicting ideological sources and ambitions of the reforms.

Finally, there is *naivete*, naivete about the nature of the private sector as well as naivete about the nature of the market, the cherished models upon which so many of the reforms are posited. If we compare an idealised view of the private sector and the workings of the market with a bilious perception of the public domain it is scarcely surprising that demands for reform should emerge. A more measured view of both would, however, lead us to prudence.

Public administration merely reflects the many contradictions and dilemmas which are inevitably provoked by the interactions of market, state and society. Ultimately, its rationale lies in its overarching and integrative functions. It should be judged not by the narrower criteria of the private sector, but by its capacity to provide ballast, to provide a semblance of coherence, to provide an occasional steering ability, but above all, to provide a degree of legitimacy to governance, particularly when it is under pressure, as it is today. At present, the public administration is the messenger boy of the political system with problems: he is the bearer of unpleasant news. There may be a case for improving his efficiency. There is little real justification for criticising and undernourishing him and there is none for shooting him. And that is what we are in danger of doing.

Note

* This article was the opening lecture at the 1995 EGPA Conference.

CHAPTER THREE

Public Management in the United States and Europe

Walter Kickert
Erasmus University Rotterdam

1. Introduction

Since the end of the 1970s, the entire Western world appears to have moved into an era of severe administrative reforms. Furthermore, these reforms apparently display certain common characteristics. They all tend to be more or less managerial reforms. The trend in the direction of new public management is apparent in the United States, Great Britain, and other Western European administrations, but on the other side of the globe as well, in Australia, New Zealand, and other 'Western' countries. Trend reports on developments of administrative reforms of the OECD (1990, 1993) confirm that most developments point in the same direction, which is the introduction of ideas, models and techniques of public management, that is, the adoption of business management techniques, a greater service and client orientation, the introduction of market mechanisms and competition in public administrations.

The adoption by many Western administrations all over the world of a same kind of new public management, is highly remarkable and in fact quite surprising. For the principles of business management might to a large extent be universally applicable all over the world, as business firms all operate on the same worldwide market, universality does definitely not hold true for public administrations. Various states and administrations throughout the world fundamentally differ in economical, socio-political, cultural, constitutional and institutional senses and so do the ways in which these public administrations are managed. Even within the relatively small subset of Western countries, the administrative differences are enormous. The differences in states, governments and administrations between the United States and Europe and within Europe itself, make the common adoption of the same kind of public sector management indeed quite surprising, to put it mildly. Unlike the natural sciences, it is not possible to derive a universally valid general theory of Public Administration which holds true anywhere and anytime. This holds true for the science of Public Administration in general as well as for the subfield of public management. After all, it is not odd that in the 'motherland' of business management, 20th century United States, such a development has also penetrated the public sector. But it is remarkable that a country such as Great Britain with its long, unique tradition of a highly valued and esteemed civil service, the higher civil servant as the traditional Oxbridge educated 'gentleman amateur', must suddenly give way to a new businesslike 'public manager' (see the contribution of Rhodes in this volume). Also remarkable is that continental European states like Germany and Austria, with their strong *Rechtsstaat* tradition and a *Juristenmonopol* in their administration, in the 1980s and 1990s have adopted managerial reform models (see the contributions of Jann, Reichard and Strehl). This volume witnesses a public management trend in a number of other European countries too. Will the Anglo-American trend of public management spread over the entire Western world ...?

In this chapter attention will be paid to public management in the United States and Europe, both in the sense of management developments in the practice of public sector reform and in the sense of theoretical developments in the science of public sector management. First, attention will be paid to the practical relevance of public management, that is, managerial developments in administrative reforms throughout the Western world, particularly in the United States and Europe. Next, scientific developments of public management will be discussed as they have occurred, predominantly, in the United States. Since the early 1980s, the topic of public management has experienced a strong upheaval in the North American study of Public Policy and Administration. Because the study of Public Administration (PA) depends on the empiry of administration (lower-cast pa), North American ideas, models and theories cannot simply be transposed onto totally different types of states and administrations. At the very least, differences in state and administration need to be considered before an idea of public management is transferred to another country. What do these differences between the United States and Europe and within Europe mean for the application of the science of public management to Western Europe? We will conclude with some thoughts about a possible European alternative perspective of public management.

2.   Managerial Reforms Throughout the West

The Necessity of Reforms

There are several explanations for the fact that the 1980s and 1990s have been the 'golden age' of administrative reform throughout the Western world (Wright, 1994). The most obvious is the financial-economic need to reform. The economic recession after the oil crisis of the 1970s resulted in enormous deficits of the public budgets and the Western welfare state proved unaffordable. The need to cut back in the public sector and especially the enormous size of the inevitable retrenchments, form the major explanation for the necessity of drastic reforms in the structure and functioning of Western governments and administrations. Without drastic reforms, these Draconian budget cuts could not be realised. The nature of the explanation has direct influence on the nature of the reforms. In principle there are three ways of dealing with deficits (Osborne and Gaebler, 1992).

First, expenditures can be limited and public tasks can be terminated. This happened to a large degree in the United States under the Reagan administration and in Great Britain under the Thatcher cabinet.

Second, revenues, respectively taxes, can be raised. The electoral punishment President Bush experienced for breaking his election vow not to raise taxes (read my lips) indicates that such a thing is equal to political suicide in the United States. Also, under Thatcher such an increase was politically and ideologically unthinkable. But in other Western welfare states too, where politics and ideology have not developed such extremes, the tax levels were such that this option was not a realistic alternative.

That leaves us with 'a third way', that is, perform the public tasks with less money. Or, according to the subtitle of the *National Performance Review* (Gore, 1993), 'work better and cost less'. The third way thus emphasises an increase of productivity, greater efficiency, better value for money, and so on, all issues that play a central role in thinking about management. Therefore, the third way almost logically forces the public sector to move towards public management. That the golden age of administrative reforms apparently resulted particularly in managerial reforms, thus logically follows from cause and event.

New Public Management

The most widely used empirical proof for the statement that managerial reforms are the dominant trend in the Western world are the reviews of the OECD (1990, 1993) on public management developments. From these reviews, it appears that more or less the same kind of developments have occurred in all of the OECD member countries. In a recent analysis of public management reforms (OECD, 1995), it is concluded that notwithstanding differences in nature, size, and approach to reforms, a common agenda has developed, 'a new paradigm for public management has emerged, aiming at fostering a performance-oriented culture in a less central-ised public sector'. According to the OECD, this new public management paradigm is characterised by the following eight main trends:

– devolving authority, providing flexibility	– improving the management of human resources
– ensuring performance, control, accountability	– optimising information technology
– developing competition and choice	– improving the quality of regulation
– providing responsive service	– strengthening steering functions at the centre

In his inaugural address at the London School of Economics, Hood presented his widely known definition of 'new public management', based on the OECD review (Hood, 1991).

– hands on professional management	– competition
– standards and performance measures	– private sector style management
– output controls	– discipline and parsimony
– disaggregation of units	

The questions Hood raises as to the novelty of the new public management trend, namely that the 'emperor's new clothes' look remarkably like the old principles of 'classical' business management, are confirmed in a comparative study done by Pollitt (1990) of managerialism in the United States and Great Britain. Pollitt concludes that this new public managerialism mainly consists of the classic Taylorian management principles from the beginning of this century. After Taylor's *The principles of scientific management*, various management theories and schools have been developed (Koontz, 1980). There is not only one theory, model and technique of business management. The trend to introduce businesslike management in gov-ernment therefore seems not so much inspired by scientific *reason* as it is by the ideological *Zeitgeist*.

Several authors have examined the phenomenon of managerial reforms in West-ern administrations, and various more or less different typologies have been pub-lished. What they all have in common is at least the following three characteristics:

– business management techniques,
– service and client orientation,
– market-type mechanisms such as competition.

3. Managerialism in the United States

General Management Culture

The birthplace of management is the United States and the belief in the curative function of management is not a recent one. In a sense one could say it is characteristic of North American culture in general. The American historical culture can be characterised by three concepts (Bellah *et al.*, 1987): biblical, republican and individualist. Utilitarian individualism is very important in the United States. The individual citizen is guided by motives of utility, weighs costs and benefits, advantages and disadvantages and selects the most useful alternative. The German-Prussian civil obedience to government and the state and the French *étatist* attitude in which the state is assumed to defend *l'intérèt général*, is lost on the average American. Commitment to the 'public cause' is a strange concept to Americans. The European concept of 'nation state' does not exist there. Citizens primarily view themselves as individual consumers of goods and services, no matter whether these are provided by private or public organisations. According to Bellah (1987), 20th century American culture is characterised by a belief in management. In the country of the free market, business corporations have become large and successful because of their effectiveness and efficiency and this is the result of good business management. It is no coincidence that the American Frederick Taylor wrote a book on the 'principles of scientific management'.

Public Sector Management

Management thinking in American government is also not a recent idea. In the 'Progressive Era' at the end of the 19th century, a societal and political movement at the local level turned against the abuses of the American spoils system. The spoils system, initially intended as a democratic guarantee that not only politics but also bureaucracy was 'for, through and by the people', had deteriorated in the 19th century into political clientelism, nepotism and corruption within the administration. There was a widespread call for professionalisation of the local bureaucracy, the call for independent, impartial, professional expertise. In his classic article Woodrow Wilson (1887) gave voice to these concerns by separating politics and administration. The Progressive Era resulted in a plan for the appointment and training of professional city managers. That period of reform was also responsible for the passage of the Pendleton Act on civil service classification, which established, for the first time, a career civil service at the federal level. The roots of American Public Administration can be found in this period. At the time, apparently, the concept of management at the local level was considered the panacea for many evils.

The breakthrough of management thinking in American federal government is often ascribed to the Brownlow Committee for Administrative Reform of 1930 and more specifically to its member Luther Gulick, who together with Taylor and Urwick, is considered the founding father of scientific management and the inventor of the famous POSDCORB acronym.

After the Progressive Era which led to the professionalisation and rationalisation of administration, the economic depression of the thirties was a following turning-point in the development of politics and administration. Roosevelt's 'New Deal' marked the beginning of the American variant of the welfare state. An era of trust in the public sector and interest in public affairs emanated in the States. This was also reflected in the study of Public Administration. The establishment of many 'schools of public affairs' dates from this time. The post-war growth and prosperity of the welfare state – the era of Johnson's 'Great Society' – led to an increasing role of government in many policy sectors and the accompanying belief in rational government planning – take, for example, MacNamara's PPBS – which was reflected in the study of Public Administration in the rise of the 'public policy analysis' schools.

The oil crisis of the 1970s resulted in a serious economic recession and in almost all Western welfare states, in serious public budget deficits. The 1980s were bitter years of retrenchments. The Reagan administration and its explicit anti-government attitude and bureaucrat-bashing fashion, represented an extreme example of across-the-board downsizing of the public sector and programme cuts throughout all policy areas. The huge demolition of the American public sector didn't leave the PA scholars unaffected. The democratisation movement of the late sixties and early seventies had already led to a politicisation, a call for attention for social matters, attention for norms and values – as witnessed by the first Minnowbrook conference and the subsequent 'New Public Administration'. In the late seventies the moral shock of the Vietnam war came on top of this, and in the eighties the economic recession and Reagan's bureaucrat bashing as well. The necessity of cost reduction, effectiveness and efficiency was large. No wonder that the call for businesslike management became increasingly louder. The call for entrepreneurial government in *Reinventing Government* and the call for government that 'works better and costs less' in the *National Performance Review* are both expressions of a renewed attention for management in the American public sector.

4.   Managerial Reforms in Europe

United Kingdom

Great Britain does not have a historical tradition of individualist, anti-government, managerial culture. Quite the contrary, the British civil service has maintained a long, highly-valued tradition. Holding public office in British government was considered an honour. The British civil service is the example of a professional, impartial, neutral, expert bureaucratic advisors to the ministers. Furthermore, the

British higher civil service is a powerful elite in British society. Although one would not expect American style situations here, Great Britain has, probably more than the United States, become the prototypical example of a managerial, client-oriented, competitive public service since Thatcher became prime minister in 1979.

The threefold description of new public management in terms of (1) businesslike management, (2) service and client orientation and (3) market-type mechanisms such as competition, in the recent developments of the British civil service are literally reflected in successive official policy documents of the government concerning administrative reform.

The introduction of businesslike management techniques in the British civil service began with Thatcher in 1979 with the creation of the Rayner scrutinies. Rayner, who came from the private sector, presided in the cabinet office over a project group which had to support the many scrutinies in the various departments. In 1983, the *Financial Management Initiative* started, an automated information system to support financial management. In 1987, the *Next Steps* report was published in which businesslike management was proposed to improve executive service delivery agencies – higher efficiency, better quality, more value for money – by granting them more autonomy. The creation of next step agencies, only piecemeal in the beginning, has assumed huge proportions. In 1995, more than 75 percent of all British civil servants fall under a next steps agency regime.

Improving the quality and quantity of service delivery of public agencies by making them more service and client oriented, was literally the main message of Major's white paper *Citizen's Charter* in 1991.

The third characteristic of new public management – market and competition – is reflected in the massive wave of privatisations of British public corporations and agencies since 1979. Second, it is reflected in Major's policy document *Competing for Quality* in 1992. This contains a proposal to force every public organisation which provides goods or services into a market test every five years. Upon this market test, an open tender can be given out for the provision of a particular good or service. The public agency involved can subscribe but so can providers from other public or private agencies. Only if the agency involved has the best offer, will it win the competition and continue to exist.

France

With respect to state, government and civil service, France does not particularly have an Anglo-Saxon tradition. *Etatist* France has a strong central government in which the *haute fonction publique* forms a powerful elite which governs and controls the entire country from Paris. The state is considered the keeper of *la volonté général*. The *haute fonctionaire publique*, educated at one of the famous *hautes écoles* such as the *Ecole Nationale d'Administration (ENA)* and a member of one of the *grand corps* such as the *Conseil d'Etat* or the *Cours des Comptes*, not only dominates the French bureaucracy but politics as well – many top politicians are *Enarques* – and, via the *pantouflage*, also the management of large (state) corporations.

It is in this unique context that we must consider the managerial reforms which were introduced in French government by the *circulaire Rocard* of 1989. In it, three reforms were emphasised which displayed great similarity with management techniques of businesses: *cercles de qualité, projets de service* and *centres de responsabilité* (Claisse, 1992; Rouban, 1994). The first concerns a Japanese technique which became popular in Western businesses as Total Quality Management. The service delivery projects were intended to provide more autonomy to the top management of executive agencies, linked with a more concise formulation of the mission, the goals and the tasks of the service. The third reform consisted of management contracts between central government and the executive agency in which the tasks and means were specified. The goals in these contracts primarily concerned the improvement of client orientation, the shortening of waiting periods, the reception of clients and so on.

Although these are unmistakably examples of the previous definition of new public management, we will have to be aware of the specific societal and state context of France.

Germany

Germany is an example of a continental European state with a strong tradition of *Rechtsstaat, Oeffentliche Verwaltung* and *Beamtentum*. From the Second World War to the German Reunification in 1989 there was a high degree of stability in German government (Seibel, 1992). This is considered by some as an example of the enormous rigidity of the highly juridified German government bureaucracy, while others consider it a sign of flexibility and adaptiveness of the highly qualified German bureaucracy. The fact is that there were hardly any reforms during this period.

Since 1989 the German government has been involved in a gigantic operation, namely the construction of a democratic public service in the former German Democratic Republic. There is no energy at the federal level to work on anything else. Furthermore, Germany is a federal republic in which the central government plays a relatively minor role.

At the local level, there have been large-scale reform operations since the early 1990s which strongly resemble the Anglo-American new public management. The German *Neues Steuerungsmodell* (the new local governance model) was specifically copied from Dutch experiences with local government reform in the 1980s. In Germany the 'Tilburg model' – a middle size town in the southern Netherlands – is considered a useful example. The *Neues Steuerungsmodell* (NSM), about which professors Jann and Reichard write more in this volume, is essentially based upon the concern-division model so popular in business. Management responsibility is delegated to the operational units. The new governance model consists of the following characteristics (Reichard, 1994):

- output- and result-orientation;
- output budgeting and performance indicators;
- service and client orientation;
- concern-division model;
- delegation of responsibility to business units.

This fits almost completely the characteristics of new public management. Although one would not expect American style managerialism in the juridical and regulated German bureaucracy, the financial need is so enormous since the unification that a business-economic approach to the public sector has apparently broken through the *Juristenmonopol*.

The Netherlands

Far reaching reforms have also occurred in smaller European countries. The famous Swedish welfare state model was downsized during the 1980s. The need for downsizing the public sector, reducing costs and increasing effectiveness and efficiency also led to a call for better management in Sweden. In Norway, the international economic recession and the retreat of the welfare state were less severe because of the extra income from natural gas and oil fields in the North Sea. Although The Netherlands also acquired substantial amounts of money from natural gas, the Dutch government could not escape serious cutbacks. In the 1980s, local governments were especially hit. This led to far-reaching reforms according to the concern-division model with management contracts between management and executive agencies, output budgeting, performance indicators, and so on. This trend of local reform clearly possessed a managerial nature. Several Dutch municipalities were reorganised in the 1980s according to this model and apparently with so much zeal that it attracted the attention of the Germans.

There have also been several reforms at the national level. After the 'great operations' – deregulation, decentralisation, privatisation, cutbacks and reorganisation – in the 1980s, *autonomisation* has become the most important trend since the early 1990s (Kickert and Verhaak, 1995). Similar to the British next steps agencies, more managerial autonomy is granted to executive ministerial agencies. The emphasis is on the distinction between policy preparation and execution. Executive service delivery agencies are separated from and placed at a distance from the ministerial core departments. Although originally a trend with a clear managerial character, the more recent developments in the Dutch civil service reveal a shift towards less managerial issues like public governance and political control. In The Netherlands, the managerial reform of agentisation was soon followed by a politically sensitive debate about future core tasks of ministerial departments – the core department – and by a debate about a new form of 'steering at a distance' between the department and the agencies. This is not only a matter of managerialism but also a question of the politics-administration dichotomy. The seemingly neutral managerial reforms turn out to have serious value implications for the public sector.

5.   Scientific Development of Public Management in the United States

Early Development

Management thinking in American government sprang from the Progressive Era movement of the end of the 19th century and called for a separation of politics and administration and for a professionalisation of the (local) bureaucracy, culminating in the 'professional city manager plan'. This resulted in the first administrative science research and teaching centers in the United States, such as the Municipal Research Bureau of New York and later the Maxwell School of Citizenship at Syracuse University. In the early 20th century, training programmes developed at several universities in the United States for professional city managers.

The early 20th century also marks the beginning of management science. *The Principles of Scientific Management* by Taylor (1911) and the *Papers on the Science of Administration* published by Gulick and Urwick in 1937 represent milestones in the beginning of modern management science. In organisation science, the rise of a new management orientation is usually considered as a reflection of the success of the modern and dynamic, especially American, business sector and its leadership, its management. The management approach originated as an alternative to the bureaucracy approach, the idealtype of Max Weber, the first founding father of organisation theory. Notice that up till the 20th century bureaucracy was the only and standard organisational form, a model that stemmed from the European state tradition. Although Gulick's POSDCORB acronym is clearly related to the ideas on 'general management' of the Frenchman Henry Fayol (1916), management science is, in a certain sense, a characteristically American invention based on a dominant culture there. In light of the enormous importance of the natural sciences and of technology for 19th century industrialisation, it is understandable that the founders of modern management science opted for an approach much like the approach used in the natural and technical sciences. Taylor's mechanical approach to labour processes reflects the scientific spirit of the age.

Modern management and organisation science usually pretend to be generic and does not make a distinction between business and public administration. Nonetheless, it is clear that business administration was an alternative to the bureaucratic model which came from the public sector and that empirical support is primarily based on research in private business. Taylor and Gulick are therefore considered the founders of business administration. Luther Gulick was extremely interested in the public sector and, because of his membership of the Brownlow Committee on the Reorganisation of Federal Government, wielded great influence in the dissemination of the new management science in the public sector. American Public Administration also considers him a founder. In this sense, management thinking was responsible for the birth of the American study of Public Administration.

Recent Public Management Sciences

The economic recession of the 1970s heralded the end of the belief in government planning both in America and in Western Europe. People became aware that devising all sorts of policy plans would not by itself lead to spectacular results. The great expectations of Washington-based policy planners usually turned out to be dashed at the local level of implementation (Pressman and Wildavsky, 1973). People increasingly realised that the factual implementation of policy might well be more relevant than the planning and analysis of policies. There was a greater need for public managers trained in the implementation and execution of policy processes who could monitor the actual implementation of those elaborate policy plans at the local level. The attention shifted from policy planning and policy analysis to the management of policy implementation. Thus, attention for public management developed.

Public Policy and Management

The Public Policy Analysis Schools experienced that shift in attention and thus also the demand in the labour market by the end of the 1970s. The demand for policy analysts who could provide a scientific, analytical foundation for policy proposals gradually declined. Thus, the PPA schools adopted the new trend in the public sector to pay more attention to the management of policy implementation, and added the M of management to PPA. This explains the wave of administrative science publications at the end of the 1970s and early 1980s on the difference between private and public management. The modern management and organisation sciences claim to be generic and therefore equally applicable to the public sector as well. American business schools in the 1980s also established graduate programmes in public management, either separate or integrated into a generic programme. If the prestigious PPA schools wanted to secure their market for public management programmes, then a distinction was necessary from the equally prestigious Business Administration schools, if only for reasons of competition. In this period, Graham Allison, then Dean of the Kennedy School at Harvard, published his seminal article on public and private management (1980).

The fact that public management was created at the prestigious PPA schools, which often had close ties with the bureaucratic and political upper echelon of the public sector, explains the relatively substantial attention for public management at the level of top executives, that is, for strategic top management in the public sector. In the writings of a typical representative of this stream, the distinguished scholar and practitioner Laurence E. Lynn of Chicago University (Lynn, 1981,

1987, 1996) one not only sees an emphasis on strategic top management reflected but also the relatively flowing change from strategic policy making into strategic management. Public management is approached from the (strategic) policy sciences and rarely from the generic management and organisation sciences.

A second characteristic of the public management approach at the former PPA schools is the case study method which originally came from the Harvard Business School and in particular the case-method of 'best practices'. Robert Behn (1991) of the Woodrow Wilson School at Princeton and Barzelay (1992) from the Kennedy School at Harvard are typical representatives of this best practices approach in which the emphasis is on cases of good, best and excellent public top managers. Their writings particularly use inductive reasoning from these excellent practices to derive the 'principles of excellent public management' (Denhardt, 1993).

Management of Implementation Networks

The awareness that policy implementation mattered more than policy planning is not a notion of the PPA schools alone. In the 'traditional' PA schools as well, the disappointment with policy planning and governmental steering of the 1970s increased and more attention was created for the implementation of complex policy programmes. A stream which found a large group of enthusiastic followers in the 1970s and 1980s was the Intergovernmental Management School (IGM) of which Deil Wright (1988) from Chapel Hill, North Carolina is a renowned and distinguished representative. In this approach of policy implementation, more emphasis is placed on complexity and interorganisational networks as, for instance, in the work of Larry O'Toole (1986).

However, some administrative scientists point to the fact that the traditional PA science had a public management orientation since the very origin of PA is related to management science. Some therefore consider the modern trend of public management as an 'unnecessary separatism' (Newland, 1994). In a recent review of the science of public management Larry Lynn (1996) made an admirable attempt for mutual communication and debate between the two scientific communities which constitute the major watershed in American Public Policy and Administration, that is, the traditional schools of public affairs and administration on the one hand, and the schools of public policy analysis and management on the other.

Public Management and Organisation Science

A third stream among the many and varied American approaches to public management is the attempt to create a specific public sector oriented management and organisation science from generic management and organisation science. Many textbooks in public management and organisation (Heffron, 1989; Harmon and Mayer, 1986) are in fact more or less adaptions of the more usual generic overview of the various organisational schools in the 20th century as is also presented in the usual textbooks at business schools. Some PA scholars like Barry Bozeman (1993) from the Maxwell School at Syracuse and Hal Rainey (1992) from Athens, Georgia, who both have a background in generic management and organisation science, attempt to create a distinct and specific public management science. More clearly than in the other streams mentioned above, we can see the body of knowledge of generic management and organisation science reflected in their work. The quite comprehensive textbook on management of public organisations of Hal Rainey (1992) uses a chapter contents that closely reflects that of business management textbooks on management and organisation. Per topic, Rainey presents an almost complete overview of what research has been done and published about the public sector. A marked difference with the strategic and excellent public management approach is that in this stream, the generic body of knowledge is clearly known and used as a starting point. An additional difference is that it does not use case studies and is aimed not only at best practices of top executives in the public sector, but it is more in line with normal organisational sociology and conducts empirical research according to current social scientific methodology.

Public Management at Business Schools

The study of public management in American public administration science is not the monopoly of the former public policy schools. The increasing need for public management within the American public sector in not explained by the decreasing need for policy analysts, but rather by the necessity to cut expenditures, to improve effectiveness and efficiency and as a consequence to adopt a more businesslike management. Effectiveness and efficiency, productivity, value for money and production quality are all terms primarily associated with business management. The eighties also exhibit the foundation of separate graduate programmes of public management at business schools such as Stanford and elsewhere. Public management courses originate at generic management programmes like the School of Organisation and Management at Yale, the Sloan School at MIT and elsewhere where private and public management are studied together. Although eminent scholars of organisation and decision making, such as the Stanford-based Jim March (1988), have undoubtedly made great contributions to the field of public administration, generic management and organisation science is nevertheless dominated by a one-sided attention for the private business organisations.

6.   Paradox of American Public Administration

Dominant Worldwide but Highly Unique

A survey of the development of administrative sciences in Europe (Kickert and Stillman, 1996) clearly shows that the American policy and administrative sciences take a dominant position in the professional field. The orientation of Dutch, German, British and Scandinavian PA scholars on the Northern American study of Public Administration is striking. This is not surprising because at the time when the European policy and administrative sciences were resurrecting in the post-war welfare states of the sixties and seventies, this field was more than half a century old in the United States. The sheer quantity of the accumulated body of knowledge in the United States and the eminent quality of its many renowned PA scholars implied that the American field became the 'wise big brother' to admire.

Contrary to the natural sciences where the researcher's nationality does not matter, the administrative sciences do, of course, depend upon the nation's characteristics, for the state, government and public administration are the very object of study and this object differs considerably between countries. The administrative sciences are logically dependent upon their object. As stated in the introduction, it is not possible to derive a universally valid general theory of public administration which holds true anywhere and anytime.

In a number of respects which are highly relevant from an administrative science point of view, the United States of America is exceptionally unique, to put it mildly. The concept of nation state does not exist there, the government, particularly central government, is viewed with the greatest suspicion, even in the American constitution which created the checks and balances in order to prevent government from usurping too much power. In public opinion polls, politicians score about as high as the mafia. Bureaucrat bashing is a most popular sport in the States. In view of the dominant culture of utilitarian individualism, American citizens primarily behave like individually calculating consumers of goods and services, no matter whether these are provided by private commercial firms or by public agencies.

The conclusion seems legitimate that one should be extremely careful and cautious in the proclamation of American Public Administration and Public Management elsewhere in the world. States, governments and administrations differ too much between the United States and Europe and within Europe itself, to be able to simply imitate and transpose the American theories of public management onto the various European public sectors.

Types of States and Administrations in Europe

Usually, the European states and administrations are distinguished according to a typology which consists of three main types. First the Napoleonic type of states, with the post-revolutionary France as the main example. Spain and Italy are typically considered to belong to this type and so does Belgium. Second, the Germanic type with its Prussian and Habsburg roots, in which post-war Germany and Austria can be placed. Third, the Anglo-Saxon type with England as the main example. The smaller Northern European states such as the Netherlands and the Scandinavian countries are usually considered a mixed form of the Anglo-Saxon and Germanic types of state.

One might, however, follow a different line of argument in categorising European states. The large European states like France, Britain and Germany are all highly unique and highly dissimilar. There are many more small states in Europe than the few large ones and most of the smaller continental European nations are highly similar in three not totally irrelevant respects:

- *State and politics*. They all have a consociationalist type of consensus democracy (Lijphart, 1984). Contrary to the majoritarian Anglo-American two-party system of democracy, they have a multi-party system with proportional elections where governments consist of coalitions between more parties. The search for compromises and consensus is a main ingredient of their political culture. The search for consensus in the post-war *Grosse Koalition* in Austria, in the *Proporz* system of division of seats in government in Switzerland, in the coalition governments between the Flemish Christian-democrats and Wallonian socialists in Belgium, in the varying coalitions between the social-democrats, Christian-democrats and conservative liberals in The Netherlands, in the multi-party coalition cabinets in Denmark and Norway which sometimes do not even have a parliamentary majority, these forms of consociationalism explain the political stability in these societies.
- *State–society relations*. They all have a neo-corporatist type of democracy. Contrary to the American pluralist type of democracy, in a neo-corporatist type of democracy interest representation takes place by a few well-organised groups which are recognised by the state and to which many public tasks and state authority has been delegated (Williamson, 1990). Sweden has a social-democrat type of corporatism, The Netherlands a typically confessional type, Belgium a linguistic, regional and confessional type, Austria again another type, but all are variations of the same basic type of neo-corporatism.
- *Society*. They all have socio-political cleavages and fragmented political and social subcultures. Austria has its Christian and socialist *Lager*. Switzerland has its regional and linguistic fragmentation into various *Kantons*. Belgium has the linguistic cleavage between Flanders and Wallonia and the political cleavage between socialists and Christians. The Netherlands has a 'pillarisation' as a consequence of its confessional history into protestant, catholic, socialist and liberal-neutral pillars. The theory of consociationalism, later renamed consensus democracy (Lijphart, 1984) originated from the question of how these countries with their fragmented societies and hence potentially unstable political democracies could nevertheless end up to be highly stable politically.

The whole range of countries from the far North to the middle of continental Europe – Finland, Sweden, Norway, Denmark, The Netherlands, Belgium, Switzerland, Austria – all have these three characteristics in common, albeit in more or less degrees and in different variations. The Netherlands – in population and economy the largest of the small European countries – is an extremely clear and highly institutionalised example of the three characteristics.

7.   Scientific Development of Public Management in Europe

France

In France government and administration are highly dominated by the legalistic perspective of constitutional and administrative law, so public administration is mainly inhabited by lawyers. France is the cradle of a separate state and administrative law (Koopmans, 1978). The resurrection in the early sixties of a separate study of public administration in France (Chevallier, 1996) was thus primarily the formation of an identity *vis-à-vis* administrative law. In addition to the enormous influence of organisational sociologists such as Crozier and Friedberg on the development of a French *science administrative*, the concept of *management public* played a large role.

   In the 1960s, the *Institut de Management Public* was created in Paris. Under the influence of the American (business administration) management and organisation sciences, concepts such as *gestion publique* and *management public* were introduced to government as an approach differing from the juridical. Although the influence of businesslike thinking is undeniable, in France these concepts mean more than only effectiveness, efficiency, productivity, and so on. In the French scientific body of knowledge on *management public* (Laufer and Burlaud, 1980; Santo and Verrier, 1993), broader concepts such as public governance and the legitimacy of the state play a major role, concepts that one will not find in the usual American literature on management. One should not forget that the French government in the 1960s and 1970s experienced a period of growth of the welfare state. The current context of state retreat, public sector retrenchments, budget cuts and the necessity to 'work better and cost less' that has led to the recent rise of management thinking in the public sector, was lacking in France of 20 years ago. Business-economic thinking in terms of effectiveness and efficiency did not dominate.

Germany

Legalistic thinking also dominates within German government. Following France, Germany has a written constitution and an elaborate system of administrative law. Germany has a strong legal tradition of *Rechtsstaat*, *Oeffentliche Verwaltung*, and *Beamtentum*. In Germany too, the resurrection of a separate study of administration after the Second World War (Seibel, 1996) heralded a separation from administrative law. Although some influence of American business management and organisation theory could be seen in Germany in the 1970s, leading to publications about

Management im Oeffentliche Verwaltung, the heyday of management thinking in German administration dates from the early 1990s. The large scale reforms of *Lokale Verwaltung* led to the *Neues Steuerungsmodell* (Reichard, 1994) that, in brief, is a corporate concern-division model and a typical business-economic approach. This last fact is explicitly clear in Budäus' recent book about public management (1994). Here, the scientific angle of public management is based on the micro-economics of the public sector. The conceptual frame of reference of a public management derived in Budäus (1994, p. 49) consists of concepts such as planning, organisation, leadership, personnel, and control – highly similar to POSDCORB – and is closely related to the early 20th century American approach to management.

Great Britain

There is no lack of overviews and analyses of the modern trend of new public management in British government (Hood, 1991; Pollitt, 1994). Although the term 'management' is very American, the term 'new public management' is a British invention. Administrative reforms in Great Britain almost appear to be the prototypical example of the main characteristics of such a new public management. A science of public management seems however hardly developed in Great Britain. There is little interest for public management at British universities. After all, the study of public administration in Great Britain is mostly embedded in political science. In this branch of science, there is already minimal respect for the art and craft of public administration and certainly no attention and appreciation for the nuts and bolts of practical management and administration. Interest for public management has to be found in the circles of the 'new universities', the former polytechnics (Lawton and Rose, 1991; McKevitt and Lawton, 1994). These are, however, more practice oriented than science oriented.

The Netherlands

Previously, The Netherlands had a strong juridical tradition in government. The Netherlands fits the continental European tradition of constitutional and administrative law. The Netherlands also has a Council of State in which government action is put to the test according to administrative law. The post-war rise and growth of public administration was a separation from administrative law. The rise of administrative sciences in The Netherlands (Kickert and Van Vught, 1995) was related to the post-war rise and expansion of the welfare state. The enormous increase in public tasks implied that government became actively involved in sectoral policy making. Government was in need of new instruments in addition to the usual legislation and regulation, such as budgeting and planning. The welfare state was in need of further scientific support for the rationalisation of its policy making. Hence, the rise of the Public Policy Sciences (Kickert, 1996).

In many fields welfare arrangements had to be built, extended and maintained, preferably by means of integrated planning. The seventies were the glory days of integral policy planning. The oil crisis put an end to the unshakable belief in government planning and control. The planning euphoria of the 1970s was replaced by a planning aversion in the 1980s. In The Netherlands, the economic crisis and budget deficits led to a fundamental debate about the future restricted steering role of government and about the limitations of government. Government was no longer considered capable of unilaterally steering society. Government was only one of the co-directing actors in a complex of various social actors. Thus, emphasis was placed upon the limitations of planning and governance. At the end of the eighties, Dutch PA research became less oriented on studying the limitations, boundaries and failures of government, and increasingly oriented on exploring the possibilities of new forms of government steering within the recognised limits of complexity. Insight into the complexity of interorganisational policy networks was considered a possibility for improving government steering. The research on public governance in a state of complexity forms a context for the Dutch study of public management.

In The Netherlands sporadic attempts were made to develop a theory of managing public organisations (Kooiman and Eliassen, 1987). Dutch scholars interested in public management and organisation all emphasise the importance of public governance in complexity (Bekke, 1993; Kooiman, 1993; Kickert, 1994b).

8.   An Alternative to Anglo-American 'Managerialism'

Public management is broader than the businesslike interpretation of management and the internal running of the government's business. Public management is more than business management, client orientation and market competition. Public management is not merely a matter of effectiveness and efficiency, but it is also a matter of legality and legitimacy and of other value patterns than strictly businesslike patterns. Public management is not only internal but also and primarily external management in a complex socio-political context (Kickert, 1994a, 1994b).

Rechtsstaat, *Democracy and Public Values*

In the public sector, the management of organisations occurs within the context of *Rechtsstaat* and political democracy. The 'environment' of public management consists of the societal, political, juridical and economic context of state and administration. The principles of democracy and legality should be the starting points of any consideration of public organisations. The criteria which a democratic nation should meet, such as democracy, efficiency and professionalism (Dahl, 1970), can well be mutually conflicting. For a large degree of democracy, a sacrifice in the degree of rationality and efficiency must be made. A public organisation is not a commercial business firm. Without denying whatsoever the great importance of effectiveness and efficiency in the public sector, other norms and values play a role as well; values such as liberty, legality, legitimacy, equity and social justice.

For instance, Hood (1991) distinguished three different value patterns. In the first pattern, government is supposed to be lean and purposeful. Effectiveness and efficiency, parsimony and performance orientation play the main roles. In the second, honesty and fairness are the central values. In government, social justice, equality, legitimacy and proper discharge of duties are central principles. In the third pattern, robustness and resilience dominate. Government must be reliable, robust, adaptive, secure and confident and must be able to survive catastrophes.

Harmon and Mayer (1986) also distinguish other norms and value patterns for government. The first pattern consists of efficiency and effectiveness concerning the functioning of government itself and the production and distribution of goods and services. The second pattern includes rights and the adequacy of the governmental process concerning the relation between government and citizens. The third pattern consists of representation and power checks concerning public scrutiny of the functioning of government. These last values are also reflected in the twelve commandments of the 'ethical code' which the American Association for Public Administration (ASPA) drew up on the basis of basic notions of honesty, justice and equality.

Public Governance

In public management, interaction with the socio-political environment plays an important role. It is not primarily an internal organisational matter, but a complex and externally oriented activity. Public management is the governance of complex networks, consisting of many different actors like parts of national, regional and local government; political and societal groups; pressure, action and interest groups; societal institutions, private and business organisations. The management of such public networks is a form of external government 'steering', steering having a broader meaning than strict administrative control but being broadly defined as 'directed influencing'. Public governance is the directed influencing of societal processes in a complex network of many other co-directing actors. These actors have different and sometimes conflicting objectives and interests. Government is not the single dominating actor which can unilaterally impose its will.

Context, Complexity and Governance

In the governance of complex public sector networks three aspects are of major importance. The *context*, defined as the environment, the *complexity*, defined as the number and variety of the system's elements and the relations between the system elements and *governance*, defined as directed influencing. The specific context of the public sector implies a high degree of complexity – a network of many different actors – and this complexity implicates a different form of governance, neither central, nor top-down. Context, complexity and governance are interrelated in a certain line of argument.

- *Context.* Public management cannot be isolated from the societal and political context, neither generally, from the context of political democracy and legal state, nor specifically, from the context of the specific policy sectors with their diversity of political, social, public and private actors. Management and organisation within the public sector cannot be isolated from this context. An outside-in approach is to be followed.
- *Complexity.* The specific context of administration, the specific policy sector, leads to the second aspect, the complexity. Public management is the governance in complex networks in a specific societal sector. The participants in such a network are, besides manifold government (which even at the national level is no monolith but often consists of many divisions, directorates and departments apart from the various regional and local governments), the multitude of advisory and consultative bodies in typically consociational democracies and the typically neo-corporatist intermediate layer between state and society. Besides the formal official political actors such as parliamentary committees and party representatives, a great number of other participants can be involved. In addition to this impressive list of various actors in the public domain, actors from the private sector also play a part in many policy processes such as firms, project-developers, building-contractors, and so on. A large number of actors with large differences and a multitude of differing relationships, means high complexity. A theory on public management will have to deal with this kind of complexity.
- *Governance.* In a network of many different actors, with different and often conflicting goals and interests and with diverging power positions, no single dominant actor exists. Such complexity means negotiating, pushing and pulling, giving and taking and implies a different form of governance than mono-centric, mono-rational, hierarchical top-down control by an omnipotent government (Hanf and Scharpf, 1978). On the other hand, public governance in complexity is not identical to the extreme opposite of hierarchy, that is, total autonomy of actors. Networks are characterised by the many dependencies and relationships which exist among the actors. The economic model of the market with free competition, in which buyers and sellers are autonomous and only the 'invisible hand' of the price mechanism functions, or the mathematical model of game theory in which all participants are making decisions in a completely independent way, are not applicable in public policy networks.

Network Governance Between Hierarchy and Autonomy

The distinction between a multi-actor network and completely autonomous actors is not without meaning. It means that actors in a network are not entirely independent. It also means that, although actors are not hierarchically sub- or superordinate, they are not completely equivalent. Government will always maintain a different position than other societal public and private actors. Government cannot dominate and unilaterally dictate in a hierarchical manner, but at the same time, it is not a complete horizontal equivalent to all other actors. This is not a normative view, but an empirical observation. The question here is not whether government should play a stronger steering role. Such a normative model of *harder* government steering, for instance in the complex environmental policy area, is not inconceivable. It would however imply a return to some form of hierarchical top-down steering by government. While the denial of the possibility of such a role was the very starting point of the network approach. It is not a normative statement but an empirical observation that the role of government in complex networks is special and unlike the roles of the many other actors. This does not imply a return to top-down control. It does imply that full horizontality and total autonomy of actors is an unrealistic model of a public sector network.

The concept of network governance lies somewhere in the grey space between both extremes of hierarchy and market (Thompson *et al.*, 1991; Koppenjan *et al.*, 1993; Kickert *et al.*, 1997).

9.   Conclusion and Discussion

A closer look at the Anglo-American trend of public management which seems to spread over the entire Western world, has revealed that its roots lie in the North American culture of business management. We have tried to argue that the transposition of businesslike management, customer-orientedness and market competition onto the public sector might well be dubious. Actually the argument amounts to two main lines of reasoning.

The first main counter-argument against transposing or imitating business management is the fundamental difference between the private and the public sector, implying that private and public management can only be 'alike in unimportant aspects' (Allison, 1980). The fundamental differences are apparent both in their environments, the relations between organisations and environment and in their organisational characteristics, to mention a few dimensions that are considered crucial in generic management theory.

The second counter-argument was that one should be extremely cautious in the transposition of American public management methods onto other parts of the world, especially onto continental Western Europe. States, societies, politics, governments and administrations differ too much between the United States and

Europe and within Europe itself, to be able to simply imitate and transpose the American theories and methods of public management onto the various European administrations.

The alternative to the Anglo-American public management, presented at the end of the American and European *tour d'horizon*, should be nuanced, however. One should avoid constructing unnecessary gaps between scientific communities. For the sake of argument the distinction between American and European administrations and the consequent differences in the respective sciences of administration, has been emphasised. Differences should not prevent scientists from learning from each other. Likewise it is not in the least the intention to create an unnecessary gap between the sciences of business and public administration. Both scientific areas can learn a lot from each other and are actually doing so. The main and simple reason for some nuances and modesty is that it will have become clear that we are not yet able to offer a sufficiently adequate alternative. Only a rough and sketchy outline, a conceptual exploration of a theory of management – preferably called governance – that is specific for the public sector, has been offered here. The alternative to 'managerialism' is not as elaborate, well developed and practically applicable as the many readily available managerial methods and techniques.

However, we have shown that from a historical and international comparative point of view, the fact that Western governments are nowadays urged to adopt a businesslike management style deserves some nuancing too.

References

Allison, G.T., 1980. 'Public and private management: are they fundamentally alike in all unimportant aspects?'. *OPM document*, vol. 127(51)1, pp. 27–38.

Barzelay, M., 1992. *Breaking through bureaucracy*. University of California Press, Berkeley.

Behn, R.D., 1991. *Leadership counts*. Harvard University Press, Cambridge.

Bekke, A.J.G.M., 1993. *De betrouwbare bureaucratie*. Samsom H.D. Tjeenk Willink, Alphen aan den Rijn.

Bellah, R.N. *et al.*, 1987. *Habits of the heart: individualism and commitment in American life*. University of California Press, Berkeley.

Bozeman, B. (ed.), 1993. *Public Management: the state of the art*. Jossey Bass, San Francisco.

Budäus, D., 1994. *Public Management*. Edition Sigma, Berlin (in German).

Chevallier, J., 1996. 'Public administration in etatist France'. *Public Administration Review*, vol. 56(1).

Claisse, A., 1992. *Administrative modernisation in France*. Acquaparte.

Dahl, R.A., 1970. *After the revolution*. Yale University Press, New Haven.

Denhardt, R.B., 1993. *The pursuit of significance*. Wadsworth, Belmont.

Fayol, H., 1916. *Administration industrielle et generale: prevoyance, organisation, commandement, coordination, controle*. Dunod, Paris.

Gore, A., 1993. *Creating a government that works better and costs less*. Penguin Books U.S.A., Inc., New York.

Gulick, L. and L. Urwick, 1937. *Papers on the science of administration*. Institute of public administration, New York.

Hanf, K. and F. Scharpf, 1978. *Interorganisational policymaking*. Sage, London.

Harmon, M.H. and R.T. Mayer, 1986. *Organisation theory for public administration*. Scott Foresman, Glenview.

Heffron, F.A., 1989. *Organization theory and public organizations*. Prentice Hall, Englewood Cliffs.

Hood, C.C., 1991. 'A public management for all seasons'. *Public Administration*, vol. 69, pp. 3–9.

Kickert, W.J.M., 1994a. 'Public governance in the Netherlands: an alternative to Anglo-American managerialism'. Accepted for publication in *Public Administration*.

Kickert, W.J.M. (ed.), 1994b. *Veranderingen in management en organisatie bij de Nederlandse Rijksoverheid*. Samsom H.D. Tjeenk Willink, Alphen aan den Rijn.

Kickert W.J.M., 1996. 'Expansion and diversification of public administration in the post-war welfare state: the case of the Netherlands'. *Public Administration Review*, vol. 56(1).

Kickert, W.J.M., E.H. Klijn and J.F.M. Koppenjan (eds), 1997. *Managing complex networks: strategies for the public sector*. Sage, London.

Kickert, W.J.M. and R.J. Stillman (eds), 1996. 'Changing European states; changing public administration'. Symposium in *Public Administration Review*, vol. 56(1), pp. 65–105.

Kickert, W.J.M. and F.O.M. Verhaak, 1995. 'Autonomizing executive tasks in Dutch central government'. *International Review of Administrative Sciences*, vol. 61(4), pp. 531–49.

Kickert, W.J.M. and F.A. van Vught (eds), 1995. *Public policy and administration sciences in the Netherlands*. Prentice Hall, London.

Kooiman, J. (ed.), 1993. *Modern governance: new government-society interactions*. Sage, London.

Kooiman, J. and K.A. Eliassen (eds), 1987. *Managing public organisations*. Sage, London.

Koontz, H. (ed.), 1980. *Management: a book of readings*. McGraw-Hill, New York.

Koopmans, T., 1978. *Vergelijkend publiek recht*. Kluwer, Deventer.

Koppenjan, J.F.M., J.A. de Bruyn and W.J.M. Kickert (eds), 1993. *Netwerkmanagement in het openbaar bestuur*. VUGA, Den Haag.

Laufer, R. and A. Burlaud, 1980. *Management public, gestion et légitimité*. Dalloz, Paris.

Lawton, A. and A. Rose, 1991. *Organisation and management in the public sector*. Pitman, London.

Lijphart, A., 1984. *Democracies: patterns of majoritarian and consensus governments in twenty-one countries*. Yale University Press, New Haven.

Lynn, L.E., 1981. *Managing the public's business*. Basic Books, New York.

Lynn, L.E., 1987. *Managing public policy*. Little Brown, Boston.

Lynn, L.E., 1996. *Public management as art, science and profession*. Chatham House, N.J.

March, J.G., 1988. *Decisions and organisation*. Blackwell, Oxford.

McKevitt, D. and A. Lawton, 1994. *Public sector management*. Sage, London.

Newland, C.E., 1994. 'A field of strangers in search of a new discipline: separatism of public management research from public administration'. *Public Administration Review*, vol. 45(5), pp. 486–88.

OECD, 1990. *Public management developments survey*. OECD, Paris.

OECD, 1993. *Public management developments survey*. OECD, Paris.

OECD, 1995. *Governance in transition: public management reforms in OECD countries*. OECD, Paris.

Osborne, D and T. Gaebler, 1992. *Reinventing government*. Addison Wesley, Reading.

O'Toole, L.J., 1986. 'Policy recommendations for multi-actor implementation: an assessment of the field'. *Journal of Public Policy*, vol. 6(2), pp. 181–210.

Pollitt, C., 1990. *Managerialism and the public services: the Anglo-American experience.* Blackwell, Oxford.

Pressman, J.L. and A. Wildavsky, 1973. *Implementation.* University of California Press, Berkeley.

Rainey, H., 1992. *Understanding and managing public organisations.* Jossey Bass, San Francisco.

Reichard, C., 1994. *Umdenken im Rathaus.* Edition Sigma, Berlin.

Rouban, L., 1994. 'France in search of a new administrative order'. *International Political Science Review*, vol. 14(4), pp. 403–19.

Taylor, W.F., 1911. *The principles of scientific management.* Harper, New York.

Thompson, G.J. *et al.* (eds), 1991. *Markets, hierarchies and networks.* Sage, London.

Santo, V.M. and P.E. Verrier, 1993. *Le management publique.* Presses Universitaires de France, Paris.

Seibel, W., 1992. *Administrative modernisation in Germany.* Acquasparte.

Seibel, W., 1996. 'Administrative science as reform: German public administration'. *Public Administration Review*, vol. 56(1).

Williamson, P.J., 1990. *Corporatism in perspective.* Sage, London.

Wilson, W., 1887. 'The study of administration'. *Political Science Quarterly*, vol. 2, June 1887.

Wright, D.S., 1988. *Understanding intergovernmental relations.* Brooks Cole, Pacific Grove.

Wright, V., 1994. 'Reshaping the state: implications for public administration'. *Western European Politics*, vol. 17, pp. 102–34.

Part Two

**Management Reforms in Western
Europe: Successes, Nuances
and Failures**

CHAPTER FOUR

Reinventing Whitehall
1979–1995

R.A.W. Rhodes
University of Newcastle-upon-Tyne

1. Introduction

The past fifteen years were a permanent revolution for the British civil service. Its famed, perhaps notorious, ability to frustrate reform foundered on the energy and commitment of the longest serving government this century. The government did not go away by losing either an election or its enthusiasm for reform. It displayed remarkable perseverance and Margaret Thatcher made no secret of her disdain bordering on outright hostility towards the civil service.

This chapter explains why British Public Administration was 'reinvented', describes the major changes between 1979 and 1995, discusses problems posed by the changes and concludes with a general assessment. I do not provide a history of the past fifteen years. I identify and focus on key trends (for a full account see Rhodes, 1997).

2. Explaining the Changes

Wright (1994, pp. 108–10) identifies five types of administrative reform in Western Europe: continuous adjustment, responses to specific political crises, pragmatic structural change, reform as its own cause and comprehensive programmes. Although the British government is expert at inventing retrospective rationales for its administrative reforms, none the less the many and varied changes are linked by the consistent aims of pushing back the boundaries of the state and cutting public spending. So, as a starting-point, British administrative reform is distinct because it is comprehensive. Whether the aims were realised is a central theme of this chapter. The pressures for change in Britain were common to Western Europe (Wright, 1994, pp. 104–8). Six factors fuelled administrative reform:

- Economic depression and fiscal pressures leading to budget deficits.
- The New Right's ideological distrust of 'big government' and accompanying determination to redraw the boundaries of the state.
- Europeanisation which further increased regulation and introduced new administrative pressures (for example, regionalisation).
- Public disenchantment with government performance. Government does too much and whatever it does, it doesn't work.
- International management fashions, especially the new public management (NPM).
- Information technology which made it easier to introduce NPM.

But if these pressures are common, why was the pace of change in Britain greater than elsewhere in Western Europe? Three factors were of overriding importance. First, Margaret Thatcher pushed through reform of the civil service. The phrase 'political will' is commonly used to explain the government's determination. 'Strong, directive and above all persistent, executive leadership' is longer but more accurate.

Second, there are few constitutional constraints on that leadership, especially when the government has a majority in parliament. Parliamentary sovereignty means that once the government decides on a change, it can use its parliamentary majority to pass legislation; there are no constitutional impediments. Also, central administrative reform in Britain does not require a statute, only the exercise of Crown Prerogative, or executive powers.

Finally, the government evolved a clear ideological strategy to justify and 'sell' its various reform packages. It attacked big government and waste, used markets to create more individual choice and campaigned for the consumer. Under John Major, the rationale for reform became more elaborate. Osborne and Gaebler (1992) are the source of the phrase 'reinventing government' and they trumpet the era of entrepreneurial government. British government cites their work to justify its policies (Butler, 1993; Waldegrave, 1993).

Whatever the specific form of the rationale, one theme remains constant, to cut public spending. This imperative drove the search for management reform. Although a commonplace of the academic literature, it is worth stressing that administrative reform is always political. The Conservative government's determination to reform the civil service was rooted in the political decision to cut back government and its spending and to exert effective control over the administrative machine.

3.   Key Trends, 1979–1995

The British government's programme can be broken down into six broad parts: introducing the minimalist state, reasserting political authority, extending regulation and audit, reforming the structure, reforming public sector management and transforming the culture.

The Minimalist State

The government's policies on public employment and privatisation show its determination to roll back the boundaries of the state.

The government's objective of cutting public spending proved difficult to realise. It averaged about 43.5 percent of GDP throughout the 1980s, although there was a small fall in the early 1990s. There was a small but steady decline in total public employment between 1979 and 1991. There was a larger decline in the size of the civil service. Its numbers fell from 732,000 in 1979 to 533,350 at 1 April 1994, a fall of some 27 percent, with further cuts planned to under 500,000 (Cm 2627, 1994, p. 3). Part of the fall stems from reclassification, not cuts, but the trend is clearly downwards. Recent senior management reviews promise large cuts, for example, 26 percent in the Treasury, 35 percent in the Department for Education and Employment and 29 percent in the Department of the Environment.

Privatisation is one of the government's success stories. Since 1979, 50 percent of the public sector, with some 650,000 employees, returned to the private sector. The nationalised industries accounted for 9 percent of GDP in 1979. By 1991, it was under 5 percent and still falling, with railway privatisation in the offing.

Underlying all these changes was the government's critical stance towards public intervention. In Margaret Thatcher's own words, the Conservative government rejected the 'centralising, managerial, bureaucratic, interventionist style of government'. Government had 'to get out of the business of telling people what their ambitions should be and how exactly to realise them'. 'Optimism about the beneficent effects of government intervention had largely disappeared'. Government had 'to put its faith in freedom and free markets, limited government and strong national defence'; in 'the creative capacity of enterprise' (Thatcher, 1993, pp. 6, 14, 92, 15 and 45–6). Intervention, centralisation and managerialism were prominent, even distinctive, characteristics of Margaret Thatcher's stay in office. The minimal state stayed both large and active.

Reasserting Political Authority

Britain has entered the era of the 'macho-minister'. The manipulative, scheming Sir Humphrey Appleby of television fame gave way to the 'can do' managerialist who did not substitute his or her policy goals for those of the minister but put the minister's policies into practice. Ministers knew what they wanted and were determined to prevail. There are several strands to the changes in the political control of the civil service.

First, the government curbed the civil service trade unions. In 1981, nine separate civil service unions went on strike in support of a pay claim. The government simply waited for the return to work. The unions claimed the government increased the original offer but the strike signalled the end of their influence. Civil service pay was based on comparability with the private sector. The Megaw Report (Cmnd

8590, 1982) recommended an end to such comparability for job evaluations which took account of evidence about the supply and retention of staff. The report took apart the existing pay system in which the Pay Research Unit, a body independent of government, decided a large block of public spending. Afterwards, the Treasury was able to set a cash limit which became the effective ceiling on public sector pay increases and pay was a matter for the market-place.

Second, fears about 'politicising' the civil service were regularly voiced. They arose initially in 1981 when Margaret Thatcher 'retired' the head and deputy head of the civil service, Sir Ian Bancroft and Sir John Herbercq. They surfaced again in 1985. Between 1979 and 1985, 43 permanent secretaries and 138 deputy secretaries left the service. The prime minister is consulted about all appointments to these grades. Thatcher's appointments led Hugo Young to describe the service as 'a thoroughly Thatcherised satrapy' (quoted in Hennessy, 1989, p. 631) and the Royal Institute of Public Administration to set up a working group to study politicising the civil service. It concluded the appointment process was 'more personalised', depending on 'catching the eye' of the Prime Minister (in a favourable or unfavourable manner)' but promotions were not 'based on the candidate's support for or commitment to particular ideologies or objectives' (RIPA, 1987, p. 43).

As time passed, it became more difficult to hold the sanguine view that it was 'personalisation not politicisation'. William Plowden (1994, pp. 100–9) argues that 'but-sayers' lose out in promotions and the government does not get the advice it needs. There has been a key change of emphasis from advising on policy formulation to advising on how policy could be implemented. These problems are compounded by Ministers not heeding advice and a rate of policy initiation which makes it impossible to give each initiative proper consideration. There has been no overt party politicisation of the higher civil service, but we have lost 'institutional scepticism' (Hugo Young cited in Plowden, 1994, p. 104).

Finally, politicisation affected vast numbers of bodies outside Whitehall. The government makes many appointments to organisations referred to (wrongly) as quangos and more evocatively described as 'the new magistracy' (Stewart, 1993, p. 5). Weir and Hall (1994) identify 5521 quangos to which ministers make some 70,000 appointments and are responsible for functions previously carried out by civil servants or elected local authorities (for example, the Funding Agency for Schools). In total, these bodies spend some £52 billion of public money. In the home of the incorruptible public servant, patronage is rife and has grown enormously over the past decade.

Extending Regulation and Audit

As the boundaries of the state were redrawn in the 1980s, the British state sought to strengthen its capacity to regulate and audit institutions, their policies and implementation of those policies. The government substituted regulation for ownership and so multiplied the watchdogs of the new private sector monopolies. The 'audit explosion' refers to all forms of management and financial audit and evaluation with related quality assurance mechanisms and 'a distinct mentality of administrative control' which displaces trust and focuses on quantified, external, ex-post, expert forms of control (Power, 1994, pp. 8–9).

Between 1984 and 1990, the government created ten new regulatory agencies and five self-regulatory organisations besides such established agencies as the Monopolies and Mergers Commission, the Independent Broadcasting Authority and the Civil Aviation Authority. The new agencies included: the Broadcasting Standards Council with a budget of £0.4 million and a staff of 14; the Office of Telecommunications (Oftel) with a budget of £4.5 million and a staff of 120; and the National River Authority with a budget of £30 million and a staff of 6,500. But having created the regulatory state, the government did not know what to do with it. Wright (1993, pp. 255–8) identifies several specific problems. He argues that fragmenting regulation between an ever-growing number of agencies breeds: competition between regulators, conflict between social and economic objectives, diminished accountability, spill-over effects between agencies and a mismatch between national and international systems of regulation.

The regulatory state also monitors performance, using audit and evaluation in their various guises. Four trends are worth noting in this brief survey. Firstly, 'managerialism' changed existing inspectorates in British government, replacing 'professional values and needs led policies' with 'rationalistic management, designed to achieve economy and efficiency' (Henkel, 1991, p. 230). Secondly, management consultants played a prominent part in evaluating and advising government at the expense of internal evaluation by departments. The Efficiency Unit estimates that government spending on management consultants grew fourfold between 1985 and 1990, stabilised in the early 1990s and would grow by 4 percent in real terms in 1993/4 (Efficiency Unit, 1994, pp. 46–7). Thirdly, the state audit bodies were revamped and there was an explosion of audits in many different fields: 'medicine, science, education, technology, environment, intellectual property to name but a few' (Power, 1994, p. 47). The National Audit Act, 1984 created the National Audit Office responsible for auditing central government departments but with its terms of reference extended to include the '3Es'. The Local Government Finance Act 1982 created the Audit Commission to appoint the auditors of local authorities. Its terms of reference also extend beyond financial probity to encompass value for money and the '3Es' of economy, efficiency and effectiveness. Finally, performance indicators have become commonplace. This fashion started out as a way of improving managerial efficiency but spread to include making services transparent to their consumers, for example, they are at the heart of Citizen's Charters (see below p. 51).

The strict financial climate saw the Treasury become more powerful. The government introduced several changes in budgeting and financial management to strengthen its control of total spending. Fiscal stringency made discretionary financial authority meaningless (Campbell and Wilson, 1995, pp. 235–41). Financial controls paralleled management change. All departments are now introducing accrual accounting (Cm 2626, 1994) which, in the words of one agency chief executive 'is likely to create enormous upheaval for little benefit' (Price Waterhouse, 1994, p. 16).

Reforming the Structure

The government always used structural reform to support its management changes but it did not become a distinguishing feature of the management changes until the 1990s, with mass agencification of central departments.

The central idea of 'Next Steps' is agencification or creating semi-autonomous agencies responsible for operational management. The key notion is distance from the central department, so there is freedom to manage (Davies and Willman, 1991, p. 16). It is the classic doctrine in public administration of separating policy from administration. By April 1994, there were 97 agencies employing 64 percent of the civil service (Cm 2627, 1994, p. 13). Each agency has a framework document which sets out its objectives and performance targets. The chief executive of the agency is not a permanent civil servant but on contract and most are appointed in an open competition. He or she is personally responsible to the minister for the agency's performance, but the minister remains accountable to parliament for policy. Agencies now cover a diverse group of organisations and increasingly they are developing their own ways of working.

Before setting up an agency four questions must be answered:

- Does the job need to be done at all (for example, cuts)?
- Does the government have to be responsible for it (for example, privatisation)?
- Does the government have to carry out the task itself (for example, market testing)?
- Is the organisation properly structured and focused on the job to be done (for example, agencification)?

Referred to as the 'Prior Options' test, these questions also mean that an existing agency can still be privatised (Cm 2627, p. 15; Cabinet Office, 1994, pp. 12–3) because agencies are reviewed every five years. Initially, agencies were an alternative to privatisation, not a step on the way (Margaret Thatcher's written answer in HC Deb. 24 October 1988, col. 14).

In effect, there are now two civil services: in the policy making core department and in the executive agencies (Cabinet Office, 1994, p. 7; TCSC, 1993, HC 390-I, pp. viii–ix). The British civil service was never unified, it always had federal qualities, but the distinction between policy and implementation becomes ever sharper and careers more distinct. Indeed, the Trosa Report commented that 'it was not sensible to continue with two classes of people' and recommended closing the 'cultural gap' between agencies and sponsoring departments.

There is some evidence the agencies are a success. Bill Jenkins (1993, pp. 92–3) argues Next Steps has 'succeeded as a management innovation', altering organisational cultures and delivering 'real improvements in service delivery'. In a similar vein, Ian Colville and his colleagues (1993, p. 562) suggest 'outsiders ... underestimate the amount of change taking place, its effects ... took time to work through.' Patricia Greer's (1994, p. 133) study of agencies in social security concludes existing data has shortcomings but the outcome is promising, for example, agencies achieve most of their targets.

Reforming Public Sector Management

Waste was an anathema to the Thatcher government and stories abound about public sector profligacy, for example, experimental rats bred at £30 each when available commercially at £2. Such stories are often amusing but they are also important because they helped to fuel the drive to reform public management, commonly referred to as the 'New Public Management' (NPM). In Britain, NPM has two divergent strands: managerialism and the new institutional economics.

Managerialism refers to introducing private sector management in the public sector. It stresses: hands-on, professional management, explicit standards and measures of performance, managing by results, value for money and more recently closeness to the customer. It is often a synonym for the '3Es'. The new institutional economics refers to introducing incentive structures (such as market competition) into public service provision. It stresses disaggregating bureaucracies, greater competition through contracting-out and quasi-markets and consumer choice. Before 1988, managerialism was the dominant strand in Britain. After 1988, the ideas of the new institutional economics became a major source of innovation and of problems for managerial reforms. The different strands pull in different directions and are a source of conflict in British administrative reform.

Managerialism: Scrutinies to FMI

In May 1979, Margaret Thatcher appointed Sir Derek Rayner, managing director of Marks and Spencer to spearhead a drive for increased efficiency. The purposes of his efficiency scrutinies were to examine specific policies, activities or functions to make savings. Estimates of the savings vary but Hennessy (1989, p. 598) suggests that, by December 1982 when Rayner returned to Marks and Spencer, 130 scrutinies saved £170 million and 16,000 jobs a year and, by 1988, some 300 scrutinies saved over £1 billion.

The scrutinies mutated into the Financial Management Initiative (FMI) via the Treasury and its preference for improved financial delegation and financial control over management information. Launched in May 1982, FMI required departments to set clear objectives, measure performance against those objectives and critically scrutinise costs. Andrew Gray and his colleagues (1991, pp. 56–8) conclude that

FMI institutionalised cost awareness in the civil service but its implementation was patchy because departments' tasks and contexts vary. Middle and lower management gave the new system only qualified support because they have to marry their new freedom to manage with centralised Treasury control. For its successful implementation, FMI needed strong political support but, in the forceful language of Sir Frank Cooper (former permanent secretary, Ministry of Defence): 'I regard the minister-as-manager as nonsense. Ministers are not interested. It's not part of the ministerial stock-in-trade' (quoted in Hennessy, 1989, p. 609). In short, there was some change, but not a lot and it depended on whether FMI was a useful means to political ends. The Efficiency Unit's (1988) report on the achievements of FMI, colloquially known as 'Next Steps', confirmed this pessimistic assessment. The report concluded the managerial revolution was only skin-deep and recommended introducing agencies to carry out the executive functions of government and bring about real financial and managerial decentralisation (for a more detailed assessment: Zifcak, 1994; Gray *et al.*, 1991). So, we enter the era of the new institutional economics.

The New Institutional Economics

The second wave of management reform was more radical. It emphasised not only bureaucratic disaggregation (or agencification) but also competition and using market mechanisms (most notably, the purchaser–provider split and market testing) and improving the quality of services (especially through citizen's charters and responsiveness to the consumers).

The White Paper on *Competing for Quality* (Cm 1730, 1991) introduced 'market testing or competition with outside suppliers to determine who is best able to provide a particular service on the basis of best long-term value for money'. In the early stages, market testing involves identifying blocks of work in agencies to put out to competitive tender. It is a way of comparing the costs of direct service provision by the agency with cost of provision by the private sectors. The White Paper set an ambitious target to review activities worth £1.5 billion in eighteen months ending in September 1993 and failed to meet it (for a detailed discussion: Oughton, 1994; TCSC, 1994, Vol. II, pp. 159–64 and paras 1942–87). More important, market testing conflicted with agencification, or in other words the new institutional economics conflicted with managerialism. Agency chief executives see it as the main problem with market testing as an end in itself, ignoring the future of the agencies (Cabinet Office, 1994, p. 12). Campbell and Wilson (1995, p. 243) report their respondents saw market testing as a 'betrayal of trust'. Staff now feel uncertain, threatened and unrewarded (Price Waterhouse, 1994, p. 3). The Treasury and Civil Service Committee (TCSC, Vol. I, 1994, para. 195) concluded the market testing programme 'had not been conducted effectively by the Government' and needed 'a reduction in the level of central oversight'. Above all, it reasserts central control, especially Treasury control. *Competing for Quality* was a Treasury document and Jordan (1994, p. 32) concludes: 'If there is a turf battle going on between defenders of the agency approach and market testers, the tide of the battle appears in favour of the latter.'

The White Paper on *The Citizen's Charter* (Cm 1599, 1991) was prime minister John Major's 'Big Idea'. The key objectives were to improve the quality of public services and provide better value for money. The Citizen's Charter contains six principles: published explicit standards, full and accurate information about running services, choice for the users of services, courteous and helpful service, effective remedies and efficient and economical delivery of services, many of which have been revised with higher standards (Cm 2540, 1994). Sir Robin Butler (1993, p. 402) describes the Citizen's Charter as 'the culmination of the movement to output measurement'. Consumer interests now dominate producer interests: 'people power'. It is a little early for such an assessment. Christopher Pollitt (1993, p. 187) is nearer the mark when he concludes that 'it is not so much a charter for citizen empowerment as managerialism with a human face.'

Managerialism gave us '3Es'. The new institutional economics provides the intellectual rationale for a new unholy trinity: agencies, contracts and charters. Added together, they make a dramatic agenda for change in the British administrative landscape, although agencification and market testing pull in different directions.

Transforming the Culture

Management by objectives and performance measurement were the means to realise the '3Es'. Civil servants are now expected to be managers. However, the culture of Whitehall stresses policy advice, a 'safe pair of hands' and loyalty to one's department. It downgrades management, treating it as an executive process separate from policy making. The managerialist reforms of the 1980s did not challenge this culture because they too were based on this 'impoverished concept of management' (Metcalfe and Richards, 1987, pp. 16–17). Although reform of the civil service between 1979 and 1988 was the heyday of managerialism, introducing private sector management skills remains an important part of the government's programme of reform. But there is an important shift of emphasis. Changing the culture of Whitehall has become the rallying cry for those who favour lasting reform – in the rhetoric of the day, the search is on for entrepreneurial government – and there are several challenges to the 'career' civil service.

Open competition is no longer restricted to a few posts but covers all the senior civil service. Appointments to the post of chief executive are advertised and open to private sector applicants. With the creation of the Recruitment and Assessment Services Agency and the reduced responsibilities of the Civil Service Commission, departments are now responsible for 95 percent of recruitment and subject only to 'light-handed' monitoring. The White Paper, *The Civil Service. Continuity and Change* (Cm 2627, 1994) opens jobs in the senior civil service to competition (see also Efficiency Unit, 1993). From 1 April 1996, senior civil servants (Grade 5 and above) will be part of the Senior Civil Service, with written employment contracts. The most senior appointments still require prime ministerial approval and an outside appointment will have to satisfy the Civil Service Commissioners. The membership of the Senior Appointments Selection Committee now includes one outsider and will include a woman. The key question now concerns the extent of open competition, the number of outside appointments and the effect of such outsiders on the civil service ethos. However, the first steps have been taken to opening the senior civil service and the debate about the future role of the 'mandarinate' gathers pace.

Kemp (1994, pp. 595–7) argues for: a cut in numbers, abolition of the 'fast stream' method of recruiting top civil servants, making advice to the prime minister about senior appointments more open by, for example, giving select committees a role, greater conviction about open competition for top jobs and greater clarity about what senior people are supposed to do. The TCSC (1994, Vol. I, paras 210–11) called for an extension of the agency approach to policy work and for auditing such work. The Government response was cautious. It remained positive about applying Next Steps principles to policy work and it noted that departments already evaluate their policies. It made no proposals for change (Cm 2748, 1995, pp. 34–5).

4.   Problems

Undoubtedly, after 1988, the government's reforms have the potential for far-reaching change in the civil service. This section discusses the extent and effects of those changes under the headings of: fragmentation, steering, accountability and the '3Cs' of conduct, code of ethics and culture.

Fragmentation

The most obvious result of the new system is institutional fragmentation. Typically, services are now delivered through a combination of local government, special-purpose bodies, the voluntary sector and the private sector. Service delivery depends, therefore, on linking organisations. Policy implementation becomes more difficult because policy has to be negotiated with more and more organisations. Organisational interdependence is common and the government faces the increasingly difficult task of steering interorganisational networks. Fragmentation breeds independence. Agencies develop different cultures to the centre, leading to problems of communication and reluctance by agencies to accept central guidelines.

Steering

Bill Jenkins (1993, p. 94) argues the government did not strengthen strategic capacity with the other changes. Agencies work in a 'policy vacuum' and steering is 'through a system of crisis management and blame avoidance'. The core task for differentiated institutional systems is to develop the capacity for steering and consensus. Given that 'Next Steps' agencies will develop a near monopoly of expertise in their policy area, given that policy often emerges from many small decisions, it is conceivable the agency tail will wag the departmental dog. British central departments experiment with strategic planning to counter this erosion of central capability. Sir Robin Butler (1993, p. 404) echoed these sentiments when he expressed concern about individual Departments and their Agencies becoming unconnected to the overall public sector, 'with ... no real working mechanisms for policy coordination'.

The view from the agencies is different. They are less concerned about horizontal links between departments and more with their links to the core department. From the start, chief executives complained about central control and the lack of clarity over responsibility for decisions (Price Waterhouse, 1991). It remains unclear whether the sponsoring department imposes the framework agreement or it is a product of genuine negotiation. Both the Frazer and Trosa reports noted considerable frustration over detailed interference in management both from the sponsoring departments and central departments, especially the Treasury (Cabinet Office, 1991, p. 20 and 1994a, p. 29; TCSC, 1994, Vol. I, paras. 157–62). Agency chief executives still claim they have to be on their guard against departmental interference (Price Waterhouse, 1994, p. 8). The brute fact is that 'I am a civil servant and cannot say no' (chief executive cited in Cabinet Office 1994, p. 31). The sponsoring departments have not adapted to the new situation and still exercise too much detailed control over finance and personnel (Cabinet Office, 1994, pp. 32, 34 and 42).

Accountability

Fragmentation erodes accountability because sheer institutional complexity obscures who is accountable to whom for what. Special-purpose, nominated bodies have multiplied in place of central departments and elected local councils for the delivery of some services. Most important, the government confuses consumer responsiveness with political accountability. Responsive service delivery as envisaged by such innovations as *The Citizen's Charter* (Cm 1599, 1991) is welcome but it cannot replace political accountability because the consumer has no powers to hold a government agency to account. This accountability 'gap' became wider with the coming of agencies because the government introduced no new arrangements to preserve the constitutional convention of ministerial responsibility. William Waldegrave (1993, p. 20) tried to justify this inaction by drawing a distinction between 'responsibility, which can be delegated and accountability, which remains firmly with the minister'. On this view, agencies and the other reforms clarified responsibility but left 'the Minister properly accountable for the policies he settles'. In short, British government has undergone a significant decrease in political accountability. It is a major problem. It is not confined to agencies. And the damage is compounded by the government's refusal to recognise there is a problem. Most attention focuses on agencies and the constitutional convention of individual ministerial responsibility which states that ministers are accountable to parliament for all the actions of their department. To keep ministerial responsibility intact, the government distinguishes between policy and management. Responsibility (for management) can be delegated to agency chief executives. Accountability (for policy) remains with the minister. But this distinction hinges on clear definitions of both policy and management and of the respective roles and responsibilities of ministers, senior civil servants and chief executives. Such clarity does not exist and the Trosa Report found chief executives from the private sector worried about their 'precarious position' (Cabinet Office, 1994, p. 24).

The government argues the reforms introduce greater transparency in government without undermining the key constitutional principle of ministerial accountability (Cm. 2627, p. 16). The TCSC (1994, Vol. I, para. 132) rejected the government's distinction between responsibility and accountability, noting the division of responsibilities was often unclear. Other critics are more pungent rejecting the government's views as 'superficial and complacent' (Plowden, 1987, p. 127; see also Davies and Willman, 1991, pp. 24–32; and Stewart's, 1993 critique of Waldegrave, 1993). As Grant Jordan (1992, p. 13) points out 'There is a deliberate or accidental ambiguity between accountability to the Minister by the chief executive and accountability of the Minister to the House of Commons' (Greer, 1994, Ch. 6).

The ambiguity matters. In theory, chief executives are responsible for policy implementation but '80 percent ... claim to have a policy input – despite the "Next Steps" emphasis on their role of delivering a service rather than policy formulation' (Price Waterhouse, 1994, pp. 7–8). 'The chief executive of the Prison Service is the government's principal adviser on prisons policy' (Plowden, 1994, p. 128). The current arrangement allows the minister to take the credit when the policy goes well but to blame the chief executive when things go wrong; 'the separation of policy and management is advantageous to those on the policy side and disadvantageous to managers' (Davies and Willman, 1991, p. 34). There is no shortage of examples. The unpopularity of the government's policy of absent fathers paying child support is part of any explanation of Ros Hepplewhite's resignation as chief executive of the Child Support Agency. The Home Secretary, Michael Howard, sacked Derek Lewis, chief executive of the Prison Service, who complained bitterly that the Home Secretary had 'invented a new definition of the word *operational* which meant *difficult*' and sued for wrongful dismissal. There is no clear dividing line between policy and operations, undermining ministerial accountability to parliament by helping ministers avoid blame.

The '3Cs'

Managerialism and the '3Cs' are a challenge to the culture of Whitehall. The '3Cs' is a shorthand way of referring to the erosion of traditional civil service values. It refers to: conduct, code of ethics and culture.

With the spread of patronage and the government's lengthy stay in office, worries have grown about standards of *conduct*, also known as 'sleaze', in British government. Sexual and financial scandals involving ministers are great fun but perhaps less important than other forms of impropriety. Examples include: ministers misleading parliament, using civil servants for 'inappropriate' party political work, waste of public money and abuse of power (Public Accounts Committee, 1994). The cumulative effect has been 'a loss of mutual confidence and respect between Conservative ministers and many officials' and Plowden (1994, p. 139) doubts that an 'effective working relationship can be rebuilt without a change of government'.

So, interest in a *code of ethics* grew. The relationship between ministers and civil servants is written down, at least minimally. *Questions of Procedure for Ministers* (1992, p. 55) states that ministers 'have a duty' to listen to civil service advice. Sir Robert Armstrong's *The Duties and Responsibilities of Civil Servants in Relation to Ministers. Note by the Head of the Civil Service* (25 February 1985) restates the constitutional platitudes that: 'the duty of the individual civil servant is first and foremost to the Minister of the Crown who is in charge of the department in which he or she is serving'. As outlined by, for example, the Association of First Division Civil Servants (FDA) (TCSC, 1993, HC 390-II, pp. 43–4), the new code would protect civil servants from ministers. For example, it would require ministers to listen to advice from civil servants, protect the political neutrality of civil servants and provide for a Civil Service Ethics Tribunal. The TCSC (1994, paras 101–7 and pp. cxxvi–cxxvii) proposed such a code with an independent appeal to the Civil Service Commissioners (para. 108–12). The government responded promptly with a code (Cm 2748, 1995, pp. 5–6 and pp. 43–5) which reflected the Head of the Civil Service's view that existing codification would do, but agreed to the independent appeal procedure.

The civil service *culture* is a blend of values including honesty, loyalty, impartiality, propriety and a respect for intelligence with conservatism, scepticism, elitism and arrogance (Butler, 1992, p. 8; Plowden, 1994, pp. 21–3 and p. 74). Sir Robin Butler, Head of the Civil Service, stresses: the need to maintain a degree of cohesion across the service as a whole and to preserve a non-political civil service with a shared sense of the essential values and ethics that make our system work (Butler, 1993, p. 404). Managerialism, open competition, impropriety and macho-ministers add up to a dilution of this culture or ethos. The skills of the civil service have been downgraded for those of business management.

There is some evidence, not just opinion, on cultural change. The Oughton Report's (Efficiency Unit, 1993, p. 108) survey of civil servants reports there is 'a belief that the public service ethos is being eroded'. Wilson (1991, p. 335) reports only 16 percent of his sample of civil servants mentioning 'articulating long-term interests' among their sources of job satisfaction. On behalf of the FDA, MORI polled 1900 union members about work and change in the civil service (response rate 54 percent). The survey reported much dissatisfaction. More than 80 percent of respondents thought reform badly managed, undermining civil service unity, 85 percent wanted a code of ethics. (For full details of the survey see, *British Public Opinion*, August, 1995, pp. 3–4). Others are more sceptical about the erosion of the public service ethos, for example, Sir Peter Kemp doubts this revolution has reached the senior civil service (Kemp, 1994). Many commentators hedge their bets and suggest the jury is still out (Jenkins, 1993). Indisputably, opinion thrives on this topic.

5.   Assessing Change

For many commentators, managerialism and agencies have had a significant impact on the public service culture of the civil service but it is easy to exaggerate the degree to which British government has changed and now works along similar lines to private business. For example, Wright (1994, p. 123) argues the state, compared with the early 1980s is becoming: more defined, more diminished, more decremental, more divided, more disaggregated, more distant, more deregulated, more denation-alised, more defensive and demoralised and more disoriented, but then warns against exaggeration! Conversely, Sue Richards notes how much has not changed, itemising: 'fast stream' recruitment, ministerial accountability, the permanent sec-retary as sole accounting officer, the policy function, senior appointment proce-dures and the delegation of pay and conditions of work to agencies (TCSC, 1993, Vol. II, p. 278). It may be a cliché but it remains essential to distinguish carefully between the rhetoric and the reality of administrative reform.

At the heart of reinventing Whitehall is the agency experiment and at the heart of this experiment is the relationship between central departments and agencies. Any assessment must examine the core assumption underpinning agencies of 'distance', or separating policy and management. This reform could have three possible re-sults: independence, 'the twilight zone' and policy experiment.

First, 'distance' could characterise the relationship department and agency. Agen-cies would become independent operational units with the core departments focus-ing on their strategic role, on the framework for agency activities.

Second, William Robson's (1962, Ch. 6 and pp. xvi–xviii) discussion of public ownership identifies 'the twilight zone' between government power and manage-rial freedom in which ministers exercise private influence and reach 'informal understandings' as a key problem. One conclusion is we have been here before. 'Next Steps' simply reinvents the relationship between the sponsoring ministry and its nationalised industries. It never proved possible to identify a limit to ministerial influence or to draw a clear line between the responsibilities of the minister and the industry's Board. The relationship remained bedevilled by a fatal ambiguity.

For agencies this fate looms large. Core departments duplicate agency functions. Oversight remains detailed. Agency chief executives provide policy advice. There is a cultural gap between the two. There is some evidence supporting this limited change version of events. However, existing studies relied either on questionnaires or on semi-structured elite interviews. There are no case studies of the dynamics of the relationship. We know nothing about the informal understandings and the indirect influence which so characterised relationships with nationalised industries, although some witnesses to the TCSC (1993, Vol. II, para. 800) already talk of a complicity between the two. At best, 'Next Steps' is an 'evolutionary revolution' (Greer, 1994, p. 132).

Many commentators echo this summary assessment. Sir Peter Kemp (1994) concludes 'the changes do not add up to a revolution'. Campbell and Wilson (1995, pp. 294–6) argue for the death of the Whitehall paradigm, insisting the civil service no longer monopolises advice to ministers, but noting the problem of advising ministers on the adverse consequences of their policy remains unresolved. And Bill Jenkins (1993, p. 95) suggests that recent reforms reflect an enduring conflict between the old politics of central control and a new model of management promoting entrepreneurial behaviour.

The third outcome assumes the government has embarked on an exciting experiment to create different ways of delivering services. However, a policy experiment needs systematic learning: that is, it must produce information so the policy makers can identify and correct errors. The current programme of reform is not so designed. Also, change follows change with such speed that systematic assessment is impossible. This design fault is important, given the problems already identified. Organisation theory tells us there is no one best way to design organisational structure; it depends on the fit between organisation and environment. So the agency model will not fit all organisations, for example, agencies in a politicised environment (social security) will have a different organisational structure and pattern of managerial behaviour to agencies with routinised tasks and stable environments (vehicle licensing). So, some agencies will fail. Evaluation could tell us which ones and why. It is unlikely organisational design can be reduced to the agency formula. Fittingly, Sir Robin Butler described the reforms as 'a journey to an unknown destination' (Butler, 1993, p. 406). How will the government change its course in response to the problems thrown up by reinventing government? What will British government look like a decade from today?

The government pushed through its reforms with opposition restricted to the professional-bureaucratic policy networks and focused on policy implementation. All governments suffer from both implementation gaps and unintended consequences (Rhodes, 1997, Chs 1 and 3) and the Conservative government's reforms of the civil service were no exception. Incremental change continues to typify

British administrative reform. These reforms have the potential to transform the British centre but that potential remains to be realised.

References

British Public Opinion. *A newsletter reviewing the results of polls conducted by Market and Opinion.* Research International (M.O.R.I.), 1995, August, pp. 3–4. Belton.

Butler, R., 1992. 'Managing the new public services: towards a new framework?'. *Public Policy and Management*, vol. 7(3), pp. 1–14.

Butler, R., 1993. 'The evolution of the civil service'. *Public Administration*, vol. 71, pp. 395–406.

Cmnd 8590, 1982. *Report of the inquiry into civil service pay (Megaw Report).* HMSO, London.

Cm 1599, 1991. *The Citizen's Charter. Raising the standard.* HMSO, London.

Cm 1730, 1991. *Competing for quality.* HMSO, London.

Cm 2430, 1993. *Next steps review 1993.* HMSO, London.

Cm 2540, 1994. *Citizen's Charter. Second report.* HMSO, London.

Cm 2626, 1994. *Better accounting for the taxpayer's money. Resource accounting and budgeting in government.* HMSO, London.

Cm 2627, 1994. *The civil service. Continuity and change.* HMSO, London.

Cm 2748, 1995. *The civil service. Taking forward continuity and change.* HMSO, London.

Cabinet Office, 1991. *Making the most of next steps: the management of ministers' departments and their executive agencies. A report to the prime minister (The Frazer Report).* HMSO, London.

Cabinet Office, 1992. *Questions of procedure for Ministers.* Cabinet Office, London.

Cabinet Office, 1994. *Next steps: moving on (The Trosa Report).* Cabinet Office, London.

Campbell, C. and G.K. Wilson, 1995. *The end of Whitehall.* Blackwell, Oxford.

Colville, I., K. Dalton and C. Tomkins, 1993. 'Developing and understanding cultural change in HM customs and excise: there is more to dancing than knowing the next steps'. *Public Administration*, vol. 71, pp. 549–66.

Davies, A. and Willman, J., 1991. *What next? Agencies, departments and the civil service.* Institute for Public Policy Research, London.

Efficiency Unit, 1988. *Improving management in government: the next steps.* HMSO, London.

Efficiency Unit, 1993. *Career management and succession planning study (Oughton).* HMSO, London.

Efficiency Unit, 1994. *The government's use of external management consultants: an efficiency unit scrutiny.* HMSO, London.

Gray, A., B. Jenkins, A. Flynn and B. Rutherford, 1991. 'The management of change in White-hall: the experience of the FMI'. *Public Administration*, vol. 69, pp. 41–59.

Greer, P., 1994. *Transforming central government: the next steps initiative.* Open University Press, Buckingham.

Henkel, M., 1991. *Government, evaluation and change.* Jessica Kingsley, London.

Hennessy, P., 1989. *Whitehall.* Secker & Warburg, London.

Jenkins, B., 1993. 'Reshaping the management of government: the next steps initiative in the United Kingdom'. In: F.L. Seidle (ed.), *Rethinking government: reform or revolution?* Institute for Research on Public Policy, Quebec, pp. 73–103.

Jordan, G., 1992. 'Next steps agencies: from managing by command to managing by contract'. *Aberdeen Papers in Accountancy and Finance*, Working Paper 6.

Jordan G., 1994. 'From next steps to market testing: administrative reform and improvisation'. *Public Policy and Administration*, vol. 9(2), pp. 21–35.

Kemp, P., 1994. 'The civil service White Paper: a job half finished'. *Public Administration*, vol. 72, pp. 591–8.

Metcalfe, L. and S. Richards, 1987. *Improving public management*. Sage, London (2nd edition).

Osborne, D. and T. Gaebler, 1992. *Reinventing government*. Addison-Wesley, Reading Mass.

Oughton, J., 1994. 'Market testing: the future of the civil service'. *Public Policy and Administration*, vol. 9(2), pp. 11–20.

Plowden, W., 1987. *Advising the Rulers*. Basil Blackwell, Oxford.

Plowden, W., 1994. *Ministers and mandarins*. Institute for Public Policy Research, London.

Pollitt, C., 1993. *Managerialism and the public services*. Blackwell, Oxford (2nd edition).

Power, M., 1994. *The audit explosion*. DEMOS, London.

Price Waterhouse, 1991. *Executive agencies: facts and trends*. Price Waterhouse, London, edition 3, Survey Report, March.

Price Waterhouse, 1994. *Executive agencies: facts and trends*. Price Waterhouse, London, edition 8, Survey Report, May.

Public Accounts Committee, 1994. *The proper conduct of public business. Eighth report, session 1993–94*. HMSO, London (HC 154).

RIPA (Royal Institute of Public Administration), 1987. *Top jobs in Whitehall: appointments and promotions in the senior civil service*. RIPA, London.

Rhodes, R.A.W., 1997. *Understanding governance*. Open University Press, Buckingham.

Robson, W.A., 1962. *Nationalized industry and public ownership*. Allen & Unwin, London, second edition.

Stewart, J., 1993. 'Defending public accountability'. *Demos Newsletter*, vol. 35, November, pp. 5–10.

Thatcher, M., 1993. *The Downing Street Years*. HarperCollins, London.

TCSC (Treasury and Civil Service Committee), 1993. *The role of the civil service: interim report. Volume I. Report, together with the proceedings of the committee. HC 390-I. Volume II. Minutes of evidence and appendices. HC 390-II. Sixth report, session 1992–93*. HMSO, London.

TCSC (Treasury and Civil Service Committee), 1994. *Role of the civil service. Volume 1 report. HC 27-I. Volume 2. Minutes of evidence HC 27-II. Volume 3. Appendices to the minutes of evidence HC 27-III. Fifth report, session 1993–94*. HMSO, London.

Waldegrave, W., 1993. *Public service and the future: reforming Britain's bureaucracies*. Conservative Political Centre, London.

Weir, S. and W. Hall (eds), 1994. *Ego-trip: extra governmental organizations in the UK and their accountability*. Democratic Audit and Charter 88, London.

Wilson, G., 1991. 'Prospects for the public service in Britain: Major to the rescue?'. *International Review of Administrative Science*, vol. 57, pp. 327–44.

Wright, V., 1993. 'Public administration, regulation, deregulation and reregulation'. In: K.A. Eliassen and J. Kooiman (eds), *Managing public organizations*. Sage, London, pp. 245–61.

Wright, V., 1994. 'Reshaping the state: implications for public administration'. *West European Politics*, vol. 17, pp. 102–34.

Zifcak, S., 1994. *New managerialism. Administrative reform in Whitehall and Canberra*. Open University Press, Buckingham.

ACCEPTED FOR PUBLICATION JULY 1996

CHAPTER FIVE

Neues Steuerungsmodell: Local Reform in Germany

Christoph Reichard
Fachhochschule für Technik und Wirtschaft, Berlin

1. Introduction

In German local authorities since about 1990 we can observe a remarkable process of reforms and innovations: the introduction of the so-called 'new steering model' (in German *Neues Steuerungsmodell*). Under this label an increasing number of local authorities is discussing and testing different elements of a general concept for modernising local government. Besides some peculiarities which will be discussed later, the German movement of administrative reforms follows the well-known patterns of 'New Public Management' (NPM) (Hood, 1991). The typical topics of the reform debate – from state reduction and decentralisation, deregulation, privatisation, managerialism to market orientation – are now more or less the same in Germany as in other states (Caiden, 1991).

But the NPM movement reached the federal republic of Germany only about 10 years after its start in countries like Great Britain or the US. One reason for the delay in introducing NPM-oriented reforms in the German public sector may be that financial pressure caused by severe cutback measures in public finances occurred some years later in Germany than in other states. Furthermore, Germans generally seem to believe in a 'strong state' and seldom revolt against severe tax duties. Consequently, the preconditions for administrative change in Germany were weaker than in other countries. However, financial pressure became a reform initiating factor particularly at local level from 1990 onwards, partly because of the immense expenses of German reunification. Thus it is not surprising that local authorities started to redesign their organisational structures and to search for efficiency-oriented and cost-cutting measures which nevertheless allow them to provide their citizens with the relevant local services.

NPM-type reforms can be found at the federal (*Bund*) and the state (*Länder*) level only to a small extent, probably due to a smaller degree of financial pressure.

At the level of federal government up to the present there are no significant signs at all for introducing new management concepts. Although actual policy declarations of the federal government also contribute to a 'lean state', effective measures for reforming the federal administrative body in this direction are still missing. There is only one minor field where innovations at federal level can be expected: personnel management. Federal government is planning some adjustments in the civil service system (for example, performance related pay, more flexibility in career structures, and so on).

On the *Länder* level the situation is diverse. The three so-called 'city-states' (Berlin, Bremen, Hamburg) are busy attempting to design and implement new steering concepts. Particularly the city-state of Berlin is well known for introducing a comprehensive management reform approach including new accounting and budgeting procedures. A few other *Länder* governments are also showing some progress in reforming their managerial systems. The government of Baden-Württemberg is particularly acknowledged for its innovations in the field of personnel management; the government of Schleswig-Holstein is performing a series of pilot studies in the field of budgeting and controlling, following the guideline of a general reform strategy; and some limited reform efforts are visible also in the *Länder* Niedersachsen, Nordrhein-Westfalen, Rheinland-Pfalz and Bavaria. The following report will concentrate on the local level, because reform concepts and experiments are more interesting and promising here than at the state level.

2.   Hindering and Supporting Factors of Reforms

Late Start of Reform

The late start of administrative modernisation programmes in Germany can be explained by several specific factors. At first, Germany shows in its institutional structures a relatively positive framework (for example, a widespread decentralisation based on the principles of federalism and of local self administration, and a widely implemented subsidiarity principle; for details see Wollmann, 1996b, p. 3). Furthermore, administrative performance is based on a relatively well-qualified, albeit one-sided legal-oriented, civil service staff which was able to handle the growing problems and difficulties over time (Naschold, 1996). Reform pressure therefore was weaker than in several other countries.

On the other side some of the specific structural patterns and the traditional values of the German politico-administrative system must be seen as a hindering factor for modernisation. Up to the present the law-based, highly bureaucratised administrative system which follows the Weberian bureaucracy model, is still practised in Germany (Reichard, 1995, p. 59). 'The persistence of steering through bureaucratic regulation' is still a dominant feature (Naschold, 1996). In addition, administrative reforms in Germany are confronted with massive legal barriers.

Whereas in Great Britain the whole Thatcherist reform programme was possible without almost any change of law, this would be impossible in Germany. Public sector laws and regulations are a severe restriction for managerial reforms in the German public sector. The following three legal areas are particularly hindering public management reforms:

- *civil service law* because of its restrictions to performance orientation;
- *public budgetary laws* and *regulations* because of their rigid rules for budgetary planning, performing and accounting which are conflicting with managerial flexibility;
- *local government acts* and *charters* because they do not provide clear rules for separating the political and the administrative sphere.

Some German states are beginning to enlarge freedom for local authorities.They introduced certain 'experimental clauses' (*Experimentierklauseln*) in the local government acts, which allow communes to perform pilot studies for testing new steering models without being bound to all legal norms. This approach has been influenced by the Scandinavian movement of the 'free commune experiments'. The responsible ministries are expected to extend these experimental clauses to cover also the fields of budgetary law and of civil service law.

Recruitment and Training

The bureaucratic structures and values are perpetuated and stabilised by the German system of recruiting and educating public servants. This system produces law professionals who are used to thinking in their specific legalistic rationale and who are reluctant to take managerial decisions. This tends to a bureaucratic administrative culture. If we compare this situation, for example, with the British civil service where up to present the higher ranks have been educated mostly in humanities, the British officers seem to be much more open to adopt a generalist managerial behaviour than is the case in Germany. An explanatory factor may be that the British officers who do not have an adequate administrative professionalism are ready to accept the managerial abilities and attitudes when being trained, whereas the German officers – already having their professions as lawyers – are resistant to changing their basic professionalism. The opportunities for German civil servants to change their administrative culture are limited, due to the high isolation of the civil service from the rest of society. Contrary to other countries the exchange of management personnel between the public and the private sector (and vice versa) is rather unusual and seldom happens in Germany.

As a matter of fact management and leadership up to 1990 was not an important topic within the training courses at civil service academies and so on. The preparation of middle level and senior officers to behave in the way of the 'spirit of managerialism' was marginal. Educating staff in 'public management' has become a new task and topic only in the last 2–3 years (Röber, 1996; Reichard, 1994a). The 'belief system' of Germany's public sector up to the present is strongly oriented towards law and regulation, only since 1990 the mainstream debate has shifted to some extent in the direction of public management (Wollmann, 1996b, p. 21).

The rather limited success of previous reforms in the German public sector is another hindering factor. From the first experiments with planning and budgeting systems in the 1960s, through territorial reforms and the functional devolution of tasks in the 1970s, up to improvements of citizen orientation and participation in the 1980s: the bulk of administrative reforms in the German administration in the past failed or brought only limited success. It would not be too surprising if the expectations of civil servants with regard to the actual modernisation movement are not highly positive (for details of past German administrative reforms see Derlien, 1996; Wollmann, 1996a).

Change of Tide in 1990

If we look back to the 1980s we can say that up to 1990 the issue of a comprehensive modernisation of the public sector was not an urgent and pressing topic in the Federal Republic. Continuity and stability were the most important features of the German administrative system at this time (for more details see Benz and Goetz, 1996).

Around 1990 a remarkable *reversal of context factors* occurred which led to a rethinking of public sector tasks, structures and processes. Particularly local government stood under specific pressure (Röber, 1996). Some initiating factors among others were:

- strong financial pressure, partly caused by increasing social welfare payments due to high unemployment rates;
- administrators experiencing growing difficulties in managing their public institutions, partly because of the high centralisation of competencies and because of lacking steering instruments;
- growing self-confidence and customer-orientation of citizens towards public services which are provided in Germany to a large extent by local authorities;
- increasing regional competition because of European integration which makes administrative capacity and performance of local authorities to a more important location factor;
- convergence of ideological positions regarding the role of state: the future of the social welfare state and the necessity to cut back the borderlines of the state are discussed by different political parties (reforms coincide with the *Zeitgeist*);
- state and bureaucracy came under pressure from the public; criticising the inefficiency of public authorities is becoming a general fashion.

In the meantime we observe a growing conviction among politicians, administrators and even unionists that the public service will only be able to survive if it will be restructured fundamentally. If this reform does not succeed, pressure for privatisation of public services will reach a critical level.

Why New Steering Model?

Despite the described hindering reform factors Germany's administration initiated certain modernisation projects of the NPM-type. It can be assumed that the following factors had some influence on the initial push of these projects:

- strong dissatisfaction of practitioners with the traditional management structures and instruments;
- the ideas for reform came 'from below', that is, from the practitioners at local level and not from the federal government or from academics (see also Jann in this volume);
- the new philosophy satisfies all major political forces: the social democrats and with them the unions are satisfied because the 'new steering model' is seen as a possible countermeasure against privatisation; the conservatives are satisfied because the new model promises proper private sector oriented management; the 'Greens' are satisfied because – with some adaptation – the new model may be able to improve citizen/customer orientation, participation and eventually empowerment (Clasen *et al.*, 1995). As a result we find relatively broad reform coalitions including parts of the unions (for example, the ÖTV, the German public service union which since 1988 actively promotes reform projects according to its programme 'future through public service');
- dissemination and promotion of the new steering model followed a successful 'missionary' strategy of the KGST (see below);
- several quality awards for high performing administrations pushed public interest (for example, the quality awards of the Postgraduate School for Administrative Sciences in Speyer in 1992, 1994 and 1996) and the International Award for Democracy and Efficiency in Local Government of the Bertelsmann Foundation in 1993);
- increasing influences from the consultancy industry which discovered the public sector in Germany being a growing market.

3.   Four Phases of Reform

In the local government of Germany the process of managerial change took the following sequence (Pracher, 1996; Reichard, 1996).

The Phase of Conceptual Design

German local authorities in the field of managerial reforms rely to a great extent recommendations of the 'KGST'.[1] KGST elaborated from 1988 to 1991 some first recommendations for new management concepts (KGST, 1991). From 1993 on-wards a series of detailed reports followed, dealing with conceptual questions (for example, KGST, 1993). KGST published its recommendations under the label *Neues Steuerungsmodell* ('new steering model'). The new steering model is a product of a *coalition of city managers*: the main ideas and influences originate from a working group chaired by the former director of KGST (Gerhard Banner). Members of this working group were city managers, *Bürgermeister*, heads of finance and organisation departments of large cities. They suffered from internal steering deficits and were interested to reform the internal management structures of a city administration (see also Jann in this volume).

Interestingly, the main features of the new steering model are based to a large extent on experiences of the Dutch city of Tilburg. Tilburg in the early 1980s introduced a professional management model which was largely influenced by private sector corporate management concepts (Schrijvers, 1993). This so-called 'Tilburg model' had considerable influence on the development of steering models in German local authorities (KGST, 1992). In the first phase KGST elaborated its steering model close to the Tilburg model and a larger number of authorities copied its structures and instruments according to the KGST recommendations. It is not surprising that KGST as well as the implementing communes made the experience that the opportunities to transfer reform elements from the Tilburg model to the *Neues Steuerungsmodell* are rather limited, due to the different legal, political and cultural conditions of a Dutch and a German commune. In fact, the Tilburg model was used more as a supplier of reform ideas than as a source for direct transfers. However, we have to state that local government reforms in Germany have been influenced to a great deal from managerial reforms in the Netherlands, particularly at Tilburg.

The Phase of the First Pilot Communes

Immediately after publication of the first KGST recommendations some large German cities began to introduce the first elements of this new steering model. Most of the pilot communes concentrated on one or two of the main elements of the model. Well-known pilot cities at the first phase were among others: Hannover, Nürnberg, Köln.

The Bushfire of Widespread Experiments

The main ideas of the new steering model were disseminated to an increasing number of communes. Only one or two years after the first KGST impulse about 40 local authorities – predominantly large cities – were busy experimenting with certain elements of the steering model. Regionally, most of the innovations have been initiated in the German *Land* Northrine-Westfalia. On the one side this is a consequence of extremely severe financial pressure on most of the cities of this highly industrialised state. On the other side initiatives for reforms particularly came up in this state because of a difficult municipal and county charter, the so-called 'north-German dual system' which was in force up to 1995 and which experts are judging to be less effective and more conflict-generating than the charters of other states. City managers working under this charter experienced greater difficulties for proper management than in other states.

Not surprisingly, introduction of the new steering model took place almost exclusively in the 'old' parts of the federal republic and nearly nowhere in the Eastern part of Germany, the former GDR (Reichard and Röber, 1993). The main reason for the reluctance in introducing new steering models in the 'New German Länder' is that East German administration had been transformed just before into the Western structures. This transformation occurred at the same time the authorities in the West began to start their debate about managerial reforms. The time-parallelism of transformation and modernisation is a *paradox* for Germany's public administration: at the same time when the (traditional!) West German structures and procedures were transferred to the East, the West German practitioners discussed the renewal of their local government system and in fact developed the new steering model. The introduction of the traditional, 'old-fashioned' West German structures and regulations in East German authorities which followed to a large extent a blueprint approach, required much time and energy by the Eastern administrators. Being occupied with the implementation of the 'old' concepts, administrators in the East were not highly motivated (and even did not have the time) to reflect about time consuming experiments with 'new', modern management concepts. Consequently, there are remarkable differences between Western and Eastern local authorities regarding their present readiness and capacity to implement new steering models. Nevertheless, in 1995 some first signals were visible that some East German local authorities had also started to experiment with new steering models (for example, the cities of Cottbus, Dessau, Magdeburg, Potsdam, Schwerin).

The Phase of Consolidation

For the past five years several hundred communes in Germany have started experiments in the context of the new steering model. According to a survey conducted by the German Cities Association in 1995, about 70 percent of all (larger) municipalities have engaged in modernisation programmes. Dominant reform fields are budgeting/accounting, organisation and personnel, council/administration relations and management of municipal corporations. Local authorities in Germany with broad experiences in the field of managerial reforms are (in alphabetic order): Bielefeld, Bochum, Detmold, Dortmund, Düsseldorf, Duisburg, Gütersloh, Hagen,

Hannover, Heidelberg, Herten, Köln, Lübeck, München, Münster, Nürnberg, Offenbach, Osnabrück (city and county), Passau, Saarbrücken, Soest (county), Stuttgart, Wuppertal.

While a larger proportion of the communes is still in the initial phase of such experiments, some authorities have considerable experience with steering concepts over several years. Smaller communes are interested to a lesser extent in introducing formalised steering models, probably because they are able to handle their day-to-day problems without utilising sophisticated management instruments. In the last two years additionally the county administrations in Germany have become increasingly interested in implementing steering concepts within their administrations. In the meantime it seems that it is a fashion for German city managers to announce that the respective city is working with steering models. Several cities are distributing brilliant brochures about their concept. Thus, it is not easy to distinguish from outside between real managerial reforms and pure public relations declarations.

4.   Major Reform Issues

The new steering model is a mixture of quite different ingredients. Several communes in Germany understand quite different things under the same label. However, the following four issues are the major subjects in the present reform debate.

Strengthening Accountability

One of the elements of the new steering model which has been introduced in several German local authorities is the concept of *decentralised resource responsibility*. The idea behind it is the following: responsibility for resources (finance, staff and so on) should be transferred from the central service departments (treasurer, organisation and personnel department) to the sectoral units (for example, social services, housing, construction services). This process of rearranging responsibilities within a local authority, which played a dominant role from the beginning and became an essential element of the new steering model, finally leads to semi-autonomous result centres which are fully accountable for their tasks and the utilised resources. The reason for starting with this element is the following: German administration for decades practised a pattern of highly centralised responsibility for resource allocation. Responsibility for finances as well as for personnel has been concentrated in specialised central service departments. Consequently, nobody really felt responsible for the overall result, for tasks *and* for the resources. The incongruity of tasks and responsibilities led to a system of 'organised irresponsibility' (Banner, 1991). It can be assumed that such a process of rearranging competencies will be full of conflicts and will afford much time for training because the service departments will have to find their new role and are forced to accept a reduction of their powers.

Introduction of Global Budgets

Parallel to the increasing cutback of finances some local authorities changed their internal budgetary system. Instead of the traditional in-detail planning of revenues and expenditures for each department and for each budgetary item by the treasurer, a new flexible system has been introduced. The treasurer is planning only global budget figures and is prescribing these figures as lump sums within a limited margin to the different departments. The local council no longer decides on the details of a department's budget but is concentrating on the political implications of the budgetary framework. The different sectoral departments are free to allocate their funds – as long as they respect the budgetary frame – according to their respective needs. They are allowed to exchange expenditures among different budget items and to transfer unspent parts of the budget to the following fiscal year. However, the departments are forced to report regularly to top management about their activities and their goal achievements on the basis of previously defined output/performance indicators.

Several large cities in Germany – for example, Köln, München, Nürnberg – have been practising the new budgetary system for some years. They experience a more cost efficient behaviour of their heads of units, leading to remarkable cutbacks in expenditure without endangering the quality of services. It is interesting that the budgetary reform on the local level took place with only minor changes to the local government's budgetary laws. However, in the meantime several state governments have introduced certain experimental clauses (*Experimentierklauseln*) into the local government acts to give the pilot communes more freedom for experimenting with new budgetary methods.

Reforms in the Accounting System

A number of communes are implementing methods of *internal cost accounting*. The traditional public accounting system in Germany, the so-called 'cameralist bookkeeping' (*Kameralistik*), is a pure cash-based system, ignoring all aspects of accrual accounting (Lüder, 1993). This cameralist system is prescribed to communes by law. As long as this general accounting system cannot be replaced by a new system comprising cost and performance accounting as well as accrual based financial accounting and reporting, local authorities tend to introduce – as a first step towards 'management accounting' – cost accounting methods to identify cost of certain public services and to allow the internal clearing of overhead costs among service and sector units (Buschor and Schedler, 1994).

Product Orientation

Following the logic of the new steering model, managerial emphasis has to be shifted from the traditional input to an output orientation. Consequently, several pilot communes began to identify and to measure their outputs, that is, their *products*. The idea behind it is that public managers should put the product in the centre of their steering activities, asking for the costs and the benefits of a produced service. Local authorities at present make considerable efforts to formulate their products exactly, with product groups and so on. KGST is supporting the active communes in exchanging experiences with 'product catalogues' for certain policy fields like social or youth services. The aim is to develop product descriptions which are compatible in order to allow intercommunal performance comparisons among German authorities. The accuracy and detail-orientation of the ongoing product descriptions seems to be somehow 'typically German'. For example in Berlin the product catalogue consists of over 2000 products, divided into more than 8000 services. Compared with the – much less detailed – efforts for improving output orientation in other countries, the German practice seems to be influenced more from the 'spirit of bureaucracy' than by the 'spirit of managerialism'. Another critical feature is that product descriptions concentrate to a large extent on procedures and activities, neglecting outputs and intended impacts/outcomes. Administrators for decades have not been used to thinking in a result-oriented manner, therefore they have difficulties in changing their behaviour according to the new challenges.

Other Issues

Besides these four main elements of managerial reforms in the context of the new steering model, local authorities are also experimenting with some other aspects and instruments, such as:

–   improvements in *quality management* (for example, regular surveys about citizen needs, redesigning procedures for cutting waiting time and so on; the city of Saarbrücken seems to be an example for implementing TQM; see generally for this topic: Oppen, 1995, Klages and Löffler, 1995);
–   introduction of 'one-stop offices' (*Bürgerämter*): all day-to-day-services for citizens will be offered under the same roof, organised in a central citizen office or in several local offices in the different city districts. Leading cities with experiences are among others: Bielefeld, Hagen, Heidelberg and Unna. The city of Hagen is particularly well known for its trade-union led (ÖTV) partnership approach to implement its one-stop agency (Kißler *et al.*, 1994). Some other cities are implementing 'investors offices', that is, front-offices to allow investors to clear up all questions and applications at one stop;
–   *corporatisation* or autonomisation of authority units: an increasing number of organisation units of local authorities, particularly public utilities, are hiving-off into (semi-) autonomy. They transform their legal status, mostly from public law into private commercial law and become a legally independent corporation. The respective local government remains as the proprietor

but usually lacks political influence. The corporatisation strategy seems to be the German variant of privatisation: transformation of the legal status is frequently discussed under the topic of privatisation, although the public property remains unchanged.

Most of the pilot communes try to integrate the different elements of the new steering model into a comprehensive concept, including the following phases and instruments of the managerial process: on the basis of defined products, council and top management are formulating performance objectives and budgetary targets. The different administrative units are specifying their targets and are transforming them into verifiable performance indicators. The units are reporting to a central controlling unit in a quarterly feedback system. The reports will be evaluated following a comprehensive controlling concept. The whole sequence of goal setting, goal achievement and controlling is organised in a feedback-loop-oriented *management cycle*.

5. First Experiences with *Neues Steuerungsmodell*

Levels of Implementation

As already mentioned, federal and *Länder* administrations lay far behind in the whole reform process. They 'do not feel the pressure and demands from people, markets and quasi-markets as intensively as local authorities' (Röber, 1996, p. 177). The federal government particularly lacks a strategic vision and concept of administrative modernisation. It still continues to rely on the principles of the traditional civil service system (*hergebrachte Grundsätze des Berufsbeamtentums*). Some of the *Länder* – like Baden-Württemberg and Schleswig-Holstein – are more innovative and more keen to develop and to implement reform concepts. As was shown above, the major reform forces are to be found at the local level. Here it can be observed that the 'leading' cities are lying close together in their concepts and also in their degree of implementation. Some evidence can be drawn from the 'Speyer Quality Award', a quality competition taking place every two years at the Postgraduate School of Administrative Sciences in Speyer, in search for well-performing public authorities in Germany. The 1994 experience with this competition showed that a remarkable number of administrations, particularly at local level, deliver their services to the citizens at a high level of performance and efficiency. In 1994, the cities of Heidelberg and Saarbrücken were the winners of the Speyer Award. These two city administrations, like most of the other cities included in the competition, have reached a relatively high degree of integration of the different elements of the new steering model (Klages and Haubner, 1995; Klages and Löffler, 1995).

Although party differences do not much matter in the German debate about administrative modernisation, there seems to be more innovation and energy in states or communes ruled by social democrats. One reason explaining this might be that social democrats are to a higher extent motivated for reforms because they follow the principle 'modernisation instead of privatisation'.

The new steering model caused a remarkable marketing and publicity boom: for five years there has been no week in Germany without a seminar or conference dealing with these questions. Professional commercial conference agencies seem to make good profits in this market and the consultancy firms are more and more involved with public sector consultation. Publishers also discovered the new market: a large number of books and magazines (typical title *The Innovative Administration*) have been distributed in the last few years. Last but not least, even the communes themselves discovered the market and created profit-oriented consultancy units (for example: the newly founded consultancy firm of the city of Herten).

Astonishingly the academic community has not been very involved in the development of the new steering model. In the first five years the debate about steering models was driven exclusively by practitioners. Neither the political or administrative sciences, nor the management or law sciences made the necessary contributions to this new field (see Reichard and Wollmann, 1996 for some first critical and evaluative remarks to the NPM debate in Germany and abroad). Unfortunately there do not exist any empirical evaluations of the impact of the new steering model on administrative performance. It was not until 1995 that the first critical comments on the German developments came out (see König in this volume; additionally: Grunow, 1996; König, 1995; Laux, 1995). Besides other doubts some critics ask what makes NPM really *new*. They say that some elements of the new steering model are the rediscovery of pre-known reform concepts (for example, MBO, delegation of authorities, decentralisation, accrual accounting, block grants or output budgeting). Although most of the steering elements in fact have been well-known for decades, it must be stated that the mixture of these elements and their integration into one comprehensive steering model seems to be rather new and functional. Furthermore, the new steering model fits well into the present framework conditions of the public sector.

Experiences with Implementation

At the beginning of the modernisation movement, most authorities started with decentralising authorities or with elaborating controlling systems. Later on, due to increasing financial pressure, authorities began to implement budgeting systems, expecting that they could cut down expenditures to some extent. Nowadays we can observe some convergence: communes try to start from the beginning with a more integrated and comprehensive steering concept.

A frequently discussed question in Germany is whether *area-wide* or *pilot* implementation should be preferred. Nearly all communes opted for pilot studies as the first step of innovation. They started their experiments by introducing one of the above-mentioned elements in a well-selected pilot area. The reason for pilot studies was the high risk of the experiments and the opportunity for learning and for corrective measures in the pilot case. On the other hand there is evidence that some communes were overstretched in managing their organisation in two completely different ways, following in some units the 'new' and in others the 'old' steering concept.

The units in local authorities which were selected for starting with the first experiments were mostly *small* departments without any conflicts. Authorities decided to select small units which often were not in the centre of the political struggles of the council (for example, theatre, museum, parks and gardens department, music school, swimming-pools and so on). Up to the present there are few experiences of successful implementation in large and conflictive departments like social services, housing or education. Although a small and 'exotic' pilot unit may be adequate for gaining first experiences, it must be argued that 'the battle won't be won' as long as managerial reforms do not reach the core departments where struggles and conflicts are concentrated and the biggest problems ought to be solved.

Implementation strategies of local authorities differ considerably in the degree of *participation* of their employees. Some authorities tried to introduce steering elements in a rather autocratic top-down way. There is some evidence that these authorities were not highly successful with this strategy. Some other authorities selected a careful participative approach, investing much time and energy to inform and convince their own employees. Few cities started with a quality circle campaign which motivated the members to identify themselves with the reform issues. Some cities at the initial phase of the process agreed with the representatives of the work force (union and employees council) upon an arrangement which commits both sides to the modernisation targets and to some social preconditions of the process (no dismissals during process, participation of representatives within the project teams and so on.).

Another topic of discussion regarding the implementation strategy is the degree of involving *politicians* (primarily members of the respective councils and committees) into the process. In a number of cities the new steering model has been introduced in a rather technocratic way, almost excluding the political sphere. It was an attempt to install managerial reforms in the administrative body of an agency without tangling the politicians. Some first lessons of experience show us that such attempts were not very successful. Public management includes the political sphere. Politicians have to play a new and active role in the new steering model; they have to formulate the strategic and overall goals of the commune and they have to control its activities with regard to these strategic issues.

In summarising the first experiences with the implementation of new steering models in local authorities it is possible to conclude the following lessons. The *failures and deficits* listed below are frequent and common:

– politicians as well as top management are not adequately committed to the goals of the change project and do not support the process over the whole period;

- politicians do not formulate clear-cut goals for the whole reform project;
- conflicts among politicians, managers and the workforce (employees council and union) are slowing down the progress;
- lack of careful and comprehensive planning of the whole reform project (that is, a project budget, a time schedule, a project organisation with steering groups and so on);
- unrealistic time pressure (overcharging of employees, too high expectations within a limited time frame);
- contradictions between the reform project and necessary cutback measures which can demotivate the participating employees;
- lack of qualification measures for those employees which have to work with the new steering instruments.

A *power balance* of supporters and hinderers in the German public sector causes the following result (Naschold, 1995): although the power and influence of reform-oriented actors has increased in the last few years, it must be stated that the traditionalists within the public sector organisations still have the majority. This contrasts with the power balance in several other countries – for example, in Scandinavia – where the reformist coalition seems to have the majority. The sceptics among administrators have been astonishingly quiet in the past, but with the first disillusions they are expected to raise their voice. One actual example is some lawyers and their associations who claim that several elements and procedures connected with the new steering model are illegal.

6.   Comparison between *Neues Steuerungsmodell* and NPM

If we compare administrative modernisation programmes in different countries from the perspective of a contingency approach, it must be expected that these programmes differ remarkably because of their divergent legal, political and cultural context. Different countries are initiating their reforms from quite a different starting point; these countries are trying to reach quite different reform goals and they are dealing with particular framework conditions. Thus, administrations in different countries are forced to design and to implement their modernisation concepts according to these divergent problems, goals and conditions. This argument leads to the general question of this volume as to whether a concept like NPM, which is primarily tailored for the problems and needs of the Anglo-Saxon administrative culture, is suitable and applicable in the different contexts of continental European states (for discussion of this argument see Kickert and König in this volume).

German Specificity

From this perspective it seems to be quite normal that the new steering model as the German variant of NPM follows a *specific* German pattern. There are first, certain context features worth mentioning, second, certain 'typical' weaknesses of the model to be discussed, and third, particularities of the implementation process to be analysed. The following more impressionistic features try to paint the picture:

1. *The specific legal system* of Germany with its *distinction between civil and public law* which is not common in the Anglo-Saxon culture, is causing difficulties in adapting the new managerial thinking: whereas the rules and regulations for contracting, purchasing, selling and so on, in Great Britain or in the US are similar in the private and in the public sector, and administrators are therefore somehow familiar with contracting procedures, this is not the fact in Germany. Contracting is strange and new for German administrators and the administrative law does not provide adequate regulations. This explains to some extent the existing difficulties with contract management.

2. The German NPM-variant is *not to the same extent ideology-driven* as in Great Britain, the US and some other Anglo-Saxon states. Whereas the neo-con-servative 'New Right' movement was of considerable influence on the British and US governments, it played a much smaller role in Germany. Moreover the theoretical influence coming from the 'Public Choice' school was not very remarkable in Germany. Thus, the normative favouritism for markets and private sector solutions was not as high as in Great Britain or the US.

3. 'Agencification' took place in Germany in a different way compared with the Anglo-Saxon or the Scandinavian countries. Although we can observe only limited attempts to subdivide ministries into semi-autonomous bodies (agencies) under the control of the core department, there is a remarkable trend in Germany on a municipal as well as on a *Länder* level for *organisational privatisation*: administrative units have been transferred to private-law-based institutions (corporatisation) or to indirect administration (*mittelbare Verwaltung*) with an autonomous legal status. This is part of a general trend towards a greater diversity of para-governmental organisations.

4. Managerial reforms in Germany concentrate to a great extent on *internal structural changes*. The reforms are dealing predominantly with restructuring authorities (decentral resource responsibility), with implementing output- and product-oriented steering cycles and controlling systems and with innovations of the internal accounting system. They seem to have a *structural bias*. In several other countries, particularly in Scandinavia, reform efforts are much more oriented to external goals. Reforms in these countries deal to a larger extent with improvements in the administration/citizen/relations, with strengthening market-type-mechanisms and (quasi-) competition and with decisions about contracting out and competitive tendering (Banner and Reichard, 1993).

5. Contracting out of public services under competitive conditions in Germany is still a rather untouched topic. The idea of designing a local authority along the model of an *Enabling Authority* with clear cut client/provider relations seems to be quite strange and unknown. However, it has to be mentioned that primarily in the field of service delivery the German administration has some kind of an 'enabling function' due to the subsidiarity principle. A large number of public services traditionally will be contracted out to third sector organisations.

    The limited scope of the German modernisation programme can be explained from its *lacking a competitive context* (Naschold, 1996). There is empirical evidence from abroad that creating an environment which supports internal as well as external competition is an important prerequisite for increased effectiveness and productivity of the public sector. Adequate measures to create such an environment could be:

    – introduction of market competition in certain public services,
    – competition among public administrations and/or public enterprises,
    – frequent performance comparisons among public sector organisations, based on agreed performance indicators (benchmarking) and
    – quality surveys for citizens/customers and citizen panels as regular feedback instruments.

    With regard to interadministrative performance comparisons there are some interesting ongoing experiments in several local authorities worth mentioning. Sponsored by the Bertelsmann Foundation these authorities collaborate continuously within a network to exchange and compare their cost and output figures (quasi-competition). The main policy fields of comparisons are at present local culture (museums, theatres and so on) and citizen administration.

6. The field of *quality management* is also widely underdeveloped in the German reform debate (Oppen, 1995). Only a few local authorities are experimenting with concepts of 'Total Quality Management'. There is some limited discussion about the value of quality audits (ISO 9000 and so on). The description of clear quality indicators is still at the beginning. Only very few authorities regularly perform citizen panels or are distributing customer questionnaires (for example the city of Duisburg).

7. Another underdeveloped topic in Germany's modernisation programmes is the field of *personnel management*. Most reform concepts underestimate the necessity of personnel development and of improving leadership behaviour. There is evidence that even excellent management concepts would not function in practice, if the *new* knowledge and behaviour related to such concepts cannot be transferred into the heads of the employees. Therefore, immense efforts must be undertaken to recruit the right management staff, to qualify existing staff, to set attractive incentives for change, to improve leadership

behaviour of superiors and generally to develop the human resources of the authority.

Personnel management in the German civil service up to now has been oriented towards the traditional values and principles of the Prussian civil servant (*Beamter*). The energy to invest in human capital and to implement modern personnel management concepts and instruments is limited. Unfortunately, personnel reforms in Germany suffer from legal restrictions in the field of civil service laws. These laws, which are centrally regulated by the federal government, don't allow performance related pay, they impede opportunities to motivate employees with other incentives and to take flexible personnel decisions. Reforms have been hanging since the early 1970s, when attempts to create a uniform, integrated civil service, based on clear structures and motivating incentives failed. Experts are claiming at least for opening and experimental clauses (*Öffnungsklauseln*) in the civil service law to allow controlled deviations and experiments in the field of personnel management.

Nevertheless, in 1994 and 1995 some early movement towards reforming the rigid civil service system of Germany can be observed. The following topics are under discussion (Röber, 1996):

- the traditional dual civil-service system (*Beamte* and *Angestellte*), particularly the cost-efficiency of the two service variants (for example, cost of the respective pension schemes);
- recruitment and training, particularly in moving from the traditional legal-oriented education to a training of 'public managers' (the first curricula in public management have been in operation for four years in several universities and graduate schools, for example, in Berlin (Bischoff and Reichard, 1994));
- performance-oriented incentive systems, particularly pay scales;
- instruments for management development, career planning, appraisals, and so on.

A few state administrations (for example, Baden-Württemberg) and several municipalities (for example, the city administration of Duisburg) are performing pilot studies in these fields. Unions are partly supporting these reforms.

In summary, the German new steering model, as experienced in several local authorities, is comparatively strong in reforming the internal organisation structures and the steering and controlling systems, but it is relatively weak in redesigning the external relations of communes, in opening themselves towards market incentives and furthermore in managing and developing the human resources. Reflecting the whole modernisation programme of the last years, the following characteristic features of the 'German way' can be recapitulated (Klages and Löffler 1995, p. 378; Röber, 1996):

- preference of internal modernisation instead of task reduction or privatisation;
- predominance of providing functions together with a low level of 'enabling activities' of the state;
- internal decentralisation in state administrations instead of 'agencification';
- structural reforms instead of cultural change;
- conservation of the particular status and privileges of the civil service;
- limited orientation towards citizen needs and expectations;
- pragmatic, incremental, step-by-step, home-made reform measures following a way of partial, evolutionary and continuous improvements;
- discrete single reform measures instead of an on-going learning process;
- reform initiatives 'from below', from single local authorities with neither general support programmes from the central level (like the Scandinavian Free-Commune-Experiments), nor centralist pressure for change like in Great Britain;
- reform promoters mainly located in core departments, limited commitment of politicians (partly because administrative reform is not an important political issue and is not pushed by the strong political will of the government).

7.   Questions about *Neues Steuerungsmodell*

Until now the scientific community in Germany has not dealt intensively with analytical and empirical questions concerning the new steering model (see Jann in this volume; some first judgements can be found in Reichard and Wollmann, 1996). Some researchers doubt whether the whole NPM concept of an 'entrepreneurial management' is adequate for the public sector (Wright, Rouban and König in this volume), others are doubtful about the innovative content of NPM concepts and about real reform impacts (Grunow, 1996; Laux, 1995).

Having in mind the dissatisfying state of the art in NPM research in Germany, it is only possible to raise several questions on possible effects and frictions of the new steering model which are currently under discussion. The following *open questions* seem to concern not only the German reform programmes but are to some extent valid also for other NPM cases.

- Will this concept be compatible with the existing *administrative culture*? Can we expect a change from the traditional bureaucratic values into a managerial culture? Isn't administrative culture resistent against change?
- Will the concept be compatible with the existing *political rationality* and behaviour? Will politicians be ready to behave in a rather economic rationality, to govern by means of political, strategic targets and to avoid isolated detailed interventions into the apparatus?
- Is a clear-cut *division* between the *political* and the *administrative* sphere feasible and is such a role separation at all desirable?

- Isn't there a danger of a greater *political patronage* within the fragmented decision making structure of a local authority? Do we have to expect an increased *separation* of sectoral-oriented policy networks?
- Can we expect that managers of the central services departments will accept their *new role* of internal service-delivery and will renounce interference into detailed resource decisions? On the other side: can we expect that managers of the sector units will decide in an autonomous and self-responsible way and to manage and control effectively their own units?
- Don't we have to handle massive problems with *performance measurement* if we intend to measure all outputs (products) in quantitative terms? Do we expect goal deviations because of a preference of quantifiable goals?
- Is the reduction of a *citizen* to its role as *consumer* of public services a too narrow view? Do we exclude other roles of a citizen (for example, the elector, the participator, the civic problem solver)?
- How realistic is the belief in the universal *power of the market* after years of experiences with market failures? Can we expect a sustainable public management system if we continue to transfer *private sector*-based corporate management concepts into public management? Is the *managerialistic* view of public management the right perspective or does it need to broaden the perspective towards a concept of *public governance* (see Kickert in this volume)?

Such questions do not play a significant role in the daily struggles of German local authorities when they are experimenting with 'new steering concepts'. Nevertheless it will be impossible to avoid discussing these questions and developing the existing concepts of public management further to make them feasible and sustainable in the long run.

Note

1. KGST is the association for managerial reforms in local government, situated in Cologne. Nearly all German local authorities are members of this association. The KGST is elaborating studies and recommendations for its members in the field of public management, organization, budgeting, cost accounting, data processing etc. KGST is distributing about 20–30 reports on specific topics per year to its members. Additionally KGST is performing training seminars, workshops and conferences. Since 1994 KGST has its own consultancy firm, the 'KGST-consult GmbH'.

References

Banner, G., 1991. 'Von der Behörde zum Dienstleistungsunternehmen'. In: *Verwaltungsorganisation und Personalführung (VOP)*, pp. 6–11.

Banner, G. and C. Reichard (eds), 1993. *Kommunale Managementkonzepte in Europa.* Köln.

Benz, A. and K. Goetz (eds), 1996. *A New German Public Sector?* Dartmouth.

Bischoff, D. and C. Reichard (eds.), 1994. *Vom Beamten zum Manager?* Berlin.

Buschor, E. and K. Schedler (eds), 1994. *Perspectives on performance measurement and public sector accounting.* St. Gallen, Switzerland.

Caiden, G.E., 1991. *Administrative reform comes of age.* Berlin – New York.

Clasen, R. *et al.*, 1995. *Effizienz und Verantwortlichkeit. Reformempfehlungen für eine effiziente, aufgabengerechte dund bürgerkontrollierte Verwaltung.* Gutachten im Auftrag der Bundestagsfraktion Bündnis 90/Die Grünen. Ms Berlin.

Derlien, H.-U., 1996. 'German administrative reforms in perspective'. In: A. Benz and K. Goetz (eds), *A new German public sector?* Dartmouth.

Grunow, D., 1996. 'Qualitätsanforderungen für die Verwaltungsmodernisierung: Anspruchsvolle Ziele oder leere Versprechungen?' In: C. Reichard and H. Wollmann (eds), *Kommunalverwaltung im Modernisierungsschub?* Basel, pp. 50–77.

Hill, H., and H. Klages (eds), 1995. *Lernen von Spitzenverwaltungen.* Speyer, Germany.

Hood, C., 1991. 'A public management for all seasons?'. *Public Administration*, pp. 3–16.

KGST, 1991. 'Dezentrale Ressourcenverantwortung: Überlegungen zu einem neuen Steuerungsmodell'. *Bericht*, vol. 12.

KGST, 1992. 'Wege zum Dienstleistungsunternehmen Kommunalverwaltung: Fallstudie Tilburg'. *KGST-Bericht*, vol. 19.

KGST, 1993. 'Das Neue Steuerungsmodell'. *Bericht*, vol. 5.

KGST, 1995. 'Das Neue Steuerungsmodell – Erste Zwischenbilanz'. *Bericht*, vol. 10.

Kißler, L., H. Bogumil and E. Wiechmann, 1994. *Das kleine Rathaus.* Baden-Baden.

Klages, H. and O. Haubner, 1995. 'Strategies of public sector modernization: three alternative perspectives'. In: G. Bouckaert and A. Halachmi (eds), *Challenge of management in a changing world*, San Francisco, pp. 348–76.

Klages, H. and E. Löffler, 1995. 'Administrative modernization in Germany – a big qualitative jump in small steps'. In: *IRAS*, pp. 373–83.

Klages, H. 1996. 'Quality improvement in the German local government'. In: C. Pollitt and G. Bouckaert (eds), *Quality improvement in European public services.* London, pp. 69–81.

König, K., 1995. '"Neue" Verwaltung oder Verwaltungsmodernisierung: Verwaltungspolitik in den 90er Jahren'. In: *Die Öffentliche Verwaltung*, pp. 349–58.

Laux, E., 1995. 'Über Verwaltungssteuerung'. In: *Archiv für Kommunalwissenschaften*.

Lüder, K., 1993. 'Governmental accounting in Germany: state and need for reform'. In: *Financial accountability and management*, pp. 225–34.

Naschold, F., 1995. 'Modernisierung des öffentlichen Sektors – Haushaltskonsolidierung, Leistungstiefe, "Prozeß-Reengineering"'. In: F. Naschold and M. Pröhl (eds), *Produktivität des öffentlichen Sektors II*, Gütersloh, pp. 21–38.

Naschold, F., 1996. *New frontiers in public sector management.* DeGruyter, Berlin–New York.

Oppen, M., 1995. *Qualitätsmanagement.* Berlin.

Pracher, C., 1996. 'New models of guidance and steering in the public administration – by the example of Berlin'. In: N. Flynn and F. Strehl (eds), *Public sector management in Europe.* Prentice Hall, Harvester Wheatsheaf, London, pp. 146–59.

Reichard, C., 1994a. '"Public Management" – ein neues Ausbildungskonzept für die deutsche Verwaltung'. In: *VOP*, pp. 178–84.

Reichard, C., 1994b. *Umdenken im Rathaus. Neue Steuerungsmodelle in der deutschen Kommunalverwaltung.* Berlin.

Reichard, C., 1995. 'Von Max Weber zum "New Public Management" – Verwaltungsmanagement im 20. Jahrhundert'. In: P. Hablützel *et al.* (eds), *Umbruch in Politik und Verwaltung. Ansichten und Erfahrungen zum New Public Management in der Schweiz.* Bern, pp. 57–80.

Reichard, C., 1996. '"New steering models" in the local government of Germany – a case study of implementing public management concepts in local authorities'. In: N. Flynn and F. Strehl (eds), *Public sector management in Europe.* Prentice Hall, Harvester Wheatsheaf, London, pp. 160–71.

Reichard, C. and M. Röber, 1993. 'Was kommt nach der Einheit? Die öffentliche Verwaltung in der ehemaligen DDR zwischen Blaupause und Reform'. In: G.-J. Glaeßner (ed.), *Der lange Weg zur Einheit.* Berlin, pp. 215–24.

Reichard, C. and H. Wollmann (eds), 1996. *Kommunalverwaltung im Modernisierungsschub?* Basel etc.

Röber, M., 1996. 'Towards public managers in Germany?' In: D. Farnham *et al.* (eds), *Public managers in Europe.* London.

Shrijvers, A.P.M., 1993. 'The management of a larger town'. In: *Public Administration*, pp. 595–603.

Wegener, A., 1996. 'Internationale Modernisierungserfahrungen: ein Fundus für Anregungen in der deutschen Modernisierungsdiskussion'. In: R. Busch (ed.), *Verwaltungsreform: Innovation, Gestaltung, Beteiligung.* Berlin.

Wollmann, H., 1996a. 'Modernization of the public sector and public administration in the Federal Republic of Germany. (Mostly) A story of fragmented incrementalism'. In: F. Naschold and M. Muramatsu (eds), *Public policy and administration in Japan and in Germany.* Berlin–New York.

Wollmann, H., 1996b. 'Verwaltungsmodernisierung: Ausgangsbedingungen, Reformanläufe und aktuelle Modernisierungsdiskurse'. In: C. Reichard and H. Wollmann (eds), *Kommunalverwaltung im Modernisierungsschub?* Basel, pp. 1–49.

CHAPTER SIX

Public Management Reform in Germany: A Revolution without a Theory?

Werner Jann
University of Potsdam

1. History of Administrative Reform in Germany

Administrative reform in Germany has a long and sad history of comprehensive concepts and great expectations versus institutional inertia with – at most – incremental change. Public administration in the Federal Republic of Germany has been the object of nearly permanent reform initiatives (König, 1995; Laux, 1995; Wollmann, 1995), but at least until the recent developments identified with the label 'New Public Management' (NPM), there were no deliberate departures from the classical Weberian concept of the hierarchical state.

After the Second World War, in the transition from the Nazi regime to post-war democracy, the German administrative system underwent remarkably little reform, both in terms of organisation and personnel. The administrative system of the Federal Republic continued the traditions of the old Reich, or, in scientific terms, the Weberian tradition of public service. If the role of the administrative state during the Nazi regime was reflected at all, it was looked upon as the abuse of a highly efficient system by an evil and criminal party and elite. The 1950s therefore saw mostly reconstruction and only very little institutional reorganisation of public administration. In fact, one of the main achievements of the post-war period was the inclusion of the 'traditional principles of civil service' (*hergebrachte Grundsätze des Berufsbeamtentums*) in the Federal Constitution (Art.33 (5) GG). These principles not only protect the traditional privileges of civil servants (pensions, lifelong tenure, alimentation instead of performance related pay), but also have been interpreted as a kind of constitutional guarantee of Weberian principles of public administration.

Beginning in the 1960s, at first prompted by the emerging new roles of the state (enlargement of the welfare state, Keynesian economics, social democratic reform agenda) and later as a reaction to fiscal stress and economic crisis, reformers

81

targeted the internal structures and processes of public administration in three major reform efforts. The results were rather mixed:

- The *territorial reform* (*Gebietsreform*) of the 1960s and 1970s resulted in larger units of local government (which were then criticised for loss of grass-root democracy), but failed in seriously redistributing the tasks and competencies between the different levels of government (*Funktionalreform*).
- The ambitious *modernisation of the machinery of (central) government* (*Projektgruppe Regierungs- und Verwaltungsreform*, 1968) managed to install some policy and evaluation capacities in the central departments, but did not alter the traditional incremental, 'negative coordination' mode of government (Mayntz and Scharpf, 1975) and the highly specialised, over-hierarchical organisation of federal ministries. Its grand rhetoric of 'long-term planning' and 'active policy making' backfired and led to a widely shared disillusion with administrative reform.
- The same is true for the attempt to reform the traditional *personnel system*, consisting of a dual structure of privileged civil servants (*Beamte*) and normal government employees (*Angestellte und Arbeiter*). An all party, blue-ribbon commission (*Studienkommission für die Reform des öffentlichen Dienstrechts*, 1970) produced eleven widely quoted volumes of research and one volume of recommendations, of which almost none was implemented.

Notwithstanding the spectacular failure of the large-scale reform agendas, there has been a steady flow of reform commissions and proposals ever since. At the end of the 1970s, when the economic and political climate had changed from reform-euphoria to consolidation, both major parties discovered 'de-bureaucratisation' as a political catchphrase (*Entbürokratisierung*, CDU, 1978; SPD, 1979). Since then each one of German *Länder* and also the federal government established at least one major commission on de-bureaucratisation and/or government reform. While most of these commissions dealt with rather mundane issues of *Rechtsbereinigung* (consolidation of statute law, Seibel, 1986), some of them came up with more controversial recommendations and gained some public notoriety (Bulling-Kommission, 1985; Kommission zur Gesetzes- und Verwaltungsvereinfachung, 1983).

Even before the recent upsurge of 'New Public Management' administrative reform was thus constantly on the political agenda. Discussions and concepts followed closely both the international discussion and the shift of the economic and political mood, dealing with – amongst others – aspects like (see Jann, 1986 for references):

- political planning (*aktive Politik*);
- programme budgeting (PPBS, MiFriFi);
- civil service reform (*Dienstrechtsreform*);

- democratic administration (*Demokratisierung*);
- citizen participation (*Bürgerbeteiligung*);
- citizen orientation (*Bürgernähe*);
- implementation (*Vollzugsdefizite*);
- evaluation (*Wirkungsforschung*);
- information technology (IuK);
- management systems (Harzburger Modell, MBO, and so on);
- leadership styles (*Mitarbeiterführung*);
- consolidation of law (*Rechtsbereinigung und -vereinfachung*);
- deregulation (*Verrechtlichung*);
- task reduction and downsizing (*Aufgabenkritik*);
- privatisation (*Privatisierung*).

Looking at these reform agendas (or at least catchphrases) three simplified conclusions seem plausible.

First, while all of these reform issues did influence and change German public administration, none of them fundamentally altered the basic structures and procedures of the German administrative state. There were incremental changes, but they were slow and small. Great expectations were regularly disappointed. Furthermore, there were no deliberate alternatives to Weberian hierarchy and bureaucracy. Reforms aimed at optimising the system, not changing it.

Second, the quick and somewhat arbitrary change of reform agendas and fads combined with political and academic 'oversell' led to widespread disappointment and disillusionment. By the end of the 1980s the field of administrative reform was characterised by ruined hopes and cynicism. At the same time the practice of administration was widely criticised. Reformers and practitioners had 'seen it all'. The most common complaints by both practitioners and academics were 'It cannot go on like this' and 'Nothing will ever change' – quite often made by the same person – followed by consensus: no more commissions, no more top-down concepts!

Third, administrative reform suffered from two characteristic features of the German political system: on the one hand it became a highly ideological debate with the two main parties on opposite sides of the agenda (on one side social-democrats favouring political planning, democratisation, citizen orientation and participation, on the other side conservatives interested in task reduction, deregulation, privatisation and so on). The fragmented and highly interdependent political system of the Federal Republic as usual prevented any one side from implementing its agenda while at the same time strengthening the power of vested interests. The result was political stalemate. By the end of the 1980s administrative reform was considered 'dead' by all professional observers.

2.   Comeback of Reform: *Neues Steuerungsmodell*

In the last few years administrative reform in Germany has made a remarkable comeback. Under the label of *Neues Steuerungsmodell* ('New Steering Model' (NSM)) it has become a household name for administrators and many politicians, a topic of numerous conferences and seminars, popular journal articles and TV talk shows. While a few years ago administrative reform was dead, today it is gradually becoming one of the most popular domestic policy issues. If it is not yet a revolution, it is certainly a quite unusual and unforeseen boom. Unlike in the US there has not, at least until now, been a bestseller (though the first attempts are on the market, see Metzen, 1994), but the speed with which the new agenda has been taken up by professionals and politicians is breathtaking. Concepts like customer-orientation, cost centre, controlling, contracting out, lean administration, or even *schlanker Staat* are everywhere:

- there are by now more than 70 percent of local communities in the 'old' *Länder* which at least claim to be engaged in some kind of NSM experience (the figure in the 'new' *Länder* is considerable lower);
- there are several *Länder* governments which actively support these experiences (Saarland, Schleswig-Holstein, Brandenburg, Berlin);
- nearly all *Länder* governments have again started new reform initiatives of their own (Hill and Klages, 1995), all of them with at least some reference to NSM; some *Länder* parliaments have taken up the issue in parliamentary Inquiry-Commissions (for example, Schleswig-Holstein, 1994);
- the Social-Democratic and the Green Party and their foundations have commissioned reports and memoranda about the subject and have held hearings (Jann, 1994; Clasen *et al.*, 1995), as have the trade unions; both parties have adopted parliamentary motions (see BTDrs 13/333) – at the federal as well as at the *Länder* level – with some quite impressive rhetoric;
- there are several new journals founded in 1995 (*Die innovative Verwaltung, Verwaltungsmanagement*) devoted nearly exclusively to the new gospel, not to mention innumerable articles in established journals. There is indeed some evidence, that no other country can match Germany in the sheer quantitative volume of – mostly normative – literary debate about NPM;
- private consulting firms have been quick to take up and spread the new message among local governments and other public agencies, there is even a brand new association of consulting firms engaged in this area;
- finally there is by now a booming industry of seminars for practitioners which, until quite recently unheard in Germany, are neither offered by public agencies nor free of charge – indeed, they are extraordinarily expensive.

As these examples indicate, there is a quite large and still growing demand for NSM and a very articulate and comprehensive public debate, which only a few years ago would have been quite unthinkable. Compared with the stalemate in the 1970s and 1980s this development has been called a 'medium miracle' (Pfeiffer, 1994). The boom has caught academic public administration and political science in universities and research centres – with few exceptions – by surprise, which in turn may be one explanation for their mostly hostile reactions and comments.

3. Characteristics of NSM

Compared with other countries, the development of NSM in Germany features some unusual characteristics: the movement originated from 'below', from local not from central government; it was pushed by practitioners, not academics and think tanks; it is not part of a simple political strategy to 'roll back the state', but rather aims at legitimising state intervention; it is not only concerned with efficiency, but with democracy and accountability; it has a strongly anti-ideological bias and aimed right from the beginning at bi-partisan support, at least at the local and *Länder* level.

The most important of these characteristics is that this time the inspiration and the message did not come from 'above' and did not address central government and its rather unusual problems, as nearly all the previous reform proposals had done. It originated from the local level and mostly from practitioners. From the beginning the main thrust of the reform was the local level, especially the organisation and procedures of local service delivery. In Gerhard Banner, the former head of the KGSt, there even emerged the German equivalent of an NPM-management guru (for details of the role of KGSt, see Reichard in this volume).

While the necessity of change was felt very strongly at the local level, and somewhat later also at the *Länder* level, because these levels are much closer to the day-to-day problems of the administrative state, the federal level has for a long time been able to ignore most of the problems. Consequently, the federal level is still engaged in a mostly party-political, ideological formulation of the issue, digging up the old trenches of the past (*Dienstrechtsreform*), even though there are now strong signs that Bonn also is joining the bandwagon (see current debates in the Bundestag about *Schlanker Staat* and the recently established expert commission of the same name).

It is not only the fiscal crisis following German reunification which propelled NSM, even though the insight 'no more money' certainly helped. The quite extraordinary success of NSM depends on widespread dissatisfaction with the status quo, especially amongst local government workers, middle and top management and local politicians. From the beginning, the German discussion concerned with the NSM stressed the shortcomings of the traditional bureaucratic way of steering large organisations. The discussion did not argue primarily in terms of micro-economic efficiency, but centred around problems of democracy, political accountability and legitimacy.

Traditional bureaucracies, so the argument went, were characterised by too much steering and control concerning details and rules (who may do what, when and how) and far too little steering and control concerning the results and objectives to be achieved. There was an abundance of legal controls and an acute shortage of concern about results. This of course coincides with the German administrative culture, which tends to view administrative issues as synonymous with legal issues (Jann, 1983).

The outcome of all this, so the argument went further, is a lack of coherent policy and finally the fragmentation and uncontrolled 'self-steering' of administrative units. Local politicians, being overwhelmed by the complexity and informational advantage of their bureaucracies, confine themselves to isolated interventions – usually narrow minded, parochial and totally disconnected with any strategic or policy issues. These interventions frustrate both politicians and managers, leading to a general atmosphere of distrust and disregard, both being convinced of the lack of competence, knowledge and the bad intentions of the other side.

In the end, there is no clear accountability and responsibility, there is a system of 'organised irresponsibility' (Banner, 1991, 1994), both inside the bureaucracy (neither central service nor service delivery departments feel responsible for results) and between bureaucracy and politicians (who always can blame each other if something goes wrong – and something always goes wrong). Citizens and voters find it difficult to identify the responsible actors.

The system is particularly unfit to reallocate resources in reaction to shifting demands and political priorities. Inside bureaucratic organisations there are invariably areas which badly need additional resources because of rising demand for public services, while other units hoard resources because they may need them later. All this (Banner, 1994; Reinermann, 1994) strongly resembles the system of a centralised command economy, which, as recent experience convincingly proved, was systematically unfit to allocate resources efficiently.

As a result bureaucratic steering and control systematically diminishes:

- a regard for scarce resources (be that money, personnel or time);
- transparency regarding costs and results;
- comparisons between better and not so good organisational units;
- incentives to perform extraordinarily well;
- organisational development;
- cooperation with external partners and
- the effective control of external, semi-privatised units.

These arguments retell well-known aspects of bureaucratic dysfunctions (for summaries see Leis, 1982; Lane, 1987; NRW, 1994; Pfeiffer, 1994). The main complaints, that bureaucracies are not interested in results, cannot contain their costs and are engaged in goal-displacement are, even in Germany, as old as bureaucracies themselves and even somewhat older than the Weberian concept of bureaucracy (Ellwein, 1994).

The interesting point is that NSM does not only look at the efficiency of public service delivery, but regards these deficiencies as problems of political guidance and control (*politische Steuerung*). Built-in deficits of democracy, political transparency and control lead to inefficiencies, not the other way round. If one accepts this argument, which very often gets lost in the rhetoric about a 'less costly, more efficient public service', NSM is, at least in theory, not an alternative, but a necessary prerequisite for democratic control of public administration.

In Germany the disillusionment with status quo procedures and solutions is quite bi-partisan. It coincides with a widespread feeling that the age-old ideological debates over *privatisation* and *deregulation* did not help to solve the inherent problems of the public sector. Professionals and politicians are fed up with the old ideological arguments. NSM is therefore widely seen not as identical or complementary with deregulation, privatisation and 'rolling back the state', but as an alternative to these strategies.

While the reform movement promises the best of both worlds to both sides, a government that works better (to the left) and costs less (to the right), it has been especially appealing to social democrats and trade unions (and recently even to the Green Party). It offers them an alternative to a purely negative strategy of fighting off claims for a reduction of public services and public standards. Modernisation is clearly seen as an alternative to privatisation.

As a result, NSM enjoys a, for German standards quite remarkable, bi-partisan support. Local governments which engage in NSM experiments usually do not encounter any sizeable difficulties in getting formal support from both the major parties and the worker-representation (*Personalrat*). The extraordinary wide consensus is even apparent in recent parliamentary Inquiry-Commissions (Schleswig-Holstein, 1994). In a way, the last few years have seen the emergence of a totally new and quite strong NSM–advocacy coalition. This coalition encompasses local and a growing number of *Länder* politicians, local government managers, private consultants, trade unionists and a rather limited number of public administration academics. Conspicuously absent are, with few exceptions, traditional political scientists, sociologists and lawyers.

4.   Elements of NSM

Like NPM in the Anglo-Saxon world, in Germany the *Neues Steuerungsmodell* (NSM) is not a coherent theory or elaborate model which can be applied in all kinds of public organisations, nor a rigorous, tested body of thought, but more a cluster of ideas, concepts and symbols, quite often not even particularly new ones.

Four Characteristics

There are by now numerous good publications and definitions of NSM (KGST, 1991, 1994; Budäus, 1994; Reichard, 1994). In the last few years the literature has been booming, even though the growth of the literature does not necessarily reflect a proportional growth of knowledge. If one uses the classical dimensions of personnel, organisation, finance and procedure, the main concepts have been characterised by catchphrases such as (Jann, 1993; Mayntz, 1995):

- from alimentation to motivation;
- from hierarchy to decentralisation;
- from cameralism to cost-accounting; and
- from rules to results.

More specifically the recipes and catchphrases described by proponents of NPM include in the area of *personnel (more motivation)*:

- performance related pay;
- teamwork and 'total quality management';
- more qualification and mobility (within the public sector and especially between the public and the private sector);
- new concepts of personal management and human resource development;
- less law and more economics and business training;
- fewer (or even abolishment of) traditional civil servants (*Beamte*);
- more professional and responsible managers;
- top-managers for a specified period only (*Spitzenpositionen auf Zeit*).

In the area of *organisation (more decentralisation)*:

- fewer hierarchical levels (*flache Organisation*);
- larger units with a larger span of control;
- less rigid organisational structures and more project oriented work;
- decentralised, semi-autonomous units with their own resource responsibility;
- one stop offices (*Bürgerämter*).

In the area of *finance (more accounting)*:

- more flexible budgeting;
- more global budgets;
- more transparency about the use of resources;
- introduction of internal cost accounting.

And in the area of *procedures (more results)*:

- output and performance oriented measurement of results (*Kennzahlen; Berichtspflichten*);
- controlling;
- contract management;
- comparison and competition between public sector units and between the public and the private sector;
- conscious decision making between *making* or *buying* services;
- product and customer orientation.

Somewhat crossing these dimensions is a final concern about a clearer and more responsible division of work between elected politicians and responsible managers, aiming at less day-to-day intervention by politicians and more strategic guidance and control.

The Term Steuerung

All these ideas, recipes and catchphrases are by now known under the label of *Neues Steuerungsmodell* (NSM). It is not just by chance that this label finally caught on. For one, there is a semantic problem. There is no easy German equivalent of 'management'. The term is, of course, well-known from Anglo-Saxon literature and business administration jargon. But for most Germans it is not quite clear what the term stands for. It has strong connotations with the private sector, so presumably it has something to do with markets and entrepreneurs. But the classical definition, 'the organisation and direction of resources to achieve a desired result' (Allison, 1979) is unknown by most Germans, at least in the public sector.

In fact, most German observers would probably equate the above definition with the concept of *Steuerung*, meaning steering, guidance and control, where there are objects and subjects of steering, intentions or objectives (desired results), instruments to obtain these objectives (resources) and finally some understanding of causal relations between steering activities and results (Mayntz, 1987; König, 1974). One of the proponents of New Public Management therefore defines management as 'steering of complex organisations' (Budäus, 1994).

What is New?

The first question to answer is, whether this really qualifies as a 'revolution'? None of the above is totally new. All these proposals are not really revolutionary, they have been known, discussed and even applied for quite some time. For one, it is the combination of a large number of elements which suggests a departure from the standard operating procedures of the German public sector. Furthermore, taken together they question 'near sacred' core elements of the traditional, Weberian concept of the public sector:

- is it necessary and useful to have a totally separate personnel system for the public sector?
- is hierarchy really the best and only way to steer large organisations and the relationship between organisations?
- does the traditional way of budgeting and accounting via cameralism offer enough information?
- is it possible to steer and control the performance of organisations primarily by rules and regulations?

5.   Criticism

Summary of Counter Arguments

In order to understand the 'revolutionary impact' of NSM one has to look at its critics. Despite, or perhaps because of, the unexpected and unusual success, at least in terms of publicity, the approach has recently come under severe criticism (Laux, 1995; König, 1995; Grunow, 1995). Critics of NSM stress its pre-occupation with concepts and visions, its affinity to commercial consultants, its naive reform-euphoria, its neo-liberal belief in the market and its neglect of the cultural premises of public administration. The main arguments of the critics seem to be:

- The whole undertaking of NSM is a *festival of visions* (Laux, 1995) consist-ing of fantastic concepts, models and promises, but very little substance and implementation. NSM is great on rhetoric, but short on substance, mostly there is just NATO (no action, talk only). The whole undertaking is more or less a fad, it is 'fast management food', it thrives on a bandwagon effect, everybody wants to join in before it is too late.
- It is also a new *marketing device* for (mostly) private consultants, who have to sell their product. Not the real problems, but the ever increasing product cycle of consultancy determines the rhetoric. As soon as local governments join the bandwagon, they become dependent on consultants. The more am-biguous the concepts and the faster they change, the better for the commer-cial consultants.
- Most of the ideas and recipes of NSM are *not new*. They are recycled, age-old concepts, sometimes with a new label. Much of it is simply common sense packaged as overly complex, jargon-laden management arcana.
- There is a *reform euphoria* sometimes bordering on pure activism (*blinder Aktionismus*) which is not interested in results but in reform for its own sake.
- Reformers forget the *lessons of the past*. They want to achieve too much and forget the very tight limits of institutional change. Organisation matters, but only very indirectly and in the long run.
- Even if there are some valid elements in NSM, the *process of implementation*

is a catastrophe and is ruining everything. Reform is mixed and sometimes confused with cut-back management, it is characterised by short-term activism, improvisation and a technocratic orientation, neglecting the legitimate interests of both politicians and employees.

- Public administration, especially local government, does not suffer from a penetrating crisis as claimed by the proponents of NPM. If there are problems, they are mostly caused by *external, exogenous developments*, such as the unrestricted demand for public services and not by internal, endogenous factors of bureaucratic organisation.
- NSM represents the unfounded *neo-liberal, economic belief* in the principal superiority of the market over administration. The victory of capitalism over communism is interpreted as the victory of the market over the state and NSM is therefore just another attempt at 'rolling back the state', another step in the *disarmament race of government.*
- NSM denies the *cultural premises of public administration* (König, 1974, 1995. The 'administrative paradigm' cannot be superseded by a 'managerial' or 'entrepreneurial paradigm'. There is a necessary functional differentiation between the public and private sector, each being organised according to its own rationality. Differentiated roles such as pupil, social service client, prisoner, and so on, cannot and should not be replaced by a concept like 'customer'. Concepts like customer or entrepreneur are inseparably connected with the paradigm of the market.
- Public and private services cannot be compared. The public sector is defined through its *obligations to society at large*, through democratic control, rule of law, justice, equity and the public welfare.
- Finally, NSM looks like re-establishing the old *politics–administration dichotomy*. For a long time the demolition of this naive dichotomy has been looked upon as one of the main achievements of political-science-based public administration. Now it is re-introduced by micro-economists who have no understanding of the intricacies of the politico–administrative system. They do not understand the peculiar rationality and behaviour of politics and politicians and the basically political nature of public administration.

Soundness of the Concept

While some of this criticism is valid, it does not shake the central concerns and assumptions of NSM. It is true that NSM is suffering from too many concepts, too much vision, too aggressive marketing and sometimes naive reform euphoria and amateurish implementation. Its proponents are far too often engaged in 'oversell' and the rhetoric often stands in sharp contrast to achievements.

NSM, like other reform agendas, is implemented in a garbage-can fashion, that is, solutions looking for problems are being used by certain actors in order to influence totally different agendas, for example, the internal distribution of power within and between agencies. But these impressions only confirm what we already know about institutional change (Olsen, 1991). Change is neither totally determined by environmental factors (competition, technological developments, performance), nor by purposeful political choice and sovereignty (human intentions, wilful design and power), nor totally by institutional autonomy and internal dynamics (robustness against changes in the environment and explicit reform efforts). The implementation process of any administrative reform tends to be complicated, continuous and conflict-laden. But these process variables do not tell us very much about the underlying soundness of the concept. If we accept that we are experiencing change, the significant question is, whether it is in the right direction or not, whether performance and/or democratic control will suffer, perhaps whether it is too slow or too fast.

The 'nothing new under the sun' argument also holds a lot of truth. NSM, at least in Germany, is used as a catch-all term for various kinds of reform proposals which have been around for many years. But this only strengthens the concept. Obviously it is not, as it is sometimes claimed, narrowly defined, but can encompass different reform agendas. Again, the question is whether these agendas work in the same direction, or whether they contradict each other.

The assertion that there is no real crisis and that if there are problems they are totally exogenous to the administrative system, lacks credibility. Obviously there are powerful external reasons for the crisis of local government in Germany, but they do not explain the current problems on their own. Local government is desperately looking for solutions, because local services, costs and tasks are out of control because the traditional internal system of steering local government is breaking down (Adamaschek, 1994).

NSM is not just naive neo-liberal market worship. There can be no doubt that the decline of communism has further undermined the belief in large-scale, hierarchical and centralised planning and problem solving. But, again at least in Germany, NSM is basically not used to 'roll back the state'. On the contrary, because it seems to offer an alternative to privatisation, it is particularly popular amongst social democrats.

6.   Administrative and Managerial Paradigms

Public and Private Sector

The major question is, and this is where criticism is most valid, whether NSM is comparable with the basic mechanisms and assumptions of the modern democratic welfare state (*demokratischer Rechts- und Sozialstaat*) or whether NSM naively transfers private sector concepts to the public sector. It is no wonder that this question raises some controversy, since proponents of NSM quite often talk about the inherent or soon to happen 'paradigm shift' and the necessary 'cultural revolution' to implement the new model. Obviously, the not always particularly modest reform rhetoric backfires.

Another way to put the question is to ask whether and how far the public sector can learn from experiences in the private sector and how big the differences between the two worlds are and should be. Figure 6.1 sketches the main concepts of both paradigms.

Figure 6.1.   Administrative and Managerial Paradigm

Administrative or public law paradigm	*Managerial or entrepreneurial paradigm*
Adherence to formalised rules and procedures	Use of resources to achieve results
Democratic control	Property rights
Hierarchy	Market
Rule of law	Rule of owner
Public welfare	Welfare of the firm
Legality	Private gain
Accountability	Autonomy
Legitimacy	Secrecy
Rules	Results
Collective action	Competition
Equity of need	Equity of market
Citizenship	Customer sovereignty
Authority (Behörde)	Firm
Risk avoidance	Risk-taking
Neutral expertise	Interest-orientation
Stability	Change
Tradition	Renewal
Voice	Exit

Obviously the NSM movement wants to diminish differences between the public and the private sector. Both in terms of personnel, hierarchy, accounting and procedures the public sector should become more like the private sector. For some critics (König, 1995) this development is dangerous and should be stopped right from the beginning.

König, like other critics, is concerned about the achievements of the modern, highly developed and functionally differentiated democratic state. If we want to keep and possibly enlarge these achievements, like democratic control, rule of law, legality, legitimacy, accountability, equity and so on; or if we want to preserve all three of Hood's core values in the public sector – frugality, rectitude and resilience (Hood, 1991) – how do we go about it? Do we refine and enlarge the concepts of the public sector, in the direction of more laws, more rules, larger and more strictly controlled hierarchies, more risk-avoidance, more stability and tradition, or do we use corresponding concepts of the private sector?

Fiction of the 'Administrative Paradigm'

In order to answer these questions we have to take a closer look at the 'administrative paradigm'. If we take the empirical findings of political and administrative science seriously, we have to accept that it no longer offers a realistic concept of the public sector. It contains more ideology than reality. Contrary to what the defenders of the administrative and public law paradigm claim (Moe and Gilmour, 1995), it is not the managerial but the administrative paradigm which rests on largely unexamined, ideological assumptions about government. The administrative paradigm is no longer a realistic description of the actual workings of the German administrative state. Accordingly it is not helpful to claim a principal incompatibility between the administrative and the managerial paradigm of public administration.

Years ago Frido Wagener (1979) described the 'pragmatic illegality' of German public administration. Thomas Ellwein (1986, 1994) stressed again and again that public administration – since the 'golden era' of the old Prussia – does not just obey rules, but decides on its own what and how much can be achieved with scarce resources. Public administration has always been 'managerial', it is used to decide how to reconcile what ought to be done and what can be done.

If we take the argument a bit further, we have to accept that the unity of public administration is nothing more than fiction (Mayntz, 1995). Our administrative system is not a large, tightly controlled hierarchy, but a complicated network. The administrative state is characterised by ever stronger functional differentiations, lacking a visible centre. Images of the classical, internal and external sovereign state are obsolete. The administrative state is not a centrally-controlled and rule-integrated hierarchy, but a more or less tightly integrated network of highly specialised organisations, firmly linked within their environment. In modern societies the success of government steering depends on the de-hierarchisation of state–society relations (Scharpf, 1991).

Modern political science has described these features for years and has developed theoretical concepts like pluralism, corporatism, federalism, policy networks, agency capture or advocacy coalitions. But both theoretical and practical discussions about the administrative state are still dominated by hierarchical images of the unitary state.

Legality, Legitimacy and Efficiency

All administrative reform, like basically all administrative theory, deals with the same set of problems:

- *legality*, using concepts like due process, equity and justice;
- *legitimacy*, concerned with fairness, democracy and accountability;
- *efficiency* and *effectiveness*, concerned with the use of scarce resources to achieve results.

Contrary to what its critics claim, NSM is not only concerned with the last of these problems. It takes up classical problems of administrative reform and empirical experiences of modern government and tries to answer them according to recent theoretical assumptions. A new theory of governance should use the rather similar concepts of management, steering and governance and integrate them with political science concepts.

The classical Weberian concept of bureaucracy claimed to have solved all three basic problems of the administrative state, offering not only a thoroughly legal and legitimate, but also the most efficient, organisation of government. This claim has been shattered by empirical evidence ever since it has been made, though whether another concept is better at balancing these three necessities of the administrative state is still open to debate. Administrative reform and the concept of public management is still hampered by a certain confusion about the nature of administration in a democratic state. Administration is not a specific category in theories about separation of power (where it is subsumed under the 'executive') nor in democratic theory (where it is assumed that the political system, if inputs are democratic, somehow manages to convert demands into outputs).

Empirical research about the role of administration in the formulation and implementation of public policies has for a long time demonstrated amongst other things (see Olsen, 1983):

- that public administration is an important actor in policy formation;
- that policy implementation is a political process of its own;
- that public bureaucracies can only be controlled very imperfectly through legislative programming, that is, that the 'parliamentary chain of command' is not a viable description of reality;
- that the administrative apparatus does not get its decision premises exclusively from the official democratic institutions, but rather through interest groups, client networks, professional standards or even its own personnel system; that is, that also the 'executive chain of command' is not a very valid description of reality;
- that we have to leave the unrealistic assumptions of mono-rationality and mono-centrism in governmental policy making and policy implementation and adopt the complexity of multi-actor and multi-rational networks (Kickert, 1995).

The reaction of political science (and American Public Administration) to these findings was to deny the possibility of any realistic separation between politics and administration. The old Wilsonian dichotomy became the hallmark of an old-fashioned, outdated and totally unrealistic science of public administration. Instead of talking about politics and administration, the concept of the 'politico-administrative system' (PAS) became in vogue (in German the shorthand RV was used for *Regierung und Verwaltung*). But in stressing the political functions of administration, the question how the administrative apparatus is 'steered' and is held accountable was not solved. The problem just disappeared through the redefinition of concepts.

Control of the Administration: Transparency

As argued above, the problem of steering the administrative apparatus is one of the central concerns of NSM (or new public management). By distrusting the steering capabilities of hierarchies and by viewing formally hierarchical inter- and intra-organisational relationships as highly problematic, as a chain of low-trust principal–agent relationships, NSM takes up empirical evidence and poses important questions.

The other side of steering is accountability. How does democratic accountability work, if the public sector is no longer hierarchically organised and does not possess sufficient information about its costs and results? How does democracy work, if all empirical findings tell us that the concept of 'overhead democracy' (deLeon in this volume), where we elect representatives, which in turn elect political heads of administrations, which in turn are supposed to control and steer these huge organisations via hierarchy, rules and procedures, does not work very well?

The central underlying theme – or even implicit 'theory' – of NSM is transparency. Whether it be cost-accounting, contracting out, performance related pay, controlling, interagency comparison, competition or even product- or customer-orientation, the concern is always about making inter- or intra-organisational relationships more transparent. When NSM asks for a new definition of the division of labour between elected politicians and permanent administrators (or managers), it does not say that there is a clear division between politics and administration, nor that there should be. It acknowledges that administrators make political decisions, it only tells us that we should no longer hide this fact behind an outdated model of political control. Instead we should try to make the relationship between principal and agent more transparent, for example, through explicit contracts. What at first looks like a simple separation between politics and administration, between policy making and policy execution, at second sight seems to be trying to achieve an organisational separation in order to actually obtain a functional integration (Kickert and Jørgensen, 1995).

For political science the interesting challenge of NSM is therefore the assumption that democratic control, accountability and legitimacy are not necessarily dependent on legally based hierarchical reporting structures, as the administrative paradigm assumes (Moe and Gilmour, 1995). In an area of big government democratic accountability must indeed mean something different from rules and regulation, hierarchy, legality and formal ministerial responsibility (Wilson, 1994).

There are still important or even crucial elements missing in this approach. Political actors have strong, institutionally rooted incentives to continue doing what NSM does not want them to do, and they have very few incentives to adopt the reforms it proposes (Moe, 1991). We do not know how to integrate politics into contract-management and competition, even though we are quite clear about the fact that governing institutions which separate the formulation of demands from the involvement in the production of solutions, lead to democratic overload and weaken the governing capacity of the political system (Sörensen, 1995; Kooiman, 1993). Instead of empowering citizens, decentralisation may strengthen local bureaucrats and public sector employees, it may even encourage corruption. The fragmentation of the public sector may become even more impenetrable, leading to even less democratic control.

7. Towards a New Theory of Administration in a Democratic State

NSM does not have a coherent theory about public administration in a democratic state, but it tackles the right questions. It asks how organisations can become more transparent, can be steered to achieve results, how organisations can learn and how they can change. If political science, as it ought to, is interested in democratic accountability, it should take up the challenge. Whether we call this concern management, steering or governance, should not make a big difference. The challenge is to overcome the sharp institutional separation within the political system between the 'input side', traditionally called democracy and the 'output side', traditionally called bureaucracy (Sörensen, 1995). Empirical observations tell us that there is an increasing institutional fusion of input and output functions in the political system, that is, the increased use of discretion by administrators, growing decentralisation, ever more powerful policy networks, politicisation of administration, and so on.

We need a new understanding of the role of public administration in a democratic state, an organisational theory of the public sector which looks at public administration as it is, not as it should be. The problem with the administrative paradigm is not its normative but its empirical soundness, it is not realistic (Diver, 1982). For the entrepreneurial paradigm in the public sector it is unfortunately sometimes the other way round. NSM in Germany has until now had a strong normative component that overwhelms the theoretical, without any clear picture of the public sector. It offers a lot of prescriptions which have a certain common sense appeal, but their basis in theory is often unclear or eclectic. These theoretical foundations cannot be clarified if we preserve the old dichotomy between both paradigms. Both seem extraordinarily unfit to describe current structures and practices and to explain the direction of change. The solution can only be in the good old tradition of dialectical combination and transformation, *Aufhebung* in the words of Hegel. Germany, because of its strong state tradition, may be a particularly promising and interesting field in which to find new theoretical models and prescriptions.

As others have noticed before, political science has to catch up with empirical and theoretical developments. The old hierarchical, Weberian theory of the state is no longer valid, instead, we need a more modern concept of governance. This new theory must take up theoretical concepts developed by business administration (learning organisation, lean management, business process reengineering, and so on), by institutional economics (transaction costs, property rights, principal–agent theory, theory of repeated games) and by political science (policy networks, corporatism, advocacy coalitions). There is until now no evidence that NSM does not fit into such a new theory of governance, indeed, there is quite a lot of evidence that it may fit much better than the classical Weberian image of the sovereign state, ruled exclusively by public law, bureaucracy and overhead democracy.

References

Adamaschek, B., 1994. *Wege aus der Krise? Wettbewerb und Selbststeuerung als Grundlage einer leistungsfähigen Kommunalverwaltung.* Bertelsmann-Stiftung Gütersloh.

Allison, G.T., 1979. 'Public and private management: are they fundamentally alike in all unimportant respects?'. Reprinted in: F.S. Lane (ed.), *Current issues in public administration*, New York, 1980, pp. 13–33.

Banner, G., 1991, 'Von der Behörde zum Dienstleistungsunternehmen: Die Kommunen brauchen ein neues Steuerungsmodell'. *Verwaltung, Organisation und Personal (VOP)*, pp. 6–11.

Banner, G., 1994, 'Steuerung kommunalen Handelns'. In R. Roth and H. Wollmann (eds), *Kommunalpolitik. Politisches Handeln in den Gemeinden.* Zeitchrift der Deutschen Vereinigung für Politische Wissenschaft. Opladen.

Budäus, D., 1994. *Public Management. Konzepte und Verfahren zur Modernisierung öffentlicher Verwaltungen.* Berlin.

Bulling-Kommission (Kommission Neue Führungsstruktur Baden-Württemberg) (ed.), 1985. *Bericht der Kommission Neue Führungsstruktur Baden-Württemberg.* Stuttgart.

Clasen, R. *et al.*, 1995. *Effizienz und Verantwortlichkeit. Reformempfehlungen für eine effiziente, aufgabengerechte und bürgerkontrollierte Verwaltung.* Gutachten, Berlin.

CDU, 1978. Entbürokratisierung.

Diver, C.S., 1982. 'Engineers and entrepreneurs: the dilemma of public management'. *Journal of Policy Analysis and Management*, vol.1, pp. 402–6.

Ellwein, Th., 1986. *Zur Geschichte der öffentlichen Verwaltung in Deutschland.* Stuttgart.

Ellwein, Th., 1994. *Das Dilemma der Verwaltung. Verwaltungsstruktur und Verwaltungsreformen in Deutschland.* Mannheim.

Grunow, *et al.*, 1995. *Lokale democratie vergeleken.* Tjeenk Willink, Zwolle.

Hill, H. and H. Klages, 1995. *Reform der Landesverwaltung*, Stuttgart/Heidelberg.

Hood, C., and M. Jackson, 1991. *Administrative argument.* Aldershot, Dartmouth.

Jann, W., 1986. 'Politikwissenschaftliche Verwaltungsforschung'. In: K. von Beyme (ed.), *Politikwissenschaft in der Bundesrepublik Deutschland. Entwicklungsprobleme einer Disziplin, Politische Vierteljahresschrift*, Part 16, Opladen.

Jann, W., 1983. *Staatliche Programme und Verwaltungskultur.* Opladen.

Jann, W., 1993. 'Neue Wege in der öffentlichen Verwaltung'. In: H. Hill and H. Klages (eds), *Qualitäts- und erfolgsorientiertes Verwaltungsmanagement. Aktuelle Tendenzen und Entwürfe, Schriftenreihe der Hochschule Speyer*, nr. 112, Berlin.

Jann, W., 1994. *Moderner Staat und Effiziente Verwaltung, Zur Reform des öffentlichen Sektors in Deutschland*, Gutachten, Friedrich-Ebert-Stiftung, Bonn.

KGSt, 1991. 'Kommunale Gemeinschaftstelle für Verwaltungsvereinfachung, Dezentrale Ressourcenverantwortung, Überlegungen zu einem neuen Steuerungsmodell'. *KGSt-Berich*, vol. 12, Köln.

KGSt, 1994. 'Kommunale Gemeinschaftsstelle für Verwaltungsvereinfachung, Das Neue Steuerungsmodell. Beschreibung und Definition von Produkten'. *KGSt-Bericht*, vol. 8, Köln.

Kickert, W.J.M., 1995. 'Public governance in the Netherlands: an alternative to Anglo-American managerialism'. MS Erasmus University Rotterdam, to appear in *Administration and Society*.

Kickert, W.J.M. and T. Beck Jörgensen, 1995. 'Conclusion and discussion: management, policy, politics and public values'. *International Review of Administrative Sciences*, vol. 61, pp. 577–86.

Kommission zur Gesetzes- und Verwaltungsvereinfachung, 1983. *Gesetzes- und Verwaltungs-vereinfachung in Nordrhein-Westfalen. Berichte und Vorschläge.* Köln.

König, K., 1974. 'Programmsteuerung in komplexen politischen Systemen'. *Die Verwaltung*, pp. 137 ff.

König, K., 1995. 'Neue Verwaltung oder Verwaltungsmodernisierung: Verwaltungspolitik in den neunziger Jahren'. *Die öffentliche Verwaltung*, vol. 48(9), pp. 349–58.

Kooiman, J., 1993. *Modern governance: new government-society interactions.* Sage, London.

Lane, J.-E., 1987. 'Introduction: the concept of bureaucracy'. In: J.-E. Lane (ed.), *Bureaucracy and public choice*. Sage modern politics series. vol. 15, pp. 1–31. London.

Laux, E., 1995. 'Zwischenrufe'. *Die innovative Verwaltung*, vol. 1, pp. 15–18.

Leis, G., 1982. 'Die Bürokratisierungsdebatte der Stand der Auseinandersetzung'. *Politische Vierteljahresschrift*, vol. 13(23), pp. 168–89.

Mayntz, R., 1987. 'Politische Steuerung und gesellschaftliche Steuerungsprobleme – Anmerkungen zu einem theoretischen Paradigma'. *Jahrbuch zur Staats- und Verwaltungswissenschaft*, pp. 89 ff.

Mayntz, R., 1995. *Öffentliche Verwaltung im gesellschaftlichen Wandel.* MS, Köln.

Mayntz, R. and F.W. Scharpf, 1975. *Policy-making in the German federal bureaucracy.* Elsevier, Amsterdam.

Metzen, H., 1994. *Schlankheitskur für den Staat, Lean Management in der öffentlichen Verwaltung.* Frankfurt/Main.

Moe, R.C. and R.S. Gilmour, 1995. 'Rediscovering principles of public administration: the neglected foundation of public law'. *Public Administration Review*, vol. 55(2), pp. 135–46.

Moe, T.M., 1991. 'Politics and the theory of organization'. *The Journal of Law, Economics and Organization*, vol. 7, pp. 106–29.

NRW, 1994. *Ausschuß für Verwaltungsstrukturreform, Auswertung der Anhörungen, Zuschriften und einschlägiger Veröffentlichungen mit dem Ziel einer Bewertung und Erarbeitung von Alternativvorschlägen für die Arbeit des Ausschusses, Landtag Nordrhein-Westfalen 11.* Wahlperiode, Volage 11/3149, Düsseldorf.

Olsen, J.P. (ed.), 1983. *Organized democracy: political institutions in a welfare state – the case of Norway.* Universitetsforlaget, Oslo.

Olsen, J.P., 1991. 'Analyzing institutional dynamics'. *Staatswissenschaft und Staatspraxis*, vol. 1, pp. 247–271.

Pfeiffer, U., 1994. *NRW 2000 Plus. Wirtschaftsentwicklung und Modernisierung des Staatssektors in Nordrhein-Westfalen.* Bonn.

Reichard, Chr., 1994. *Umdenken im Rathaus. Neue Steuerungsmodelle in der deutschen Kommunalverwaltung.* Berlin.

Reinermann, H., 1994. 'Die Krise als Chance: Wege innovativer Verwaltungen'. *Speyer Forschungsberichte*, vol. 139, Speyer.

Scharpf, F.W., 1991. 'Die Handlungsfähigkeit des Staates am Ende des zwanzigsten Jahrhunderts'. *Politische Vierteljahresschrift*, vol. 32(4), pp. 621–34.

Schleswig-Holstein, Schleswig-Holsteinischer Landtag (ed.), 1994. *Schlußberich. Enquete-Kommission zur Verbesserung der Effizienz der öffentlichen Verwaltung*. Kiel.

Seibel, W., 1986. 'Entbürokratisierung in der Bundesrepublik Deutschland'. *Die Verwaltung*, pp. 137–62.

Sörensen, E., 1995. *On the Concept of Governance*. Paper presented at the ECPR conference in Bordeaux, 27th April–2nd May 1995.

Wagener, F., 1979. 'Der öffentliche Dienst im Staat der Gegenwart'. *Veröffentlichungen der Vereinigung der Deutschen Staatsrechtslehrer*, vol. 37, pp. 215–66, Berlin/New York.

Wilson, F.L., 1994. *European politics today: the democratic experience*. Englewood Cliffs, Prentice Hall, New York.

Wollmann, H., 1995. 'Modernization of the public sector and public administration in the federal republic of Germany: (mostly) a story of fragmented incrementalism', MS to be published in: M. Muramatsu and F. Naschold (eds), *Public Policy and Administration in Japan and in Germany*.

CHAPTER SEVEN

Administrative Reforms in Austria: Project *Verwaltungsmanagement*

Franz Strehl
Johannes Kepler University, Linz

1. Introduction

This contribution is a report on and a discussion of a large scale reform endeavour at the Austrian federal level and is based on theoretical deliberations and practical experience in this project. It is intended to provide examples and learning opportunities concerning approach, strengths and weaknesses of administrative reform.

The complex and prominent reform project at the Austrian federal level is called *Verwaltungsmanagement*. In the following its development from 1987 to 1994–95, its contents, organisation, methods and procedures and the main results and further outcomes of this important and controversial project will be discussed. The notion *Verwaltungsmanagement* indicates that the focus of the reform on management orientation is necessary as well as fashionable. In 1986 a special department was organised in the Federal Chancellery and given responsibilities in the areas of federalism and reform. This was a considerable change compared to former reform endeavours: no isolated, independent projects within the ministries should be undertaken but one large, complex, integrated, and inter-ministerial project was planned. This meant the integration of a variety of sub-projects based on the same method, aiming at the same overall goals and covering basically the same contents.

The development of the project approach was based on the experiences of some ministries and on Swiss, German and British reform projects. The specific and strongly criticised feature of the project is that all 14 ministries are involved in the project simultaneously, that organisational analyses are conducted in each of them and that rationalisation and change proposals are developed within an overall strategic framework, and those proposals with high priority are implemented in a coordinated way. Based on a resolution of the ministerial council (at the end of 1989) the project was started in all ministries and was planned for a period of 5 years. The formal framework and guidelines are laid down in an official project manual. In the following the main features of the project are described.

Project Goals

- Reorganisation of task and management structures, concentration on core tasks: adjustment of competencies and responsibilities, contracting out, abolishment and reduction of tasks.
- Increasing productivity by 20 percent within four years: critical evaluation of core tasks, improving efficiency and effectiveness.
- Reducing costs of administrative procedures: development of cost and performance ratios and indicators as management instrument.
- Concentration on management tasks: relieving top executives of day-to-day overload and thus creating capacities for strategic tasks.
- Improving service functions for the citizens.

One major (planned) feature of the project was that the focus should place a stronger emphasis on results and output rather than on management by mere resource allocation (input orientation): performance and performance responsibility are the key words. However, an important precondition is the setting of goals and objectives by the politicians and chief executives in the administration. (This, being a complex and difficult task, could not be reached on a broad basis until 1994/95 and will need further great efforts in order to be realised at least partially).

Strategic Project Principles

- Emphasis not on a 'test office' but on 'offices tests'.
- Demonstration of the Federal Government that there is a serious attempt to improve the public administrative performance.
- Improving close relationships with citizens – 'the citizen as client'.
- Reforms being implemented together with and not against the civil servants.
- High degree of involvement and participation of civil servants.
- Creating synergies and a general positive 'reform climate' in the long run.
- Maintenance of ministerial autonomy: the project management in the Federal Chancellery is only responsible for project methods, organisation, results analysis and coordination.
- Organisation of the project according to the principles of project management concerning the planning, steering and monitoring of performance, time and costs and the definition and allocation of competencies and responsibilities among the participating institutions.

One of the crucial issues of the administrative reform is the way in which increased efficiency and effectiveness can be realised:

Should the central functions and competencies for the federal budget administration (Ministry of Finance) and job positions (Federal Chancellery) be strengthened within these organisations? *Or* should these functions and competencies go along with the simultaneous development and implementation of increased autonomy in the other ministries?

The department of the Minister for Federalism and Administrative Reform is organised within the Federal Chancellery and its main reform responsibility is the coordination of the relevant activities within the federal administration. Based on the Constitutional Law the responsibility for the implementation of any project lies exclusively with the ministries. The minister mainly plays the role of a promoter and sponsor. The reform project is oriented in two directions. The first direction is adaptating to changing challenges and requirements which are necessary in the long term, and the resulting concepts of development. The second stresses short term restoration with respect to economies and efficiency.

The short term dimension is rather seen as a 'therapy of symptoms' through which small scale successes can be achieved quickly. The long-term concept emphasises the analysis and removal of the fundamental causes of the deficiencies and in this respect is a slow and laborious learning process which has to overcome many obstacles in an incremental way – step by step. The emphasis is primarily on 'development' and long-term orientation in the areas of personnel and finance.

Three Phases of the Project

Phase 1:   Basic administrative analysis (1989).
Phase 2:   In-depth and inter-ministerial studies (1990–93/94).
Phase 3:   Autonomous implementation of sub-projects in the ministries (1994–ongoing).

In phase one a general analysis of the strengths and weaknesses of the ministries was conducted. The primary purpose was the identification of the main areas with high potential for improvement. The main goal was to ensure consistency of the project philosophy and goal orientation in all ministries and with all external consulting firms (laid down in two project manuals). The project directly covered 14 ministries with about 8700 civil servants. Indirectly – in all decentralised organisations – some 150 000 persons will be affected in the long run by the project results.

2.   Project Organisation

Figure 7.1.   Project Organisation

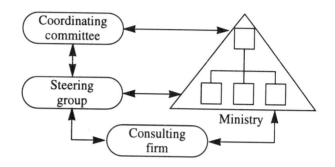

Coordinating Committee

The Federal Minister of Federalism and Administrative Reform is the chairman of the Coordinating Committee, which includes representatives from all ministries and civil servants unions. The committee has the following roles:

- a central organisational/political institution that decides on project matters and provides the basis for governmental decisions;
- provides the organisational and financial basis for the entire project,
- monitors the project;
- applies for tendering and contracting the consulting firms and for budget allocation;
- assesses and comments on the consulting firms' reports on the ministries;
- prepares and resolves reports to the government;
- decides on motions and proposals of the steering group.

Steering Group

Roles:

- coordinates the overall project and the sub-projects at the operational level in respect of deadlines, costs and goals in close cooperation with the respective ministry;
- prepares the business of the coordinating committee;
- transforms the project reports about the ministries into condensed information for the government via the coordinating committee;
- coordinates all activities concerning inter-ministerial issues.

Intra-ministerial Organisation

Project coordinator
The intra-ministerial project organisation follows the principles of a matrix organisation; the project coordinator has competencies and responsibilities which put him in a position to control the project.

The project coordinator:

- directly supports the ministerial top management regarding the project;
- directly reports to the ministerial top management (section chief and/or minister);
- is in direct contact with the steering group;
- is the representative of the ministry in the coordinating committee;
- is the 'turntable' between the project manager of the consulting firm, the ministerial project group (civil servants at different hierarchical levels within the organisational units in the ministry) and the steering group.

Ministerial project group
This group is appointed by the Minister. For the duration of the project the group members are exempted from other duties according to project workload and priorities (approximately 25 percent of regular working time). They have sound professional knowledge of the ministry. They are responsible for supporting the implementation of the sub-tasks and for the deadlines and performance of these tasks. They remain in their organisational units and work part-time on the project as required.

Personnel representation
Union representatives are involved in all decisions on important project steps and in the assessment of measures and recommendations.

External consulting firm
The consulting firm is selected by the ministry concerned and the steering group in a joint decision-making process based on criteria specified in advance. A detailed differentiating profile is developed against which the firms' proposals are measured.

In general, the firm must:

- be professionally and methodologically equipped to fulfil the contract;
- possess sufficient expertise and experience in the relevant fields;
- inform the project coordinator and the steering committee on all matters.

Problems should be solved at the lowest possible hierarchical level and should only be taken to the next level if they cannot be solved and if the topic is not only relevant for one single ministry.

3.   Reform Project Phase One

In phase one the following topics were analysed:

- organisation (goals, structure, distribution of competencies, strengths and weaknesses, relationships between central and decentralised organisations, work process analyses, inter-ministerial issues);
- basic resource/performance relations;
- costs;
- personnel and financial capacities;
- savings potentials.

These topics were worked on by the external firms and ministries in methodologically and conceptually different approaches and, not surprisingly, the results are many and diverse. The major results are a structured representation of the organisations and tasks, the identification of those areas in which a high potential for rationalisation is to be expected. Important problem areas concerning the interfaces between ministries and between the centre and the decentralised (subordinate) organisations could be defined in detail. In particular, civil servants at all hierarchical levels were invited to develop proposals and suggestions which are systematised as a basis for the in-depth studies in phase two.

In total about 3700 suggestions from all ministries were structured systematically. Two thirds of these suggestions could be realised within the ministries themselves. The others are structured according to specific themes and form the basis for in-depth studies concerning complex and encompassing problem areas which promise high rationalisation potential. They are pursued as major projects in phase two. The most important issues resulting from phase one are (*Bundeskanzleramt*, 1994, p. 11):

- More than one third of the suggestions concerned volume, effectiveness and efficiency of task fulfilment.
- About 40 percent concerned improvements of organisational structures and processes.
- 20 percent show room for improvement in information technology and the personal workplace.
- 20 percent concern leadership, motivation, pay, training.
- 10 percent concern legal matters (change of laws).

4.   Reform Project Phase Two

The analysis of phase one resulted in 9 inter-ministerial in-depth studies, seven of which were started in 1990–91. The most important sub-projects were the following.

Reduction of competence/responsibility overlapping
Overlapping of competencies/responsibilities between ministries results in considerable efficiency and effectiveness problems. The main task of this in-depth study was the analysis of existing multiple responsibilities in the top federal administration and the development of change proposals. In particular the following areas were identified: task related non-overlapping structures, optimisation of spans of control, positioning of staff units, abolishment of overlapping in the areas of budget and personnel, environmental protection, European Union and international organisations agenda, economic and cultural development, financial share management, issues of youth and family, traffic, statistics.

Leadership and personnel
Leadership and personnel are being paid increasing attention. Modern approaches to human resource management will have to be emphasised in future projects: leadership profiles, leadership guidelines, motivation issues, personnel requirements and personnel development, growing mobility of civil servants, delegation of decision making, performance orientation.

Budgeting and 'controlling' (management control systems)
Main issues are an increase in the transparency of budget planning and execution, the development of 'controlling' (that is, management control systems) and cost accounting systems.

Strategic electronic data model
The ministries provided numerous proposals for an improvement of the information technology. This sub-project focused on the development of an integrated strategic electronic data model with three major areas:

– societal conditions for the implementation of information technology (citizens' expectancies, information management in law-making processes);
– management aspects of technology (organisation, resources, internal service fee calculation);
– technical infrastructure and international standards.

Buildings and offices
A problematic feature of the federal administration is the permanent scarcity of office space and the fact that organisational units are scattered in many buildings

resulting in logistic and work process inefficiencies: by Austrian standards there is a high degree of scattering of ministerial units in 86 sites. The main goals are efficient location coordination, logistics and overall management.

Office management, technical communication, documentation
One issue is the technical state of the art in different ministries that varies to a high degree, another issue is the long duration of file work processes (transport and left undone time is almost 80 percent of the total file processing time). The project focused on the efficient completion of files under the given legal and organisational conditions which is considered to be an important element of the legality principle and openness to scrutiny of administrative action. In order to improve the situation the emphasis is on office information systems (electronic file), rationalisation and technical work place design.

Procurement
Federal procurement showed a high potential of rationalisation, decentralisation and standardisation.

Civil servants' business trips
It is interesting to note that the costs of federal business trips have developed in a way which makes it necessary to analyse the respective legal norms, organisation (application, approval, financial clearing) and management aspects as internal dimensions, and the taking advantage of the size of the federal administration as a contract partner for services like airlines, travel agencies, railways, hotels, cars, and so on, as external dimensions. The overall organisation was assessed as being too complicated and expensive and did not use (to a satisfactory degree) modern possibilities of travel management also because of obsolete technology and legal norms.

5.   Reform Project Phase Three

The main issue of this phase was the implementation of intra- and inter-ministerial projects with respect to methods, inter-ministerial coordination and financial and personnel support by the Federal Chancellery. One strategic idea was to initiate learning processes between organisational units working on the same topics and thus to foster project developments.

6.   Assessment of Content and Process of the Reform Project

Role of the Federal Chancellery

Due to the legal, historical and organisational situation the Federal Chancellery is in a rather difficult position as to reform responsibilities. In fact, it does not have formal competencies *vis à vis* the autonomy of the ministries. Several functions are unclear: concerning the reform agenda the Federal Chancellery on the one hand is in a 'staff position' (providing coordination and recommendations without direct possibilities of intervention), on the other hand it carries responsibilities and competencies for the overall federal administration concerning decisions on personnel positions. Therefore the Chancellery is identified by the ministries as very powerful and many conflicts concerning personnel development issues result. The permanent issue is the centralisation or decentralisation of personnel related competencies. The perception is one of 'Big Brother' and traditionally the reluctance to accept the Federal Chancellery's influence and control functions is rather high.

Political Priorities

Political interests and changing priorities on the highest levels tend to reduce the status and importance of management oriented reforms and to retard the respective projects. Accordingly, reform projects are allocated relatively low financial and personnel resources and, therefore, the desirable momentum is lacking. In addition, traditionally, the need and interest to really work on efficiency and effectiveness cannot be said to be highly prominent and there are no well-developed incentives to do so. There are views that success of the reform could be improved if the allocation of certain budget positions and personnel positions could be linked to the successful realisation of reform projects.

   In phase one the overall success was rather limited as compared to the expectations. One very positive effect was that many organisational units have developed a high degree of problem awareness and various projects promise further developments (in the long term).

Comments on Phase Two

In 1993 the reform project was formally closed but the sub-projects, of course, did continue. It has provided many opportunities to initiate an encompassing change in the federal administration (*Bundeskanzleramt*, 1994, p. 125). The strengths and weaknesses of the project in respect to the stated project goals can be summarised as follows:

Reorganisation of task and management structures, concentration on core tasks
The main problems were to find obsolete tasks and the self-definition of responsibilities and tasks by managers. In this highly sensitive area political and organisation–political strategies of resistance play a particular role. In the official project evaluation the conclusion was drawn that this goal has been attained in a very limited way only (*Bundeskanzleramt*, 1994, p. 127).

Increasing productivity by 20 percent within four years
It is interesting to observe that officially, as well as informally (on purpose or not), the term 'increasing productivity' is equated with 'personnel reduction'. This view which was also published in the media resulted in serious arguments and resistance by the civil servants. However, it is exactly this goal which has directed awareness towards thinking more in terms of efficiency and effectiveness and has promoted the reform climate. In some organisations modest successes could be reached.

Reducing costs of administrative procedures
At the beginning of the project cost consciousness within the administration was practically 'zero' (*Bundeskanzleramt*, 1994, p. 125). The project contributed to the development (and implementation) of cost accounting approaches in several organisations and to a growing interest in the topic. As an overall result there was an increase in cost accounting projects.

Concentration on management tasks
In connection with other project goals a very important approach on leadership and personnel was developed which contributed to a climate favourable for a new way of perceiving management and leadership tasks and leading away from the mere administration of organisations and personnel by top civil servants. But also concerning this goal, as holds true for most of the reform details, it must be said that changes occur in homeopathic doses and in small steps.

Improving service functions for the citizens
The idea that citizens (taxpayers) are not only 'addressees of legal norms' but also 'clients' having a right to receive services, is accepted and realised to an increasing degree. This is reflected on the one hand by a more intensive call for transparency of administrative costs and on the other hand by an increasing focus on themes of behavioural issues of civil servants (such as leadership, motivation, personnel development and performance).

The projects in phase two can be classified as rather promising. The most important topics, 'leadership and personnel development' and 'controlling/cost accounting', are emphasised in principle and promoted officially. However, only little progress can be identified. A major problem in the area of 'controlling' is the semantic closeness to *Kontrolle* (the traditional audit and a posteriori control). It is interpreted as a modern (fashionable) and very subtle instrument of a posteriori control combined with a priori elements which, of course, has to be declined. There was no systematic and effective promotion and marketing of successful sub-projects in diverse organisations. However, projects contributed to an improved climate, and topics can be discussed now which could not be approached before.

The Minister of Federalism and Administrative Reform has only limited possibilities in demanding the realisation of resolutions of the Council of Ministers. He has competencies of coordination but no right of order whatsoever in the ministries, and mainly has to rely on the goodwill and cooperation of the other ministers. On the one hand a reform of this dimension can only be undertaken and realised in the long term, on the other hand politicians formulate their criteria of success in the short term between election and re-election. Concerning the standpoint of unions it can be said that their overt behaviour was a rather constructive one. Of course, they wanted to score points concerning pay. One of the issues of the reforms concerning leadership and personnel development was the representatives' fear of a weakening of their traditional positions and influence because of improving relationships between supervisors and subordinates and the possibilities of direct and individual participation and co-determination.

Prospects of reform success should mainly exist at the level of interpersonal relationships between those actively and passively involved; the increasing build-up of direct contacts, incremental step by step approaches and 'snowball effects'. Frequently the view is held that cutting back resources represents the only strategy possible to foster reforms and resource allocation should be undertaken on zero-based budgeting. However, this concept presupposes specific attitudes and ways of thinking, which are assumed to be initiated and intensified by reform endeavours. Another basic reform problem is the view that innovations imply that former approaches were wrong and faults would have to be admitted.

The traditional role and structure of the civil service stands in the way of a discussion about and a reorientation of goals and performance. Legal norms are argued to be reasons for non-alterable situations, although, of course, sufficient room for manoeuvre would exist. As always a strong internal orientation of the administration is dominating; planning and fulfilment of tasks, performance and service benefits for the clients would have to be focused on much more strongly. There are also certain discrepancies between the resolutions of the Council of Ministers and their realisation within the ministries and their organisations.

Another problem is the low quantitative and qualitative personnel capacities and the scarce budget in the organisation of the Minister of Federalism and Administrative Reform as well as in the ministries themselves. One is inclined to raise the difficult question to what extent this situation results from strategically oriented intentions, sounding very reasonable in the light of a scarce budget, which can be interpreted as standing against reforms. In principle it is accepted that if reform endeavours are not supported to a high extent by top politicians and the administrative top executives who would have to foster them actively, the prospect of success tends to be zero. These issues show large room for improvement and the project

Verwaltungsmanagement was not sufficiently successful to make the reform a broadly accepted political topic (*Bundeskanzleramt*, 1994, p. 136).

The project teams in the ministries were not relieved from day-to-day business which resulted in an incompatibility of tasks and responsibilities and a considerable overload which could only be compensated by high personal commitment. In this context the problem of low (non-existing) incentives for innovative managers and civil servants was not solved at all.

The performance orientation must be seen as a goal very difficult to attain and if at all only in the long term. The traditional principle of 'resource use' (input orientation) still predominates administrative processes and the issues of efficiency and effectiveness are not at all fully treated.

However, the project also had various merits (*Bundeskanzleramt*, 1994, p. 13):

- encompassing and integrating a high quality collection of proposals forming a very valuable ground for further projects;
- establishment and advancement of project management methods;
- topics which had been taboo several years ago are now broadly discussed, issues building an important basis for ongoing work in the ministries;
- increasing the awareness concerning the necessities of implementing management know-how and promotion of a respective organisational culture.[1]

7.   Review from an Organisational–Political Perspective

The rationally planned concept and strategy of the project can be contrasted with some 'deviations'. From an organisational–political perspective there is a discrepancy between the rationality of the intended strategy and the actual project processes and results.

Specific Contingencies in the Ministries

The project is determined on the one hand by the specific conditions in the respective ministry and on the other hand by the methods and philosophy of the external consulting firm and finally by the fit or match of ministry and firm. The following determinant factors can be identified:

- basic attitudes of management and key actors towards the project;
- forms of support or resistance strategies based on the different interests in the ministry;
- actual political issues and their relevance for the ministry;
- administrative and political climate;
- role of personnel representatives (unions);
- history (success and failure) of reform projects;

- formal and informal position of the project coordinator;
- form and intensity of cooperation with the steering committee;

The ministerial interest in the project (support or resistance) depends, among others, from:

- the in-house goals which could be reached through the project;
- the in-house goals which could be threatened by the project;
- the possibilities to reduce pressure through the project;
- the possibilities to improve their own position through specific project results.

External Consulting Firm

Despite the aspiration to achieve as much unity of procedures, different approaches of the firms can be identified:

- focus on the strategic orientation of the ministry, no or little quantitative data and analysis;
- focus on quantitative data, organisational structure and processes, personnel capacity, slack resources;
- integration of quantitative and strategic aspects in combination with some dimensions of organisational behaviour;
- difference in the degree of participation of the civil servants concerned in the project work;
- top-down versus bottom-up.

Pressure

External pressure on the system

- Budget scarcity.
- Increasing complexity and dynamics of tasks.
- Increasing public pressure towards more efficiency/effectiveness.
- Political pressure from counterparts in the government.

Internal pressure

- Political (and administrative) necessity to demonstrate some success in the area of reform work.
- Pressure or support from key actors and interest groups in the political and the administrative sector.
- Increasing internal project related problems.

Different Interests

Different interest groups (stakeholders) inside and outside the public administrative system articulate very different and often conflicting requirements and subjects of change in the public administrative system (for example organisational units, key decision makers, unions, political parties, public institutions, private institutions, media). In the ministries the interest (either support or resistance) in the project depends on:

- own goals which can be reached through the project;
- possibilities to reduce pressure;
- possibilities to improve their own situation through project results.

It is difficult to implement managerial instruments in organisations and to keep them alive and well. The incentives for accepting and using them are rather poor (for example, full tenure for a large group of civil servants, no performance incentives, no performance related salary, no career incentives). The individual interests of those concerned often are in contradiction to the so called 'objective requirements' formulated by internal or external forces. This situation raises the problem of 'acceptance' in addition to the problem of the quality of propositions and solutions. The implementation of managerial instruments constitute in certain respects threats and pressures to the organisational units and interest groups concerned:

- changes of the organisational power structure: loss of power for units/ individuals;
- loss of personnel;
- reduction and/or loss of tasks;
- transparency by discovering weakness and slack resources;
- pressure towards more efficient and effective performance;
- sacrifice of beloved habits and behaviours;
- losing political games in the organisation (for example, union versus management).

Benefits or threats of a change are perceived differently in different organisational units and on different levels of hierarchy. Actors at the top differ from subordinates with whom or against whom the project is being undertaken. One basic assumption of organisational change is that those concerned or affected obtain advantages from cooperation towards a change. The offer of pay-offs for the actors is an important reason for cooperative behaviour. However, if the actor concerned is expecting disadvantages through the change (for example disclosure of slack resources, undesired rationalisation, change of task quantity or content), then this constellation can be interpreted as a zero sum game (or even 'minus sum game'). It is characterised by antagonistic and conflicting goals of the actors involved: improvements for the one actor (leader) are disadvantages for the other actor(s) (subordinates). Therefore, in organisational units the interests cannot be seen homogeneously pro or contra a change but can be different depending on the actors' subjective perspective and anticipation of costs and benefits according to their interests.

Interdependencies between the Political and Administrative System

The success of a politician who publicly announces reform concepts depends on the operative implementation of these concepts in the administrative system. In this respect the political decision makers are in a relatively weak position with regard to the administration. They are forced to legitimate their plans and concepts in public; the administration is not exposed in the same way. In particular, innovative decisions are frequently directed against the bureaucratic routines and not well received because they would make changes necessary.

On the other hand, political interest groups used the project for their own purposes announcing data or consequences of the organisational analyses, for example, in the mass media. This can be detrimental to the project's progress in organisational units, for example, if

- the timing is wrong;
- data are not sound;
- data are not accepted and confirmed by the organisational units concerned.

In general, through actions of this type the basis of confidence between ministries and the external groups is eroded easily.

The more important (interesting) the project results are (for key decision makers)...the higher are the resources allocated to the project...the higher are chances to achieve results...the higher is the project importance.

The less important (interesting) the project results are (for key decision makers)...the lower the resources allocated to the project...the lower the chances to achieve results...the lower the project importance.

This aphorism indicates that there is permanent pressure on those responsible for the project to demonstrate and prove success in the administration as well as in the political system in order to secure enough support by key decision makers (individuals and groups). The problem is that in each phase and sub-phase of the project opponents are able to develop arguments against the project with the tendency towards a self fulfilling prophecy.

It is difficult and takes much energy and time to convince a politician of a reform endeavour and to gain his/her official and real support. Based on this necessary, but not at all sufficient, precondition it is difficult to gain the support of key decision makers in the administrative units concerned to start the project.

Figure 7.2.   The 'Vicious Triangle' of Project Success

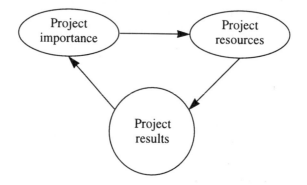

At one point in time (due to many reasons and other priorities) the political support decreases; this is being felt by the organisational members and may result in passive resistance. The increasing perception that political support decreases may lead to an increasing passive and active resistance by organisational members. As a consequence no actual project success can be reported to politicians and media, the negative pressure on the project increases and partial project failure is being programmed.

Reform Strategies

Rational strategies are used when an organisational unit concerned is convinced that the change is based on facts. Rationality means fact-oriented arguments directed towards own goal achievement. On the other hand organisational–political strategies are based on bargaining and coalition building. Decision makers observe their self-interests and try to use their power and influence respectively for resources which are of relevance for others. Some examples are: do nothing; prove that assessment results stated by the external consultant are incorrect; insist on maintaining or increasing tasks and resources required; threaten to reduce the quality and quantity of performance in key areas; influence the external consultant and not to touch specific issues, to modify results of analysis or to design and propose recommendations of a certain kind.

Other examples of organisational–political strategies are: organisational shift of solutions, 'Before we touch this *minor internal issue* we should solve those important interface problems on the overall level'; or time-shift of solutions, overt behaviour may be in favour of change, yet many *facts* and *contingencies* make action impossible for the time being. Solutions are being delayed until new priorities emerge and the old issues are not relevant any more; political threats and power play resulting in overt resistance to change in the ministries.

The traditional top-down reform strategy with little participation of people concerned and the attempt to implement completed concepts through the chains of command, results in very low motivation to cooperate and does not take advantage of the know how and expertise of those who operate in the day-to-day business and know the problems and solutions.

The split between problem recognition (awareness), planning, design and implementation of solutions is in contradiction to the requirement that organisational learning and change takes place only if the design and implementation of change are undertaken by the same actors; learning and change do not take place when certain events are caused by specific actors but other actors are affected by the consequences of these events.

An incremental approach observing the actual decision making processes in and between the ministries seems to be more promising. The most important aspects are identifying formal and informal key decision makers and interest group representatives in order to promote the change (network building) and to involve them to a high degree in all phases of the project. Furthermore one should secure a high degree of participation of key organisation members foremost in the planning and analysis phase of the project by appropriate methods. In the phase of implementation authoritative decision making may be indispensable since not all resistance can be eliminated by participation. Other important aspects are to give real time feedback about results and propositions, to take into account the different situations regarding goals, means and possibilities of agreement, and to invest much time and energy in coordinating the project, also to develop marketing efforts to support the project inside and outside the administrative system and give a chance to those concerned to demonstrate that a change means success and not that there was failure in the past.

Basically, the decision making model of 'Muddling Through' (Lindblom, 1959) and the 'Garbage Can Model of Decision Making' (March and Olsen, 1982a,b) can be applied as guidelines for strategic procedures in reform projects. For the project management concept the results and proposals of Van de Ven (1980a,b,c, 1981, 1986) are very useful.

8.   Summary Hypotheses

Hypothesis 1

Private sector management instruments can be applied to increase efficiency and effectiveness in the sector of public administration but are seen as a threat. However, they have to be adapted to the specific conditions of the public sector. In particular the complexity of decision making processes and tasks and the partial non-existence of a market have to be taken into account.

Hypothesis 2

The contradiction between reform concepts and actual administrative actions is often fabricated. It is created in order to protect internal interests which could be threatened by transparency (weaknesses concerning efficiency and effectiveness). This is one of the main reasons for resistance.

Hypothesis 3

The management instruments applied in the project are to be implemented in the long run and contribute to a reorientation from 'thinking in terms of input' to 'thinking in terms of output'.

Hypothesis 4

The interests of organisation members (active decision makers and passive concerned) implicate support for or resistance against change. The main reasons for resistance are loss of power, status and influence. The reform strategies determine the effectiveness of the reform project. They have to be developed further based on sound theory and adapted to the specific contingencies of the public sector. The basic rule is that the quality of instruments by itself does not suffice for change, acceptance by those concerned is at least as important.

$$E_R = f\,(I \times SoC)\,/\,Con$$

E_R = Overall Effectiveness of Reform Projects, I = Instruments (Quality)
SoC = Strategy of Change (Acceptance), Con = Contingencies
$\times$ = 'multiplicative' context.
If one component is very low (zero) the overall effect will be very poor (zero).

Hypothesis 5

The paradigmata of incremental decision making processes and organisational–political decision making (garbage can model of decision making) are useful to describe and evaluate processes, determinants and outcomes of the reform endeavour and to develop recommendations for a project management concept.

Hypothesis 6

The authoritative top-down strategy of change will fail in most cases, especially at the beginning of a project.

Hypothesis 7

Isolated small-scale reform projects in different areas of the administrative system (bottom-up) are learning opportunities for all the actors involved. However, no critical mass can be built up to initiate a large-scale reform process. This requires a simultaneous bottom-up and top-down 'network approach'.

Hypothesis 8

Many civil servants do have the motivation and commitment to contribute to change and innovation. However, the system has to offer reasons to activate this potential and transform it into specific actions. In this respect room for improvement is to be found especially concerning leadership and personnel policy (for example, income, income distribution over lifetime, incentives, performance evaluation, career opportunities, education and training).

Hypothesis 9

Unions and personnel representatives are not principally against change projects. Their positions in salary bargaining can be improved if they demonstrate willingness to contribute to efficiency and effectiveness. They can demonstrate solidarity if they contribute to a more balanced workload distribution among colleagues.

Hypothesis 10

External pressure on the administrative system promotes reform endeavours. The mass media play a particularly important role in the interface between the political and administrative systems and should be employed to promote the project. However, constructive cooperation with the media is very time consuming and difficult. Whoever works in the area of public administration reform should be aware that he is eternally seen as an illusionist.

Hypothesis 11

Reform projects which have failed block other projects for change in the long term because 'it has been proven once again' that reform goals could not be reached. In addition the willingness to cooperate is reduced once more. This topic might be named 'Failure as Tradition'. However, for consolation it should be stated that it is important to discuss ideas which seem impossible to realise, just to find out if this is indeed impossible.

Note

1. At the end of 1994 following parliamentary elections the position and functions of the Federal Minister of Federalism and Public Administration Reform were 'abolished'. It is to be expected that this reduction of formal power will have a negative impact on the reform endeavours at the federal level.

References

Bundeskanzleramt (Federal Chancellery), 1994. *Verwaltungsmanagement Projektbericht 1994* (project report), Graz.

Lindblom, C.E., 1959. 'The science of muddling through'. In: *Public Administration Review*, vol. 19, pp. 79–88.

March, J.G. and J.P. Olsen (eds), 1982a. 'Ambiguity and choice in organizations'. Oslo.

March, J.G. and J.P. Olsen, 1982b. 'Organizational choice under ambiguity'. In: J.G. March and J.P. Olsen (eds), *Ambiguity and choice in organizations*, Oslo, pp.10–23.

Van de Ven, A.H., 1980a. 'A process for organization assessment'. In: E.E. Lawler *et al.* (eds), *Organizational assessment: perspectives on the measurement of organizational behavior and the quality of work life*, Wiley, New York, pp. 548–68.

Van de Ven, A.H., 1980b. 'Problem solving, planning and innovation. Part I. Test of the program planning model'. In: *Human Relations*, vol. 33(10), pp. 711–40.

Van de Ven, A.H., 1980c. 'Problem solving, planning and innovation. Part II. Speculations for theory and practice'. In: *Human Relations*, vol. 33(11), pp. 757–79.

Van de Ven, A.H., 1981. 'The organization assessment perspective'. In: A.H. Van de Ven and W.F. Joyce (eds), *Perspectives on organization design and behavior*, New York, pp. 249–98.

Van de Ven, A.H., 1986. 'Central problems in the management of innovation'. In: *Management Science*, vol. 32(5), pp. 590–607. Institute of Management Science.

CHAPTER EIGHT

The State of Public Management Reforms in Switzerland

Kuno Schedler
University of St. Gallen, Switzerland

1. Summary

Reforms under the label 'New Public Management' have only a brief tradition in Switzerland. Extensive concepts which not only contain individual elements of operational control but also aim to change the politico-administrative system as a whole have only been discussed and tried out in recent times, that is, since 1993. However, business-administrative management elements were introduced in everyday public administration a great deal earlier, including financial planning, management by objectives, or personnel management instruments and incentive systems similar to those in use in the private sector. Thus a new public management system is not being introduced in one fell swoop, but rather at an evolutionary pace, although a clear 'fashion trend' towards NPM is rapidly accelerating the development while extending the scope to political control.

NPM creates particular problems in the field of direct democracy, whose structures are especially strong in Switzerland, including, among other things, a deeply rooted federalism and interconnections between all levels of government, as well as the tradition to put even details to a democratic vote if the need is seen to arise (Haldemann 1995b, p. 21). So far, it has proved impossible to establish conclusively what kind of influence the two currents will have upon each other – practical trials have not been sufficiently developed yet to yield tangible results. A further cluster of problems is presented by the traditional understanding of the constitutional state, which forms the basis of a relatively strongly established regulation of government action. Here too, no essential progress has been made in respect of a common future development.

2. Introduction

Swiss public administration is geographically torn between the Napoleonic culture of 19th century France (the Confederation with the basic outlines of today's constitution was founded in 1848) and a Germanic influence, which is not least a consequence of the fact that the majority of the Swiss population is German-speaking. Nevertheless, Swiss public administration has developed considerable independence, in terms of both structures and culture. French centralism is countered by an emphatically decentralised federalism in this country, which is in line with American rather than French traditions. Both in France and in Germany, public administration tends to be a closed system which is virtually impermeable. This is illustrated by, say, the German civil service with its career structures and the principle of tenure for life. In contrast, Switzerland's administrative system is comparatively open: the interpermeability between the public and the private sectors must be rated high both in terms of personnel and materially. This was shown by the early introduction of commercial accounting (1980s), but is also evidenced by the great number of civil servants who come from and/or move into the private sector. The non-existence of public administrative academies such as are customary in France and Germany may well represent a crucial contribution towards this permeability: there is no theoretically based and specialised curriculum for civil servants, which means that all personnel in public administration have been trained along private sector lines.

Reforms that take place in Switzerland are often unspectacular, slow and hidden from view. Schwarz (1990, p. 1) pointed out that public administration reforms in Switzerland must be likened to renovated rather than new buildings, but are constantly going on nonetheless. 'Great shake-ups' hardly ever take place and any far-reaching alterations to the political system, such as a transition from a concordance democracy to a competitive democracy, cannot be discerned although they continue to be discussed in theoretical writings (see, among others, Germann, 1994). Political rationality ensures that the vast majority of adaptations are carried out in an evolutionary manner and, as a rule, are only realised after they have gone through several stages during which political compromises were sought and found. This may be a reason for the fact that international studies hardly ever portray Switzerland as a country easily given to reforms. Another reason is the nature and quality of sources of information: it is fully justified to describe Switzerland as a developing country as regards information, particularly as regards the acquisition of information beyond the individual levels of state (Confederation, cantons, communities). The Swiss contacts for the OECD, for instance, are Federal Offices, which will not provide any information about developments in cantons and communities. Thus these elements of administrative and government reform, which are so relevant to Switzerland, are missing, which may give the impression that Switzerland is not moving anywhere at all. Nevertheless, it must be stated that NPM reforms in this country are still in their beginnings.

3.   The State of Debate in Switzerland

A Brief Historical Outline

The more recent history of public administration reforms in Switzerland has been characterised by an increasing influence of business administration and its instruments on the reform debate. A distinction can be made between various periods during which the notion of reform was weighted in a different manner. Schwarz (1990, p. 1) wrote that the 'public administration reform projects' that started in the 1960s and 1970s focused primarily on a restructuring of the *management organisation*. In the 1980s, externally analytical approaches (such as overhead cost analysis) were used in an attempt to make public administration more efficient. All these projects had a common denominator in that they predominantly aimed to change the structures, whereas the *socio-emotional elements* of public management were only tackled as a second priority, in the form of training schemes. Schwarz also indicates that the reform and reorganisation programs of the post-war period in Switzerland either referred to public administration or the government, whilst the hierarchically supreme body, *parliament*, was invariably kept out of any processes of change. Implicitly, the decisive factor may well have been the thesis whereby public administration's capability of reforming itself of its own volition was limited, which is why the political leadership had to exert the pressure requisite for reforms,[1] whereas a restructuring of political control was not necessary to the same extent.

The 1990s saw a new reform approach, whose main focus was directed not so much on structural change, but rather on the necessity of subjecting public administrative processes to an analysis. This discovery was largely the result of the partially sobering experience with the analytical approaches employed in the 1980s. Thus 'organisational development as a strategy of public administrative reform' (Schwarz, 1990) was put on the agenda, so that the main interest was not concentrated on public administration itself, or on the people working in it.

Schwarz (1990, p. 9) summarised the issues of the (state) reform debate in four categories:

- *Decentralisation*: relief of the central state from functions that could also be fulfilled by the cantons and/or communities (known as functional reform in Germany).
- *Re-privatisation*: transfer of certain state activities into the private sector.
- *Re-democratisation*: reinforcement of the position of citizens and of their representatives in the process of developing political objectives, which finds expression in citizen participation and parliamentary reforms.
- *De-bureaucratisation*: development of the efficiency of public management in the direction of the standards set by corporate management.

It is against the backdrop of this already intensive reform debate that the success of the approaches of 'New Public Management' (NPM) in Switzerland must be explained, since this philosophy provides a management model that supplies the instruments that are necessary to realise the above postulates. A reasonably broad debate of reforms along the lines of NPM, such as is being conducted in Switzerland with some intensity now, is relatively young. A conservative estimate would trace its emergence, at least in terms of the reform approaches dealt with here, back to 1993.

The notice received by foreign models in the media – particularly the Tilburg model as first propagated by Reichard (1992) in the German-speaking part of Europe – caused the initiation of an intensive discussion of the issue of public administration reform in the Berne area in the spring of 1993 (Müller and Tschanz, 1995, p. 228). At the same time, the Institute of Public Finance and Fiscal Law at the University of St. Gallen began to study international reform models. The Institute's starting point was a conference on Comparative International Governmental Accounting Research (CIGAR), in the course of which it became evident that the reforms then being conducted by New Zealand and Australia were both revolutionary and way ahead of any other country (see the conference anthology, Buschor and Schedler, 1994). In the same year, original terms such as 'contract management' (Tilburg model) or 'New Public Management' were replaced by a Swiss designation coined by Buschor: 'results-oriented public management' (*Wirkungsorientierte Verwaltungsführung*, Buschor, 1993). To date, however, this term has gained only partial currency; the prevalent designation, particularly among consultants and in the media, is still that of New Public Management.

In the following years, the reform movement that emerged was of an intensity that Swiss public administration had not experienced for many years. Hardly any research has been done into the truly decisive reasons for the new openness of public administration and political circles in Switzerland towards reforms. It may be argued, however, that it was a mixture of several factors that made the soil fertile for new ideas:

- The failure of the analytical reform efforts left in its wake, both in public administration and in politics, a number of disappointed people who had vehemently exerted themselves to improve public administration. Owing to the same failure, however, it also dawned on people that public administration can only be reformed if it is itself involved in such reforms.
- In the 1990s, the budget deficits increased with gathering speed although the economy was no longer in a phase of recession. This favoured the insight that the current problems were not economic but structural in nature and that a renewed economic upward trend would not be able to solve them. In this manner, the pressure to act was substantially increased at the beginning of the reforms.

– Private sector management had made considerable progress since the Second World War, yet this progress had only been partially emulated in public administration. As a consequence of the comparatively high degree of personnel permeability between public administration and private industry, these differences became more and more obvious and were increasingly subject to criticism.
– The complex social system of public administration has its own typical response to problems and resistance: it always finds new ways of avoiding existing incongruities. Thus various steps in the direction of results-oriented public management had been initiated but not systematically placed into a new management model. As soon as the model was presented on a broader basis, many 'intrapreneurs' in public administration availed themselves of this opportunity to legitimise their own ideas in the overall context.

The new wave of reforms increasingly directed business consultants' attention to public administration. The adoption of private sector management instruments and their adaptation to the requirements of public administration systemically called for business administrative knowledge. Naturally, this was connected with new approaches to solutions that were developed with a different logic.

Integration of the 'Traditional' Disciplines of Public Administration Theory

In the long term, a reform cannot be crowned by success if it cannot be sustained and shaped by all the relevant disciplines of public administration theory. Just as it was necessary for business administrative theory to be introduced into public administration, an interdisciplinary dialogue is now relevant to the realisation of the reforms. The critics of the new reforms rightly point out that public administration is not a group of companies. This, however, must not prevent the debate about improvements in administrative and political control instruments; rather, an interdisciplinary dialogue should aim to locate the weak points of today's political/administrative system and then to eliminate them with the help of newly developed instruments.

In this respect, both proponents and critics committed some sins in the heat of the initial euphoria. While the former overhastily tended to brand the lawyers as those to be blamed for the wretched state of affairs, the latter disparaged the reformers as naive and superficial purveyors of rush jobs who jeopardised both the state and democracy. In the meantime, the fronts have softened somewhat; open questions are usually accepted as such, and new solutions are tested on a wide basis irrespective of any scepticism.

Legal Debates

It is typical of Switzerland (as it is for Germany and Austria) that, in an international comparison, administrative action is governed by law to a very great extent. Any state action is thus founded upon the principle of legality, which has two functions (Müller 1995, p. 15):

- *Constitutional function*
  The constitutional function of the principle of legality serves to guarantee legal security and equality before the law. This ties authority action firmly to the law; extensive interpretations require a legal basis for any activity to be taken up, which can place substantial limits on the leeway enjoyed by public administration. The advantage of this function is a security of expectation, that is, everyone concerned may assume that an authority will take a certain, predictable course of action.
- *Democratic function*
  The democratic function of the principle of legality serves to legitimise administrative action. By stipulating that certain interventions and decisions of public administration require a legal basis, it ensures that such action is always backed up by fundamental democratic decisions (by parliament or by the people).

Depending on how the principle of legality is interpreted, it may turn out to act as a brake on public administration reforms. This is especially true if the legal foundations for each and every reform measure must be newly created in the democratic process. The Swiss Canton of Zürich, for instance, had faced a referendum in 1996 which proposed a whole package of such reforms. If the people rejected the proposed package, the continuation of the reform process would have been doubtful despite the immense efforts of government and public administration.[2]

In material terms, the legal edifice in which Switzerland's public administrations are integrated does not constitute an insurmountable obstacle for the first steps of NPM, provided NPM is not introduced in a dogmatic manner. Although, as mentioned above, various legal foundations remain to be created (in budgetary law, civil service law or organisation law), the current trials indicate that it is possible to work efficiently and effectively within the existing legal framework, provided this framework is not too narrowly defined and regarded as immutable.

The Swiss representatives of jurisprudence may be sceptical but, as a rule, are fairly open towards the new ideas. Thus Schweizer (1995, p. 153) wrote about budgeting principles: 'The primacy of democratic assessment, decision making and control of course also allows for differentiated competencies, ... including, in conditions that must be defined in more detail, the creation of subsystems of public budgets such as special accounts or globalised budgets (one-line budgets)'. What is called for, however, is an overall view of state resource management, complete openness and the full disclosure of financial management to inspection, matters which NPM, too, encourages rather than prevents.

Even the essence of the *principle of legality* has become a debating point, for instance in connection with proposals to promote responsive legislation. Thus Mader (1995, p. 163) points out that the Federal Office of Justice has 'displayed some liking for trial regulations and, in this connection, has also accepted a certain qualification of the principle of legality'.

Constructive criticism of the concept of New Public Management has been aired, in particular, by Mastronardi (1995, p. 1541), who regards it as a reinforcement of the performance state and economic state principles (as expressed in constitutional principles), which, however, are in opposition to the concerns of the constitutional and democratic state. If we follow Mastronardi, we will perceive a latent conflict between NPM and the two latter constitutional principles, which, to be sure, received more notice in the past than the two former principles. Mastronardi (1995, p. 1550) formulates, among other things, various prerequisites for the introduction of NPM:

–   If clear standards of competence are to be relinquished in favour of flexible contractual relationships, then legal protection of the citizens must be guaranteed to the same extent as in the traditional organisation of public administration.
–   If control of effectiveness and efficiency is to replace the democratic control of the process, control instruments must be developed which will create the necessary transparency.
–   Wherever politically relevant decisions have to be made in the managerial area, politics must not be excluded. The separation between strategic and operative decisions that has been demanded (Buschor 1993, p. 19) must be called into question – not dogmatically, but pragmatically and with political sensitivity.
–   An increase in the autonomy in the managerial field will extend the discretion available to public administration. This will intensify the need to legitimise the new processes by means of fairness. The equality of opportunity of the different groups that claim or are entitled to state services must be guaranteed.

In our view, the course of current reforms in cantons and communities has made it clear that not all areas of public administration can be equally steered according to the ideal precepts of NPM. To conceive of the new approaches as purely service-related, however, would probably not do justice to the matter. There are a number of gradations between *intervention management* in the sense of gun-carrying police officers and *performance management* in the sense of a cantonal bank in competition with the private sector and these gradations must be examined individually and specifically. In this respect, we must agree with Mastronardi (1995, p. 1552): 'The response is likely to be different for every area of public administration'.

Politological Considerations

The ideal picture of bureaucratic control, which in Max Weber's tradition also applies to Switzerland, is radically called into question by NPM. Owing to the results-oriented nature of control, the most important elements of bureaucracy are subjected to diametrical change. Haldemann (1995b, p. 20) indicates five directions:

- – deconcentration (decentralisation) instead of centralisation;
- – success orientation (deformalisation) instead of formalisation;
- – generalization (despecialisation) instead of specialisation;
- – participation (dehierarchisation) instead of hierarchisation;
- – concentration (desegmentation) instead of segmentation.

Justice, that is, equal treatment of citizens, is guaranteed by law in Switzerland. In turn, the law is legitimised through its democratic enactment in parliament and/or through the direct participation of the people. This fundamental maxim is being challenged by new ways of thinking in terms of costs, performance and effect. For this reason, some political scientists consider that Switzerland's democratic tradition will be at stake if NPM is introduced nationwide (for example, Knoepfel, 1995).

And indeed, Switzerland's outstanding feature is its direct democracy and federal structure. As a rule, the cantons enjoy a high degree of autonomy even though the distribution of competencies has become increasingly blurred. Political decisions are characterised by compromises which are often made even at the preparatory stage. Interest groups exercise an important influence here, in that their representatives are regularly members of the committee responsible for the preparation and drafting of bills. Public administration is strongly integrated in policy making and its top jobs are increasingly manned according to party-political criteria. This creates close interconnections between persons, institutions and state levels which do not only prevent a clear demarcation between policies, but also a strict separation between politics and public administration.

Some political scientists are putting up considerable resistance to NPM. Knoepfel (1995, p. 454) warns that NPM would give rise to unfulfillable expectations or cause damage to fundamental principles of the institutional structure of Swiss democracy. The main thrust of his criticism is focused on the separation of politics and public administration, which is propagated by NPM models and should also be envisaged in Switzerland. Moreover, he says, it is naive to think that politicians would let themselves be tied down to measurable objectives and indicators, since it is precisely the blurred nature of issues that makes political compromises possible in the first place. Finally, Knoepfel criticises the proposed translation of the control focus from inputs to outputs and outcomes, since politically decisive results can only be achieved by means of influence exerted on processes and inputs.

Haldemann (1995b, p. 21) locates the deficits of the Anglo-American New Public Management approach for Switzerland primarily in areas where the Swiss political/administrative system differs from those of other countries:

- characteristic differences between state levels (confederation, cantons, communities) are issues that are not taken into consideration;
- complicated distributions of functions and competencies between different levels of the state are not taken into account;
- joint planning, negotiations and decision making with bodies at the same or at a lower level are not taken into consideration;
- participation, weights of influence and networks between various active groups are not included in the debate;
- approaches suggested from below, such as the concerns of a modern civil society or personnel participation, are often forgotten in this reform discussion;
- aspects of substance and peculiarities of programs and measures are left out of the discussion;
- the state's various control media (intervention media), that is, norms (law), performance (money) and referenda (information) are not taken into consideration in a differentiating manner.

Klöti (1995, p. 411) examined the relationship between federalism and NPM and came to the conclusion that at the level of principles, hardly any contradictions can be found between the theories of federalism and NPM, since both are based on the fundamental principle of decentralised decision making. However, he located difficulties in all those areas which are characterised by interconnections between state levels. His main criticism is also aimed at the proposed separation between politics and management. He rightly emphasises that pure management decisions at federal level may well be political issues at cantonal level. This would mean that they would be rated as such and could therefore no longer be autonomously dealt with by public administration. If politics may define itself in these terms, then there is a danger that this will cause a spiral which turns a reformed (results-oriented) public administration gradually back into the old system.

Finally, Klöti points out that the incentive structures in today's public administration system run exactly contrary to the postulates of NPM. The majority of federal subsidies granted to cantons and communities are not results-oriented but take their bearings from the expenses accruing from state action; in this way, they encourage an optimisation of expenditure rather than of effects. The ongoing reform of federal fiscal equalisation, however, works on the same fundamental principles as NPM (Frey 1995, p. 436), with the consequence that the two projects now reinforce each other.

Finger (1995, p. 138) and Haldemann (1995a, p. 144) defend the Swiss approaches to NPM, stating that adaptations to Swiss specifics have already been made and that, in addition, the traditional control system was struggling with serious disadvantages, too. The state, says Finger (1995, p. 143), will forego its legitimacy without radical and lasting reforms. Haldemann (1995a, p. 147) points out that NPM is opening up great opportunities for a significant improvement in the productivity and citizen-orientation of the civil service and for an increased establishment of the state and its legitimacy in the minds of the general public.

4.   NPM in Switzerland

In this chapter, NPM reform processes are examined in more detail, on the basis of a survey of ongoing projects. Since NPM reforms are still young in Swiss practice, individual projects can only be assessed with regard to their designs and their initial steps.

In comparison with other countries, a weighty difference is discernible in all the projects: whereas in, say, New Zealand, the government assumed a clear and firm leadership and employed external consultants to provide directional support, the Swiss approach is strongly focused on the principles of organisation development. The active involvement of personnel is accorded particular weight, and even members of parliament are increasingly involved.

Project Survey

Various polities are experimenting with NPM at the same time. To understand the processes, it is important to know that reforms aimed in a similar direction were put into motion even before the emergence of reforms along the philosophy of NPM. It may therefore be said that several NPM instruments (such as commercial accounting) are already in place and need not be developed completely from scratch.

In the following section, the current NPM projects will be surveyed and briefly commented on; a more detailed description would go beyond the scope of these pages. At communal level, the survey is unlikely to be complete since the large number of communities (approx. 3000) cannot be continuously monitored. Yet it provides a picture – as of 1 January 1997 – and draws some interesting conclusions (Hablützel *et al.*, 1995).

New Public Management Projects

Various projects are being undertaken at all three state levels in Switzerland, and a whole number of further projects are at a preparatory stage. It is striking that in virtually all instances, the approach of pilot projects was used to establish the instruments of NPM, and to train personnel, management and politicians. As a rule, the legal basis is provided by experimentation clauses which enable polities to disregard existing law within the confines of exactly defined trial projects without already codifying the solutions to be tested. Here, too, though, there are exceptions to the rule.

At *federal level*, several committees and working groups are looking into the possibilities of introducing NPM at once. The actual driving force, however, is likely to be found in public administration itself where, for instance, a working group called *Handlungsspielraum* or 'Scope of Action' (a highly qualified team of directors of federal offices) have worked out proposals for the creation of more leeway for public administration. Financial pressures and the failure of previous cost-cutting efforts have increasingly prompted parliamentary committees to place NPM on their agendas. Thus an expert group was recently commissioned to examine the effects of NPM on parliamentary work and to develop new control instruments.

In a newly drafted 'Government and Public Administration Organisation Bill' (Art. 51), the legal basis is to be created for work with performance agreements and globalised budgets. The reforms are modeled on the English agencies which, albeit not legally independent, enjoy a far-reaching functional autonomy. Although the bill was rejected by the Swiss people in 1996, two pilot projects were started in 1997, and a rapid extension is planned from 1998. A second version of the same bill is likely to be exacted in 1998, so the legal background will be in place.

Table 8.1. New Public Management Projects at Federal Level

Confederation in general	'Managing by Performance Agreements and One-line budgets' * Formation of quasi-autonomous agencies and their control by means of performance agreements and one-line budgets.
Federal Military Department	'Reform of the Federal Military Department (EMD 95)' (has started) * In the course of the reduction of the army by one third, the ministry is being correspondingly reorganised and given lean structures in accordance with NPM principles.

In the *cantons*, preparations for the introduction of NPM have been going on since 1993. The pioneering work has been done by the Cantons of Lucerne, Berne and Zürich in particular. In the meantime, the number of cantons conducting NPM projects in their public administration has multiplied. With the exception of the Canton of Zürich, which does not carry out any pilot projects but aims directly at concrete realizations, all the other projects are characterized by an introductory experimentation stage which is likely to become increasingly shorter as more know-how is acquired in Switzerland.

At *local level*, it is particularly the Berne area which has been staging NPM projects. Financial pressures are likely to have been the primary motivator here, since both the Confederation and the Canton and City of Berne have for some years been conducting stringent cost-cutting programs which have not had the desired success.

Table 8.2.   Some New Public Management Projects at Cantonal Level

Canton of Aargau	'Results-Oriented Public Management' (in preparation) * Start in the Civil Engineering Office as from 1/7/1996, extension planned for 1997.
Canton of Berne	'New Public Management NEF 2000' (Start 1/7/1996) * More than 10 pilot projects involved over 2,000 personnel. The project is part of a comprehensive reform of the public sector.
Canton of Basel-Landschaft Canton of Basel-Stadt	Public Management PMA (in preparation)
Canton of Fribourg	(NPM project in preparation)
Canton of Geneva	(NPM project in preparation)
Canton of Graubünden	(NPM project in preparation)
Canton of Lucerne	'Results-Oriented Public Management WOV' (Start 1/1/1996) * 13 pilot projects, test period until 1999
Canton of Schaffhausen	'Results-Oriented Public Management WOV' (in preparation) * 10 pilot projects
Canton of Schwyz	New Public Management * 3 pilot projects
Canton of Solothurn	'Lean State' (in preparation since 1994, start second stage 1/1/1996) * First stage: incisive reorganisation, that is, reduction from 12 to 5 ministries, tightening-up of all organisations; second stage: NPM.
Canton of Thurgau	'Optima' (has started)
Canton of Valais	'Administration 2000' (first stage since 1994, second in preparation) * After a detailed overhead/cost analysis, NPM should now be introduced in a second stage with 6 pilot projects.
Canton of Zürich	'New Organisation Model in the Health Service' (in preparation) * 7 hospitals serving as pilot projects 'Results-Led Public Management of the Canton of Zurich wif!' (start 1/1/97) * No experiments; instead, direct realization in permanent organisations. Referendum in 1996.

Table 8.3.   New Public Management Projects at Municipal and Communal Levels

Canton of Berne: City of Berne	'New City Administration Berne NSB' (in preparation since 1994, start 1/1/1996)
	7 pilot projects, duration prolonged until 1999
Canton of Berne: City of Thun	'Modern Administration Thun' (has started)
Canton of Berne: Community of Köniz	'Service Company Köniz DUK 2000' (has started)
Canton of Berne: Association of Bernese Communities (VBG), Canton of Berne and 7 pilot communities	'Bernese Communities as Contemporary Service Companies' (since 1995)
Canton of Basel-Landschaft: Communities of Reinach and Liestal	(NPM project in preparation)
Canton of St. Gallen: Communities of Oberuzwil and Oberriet	'Results-Oriented Public Management WOV' (has started)
Canton of Zürich: City of Zürich	'Public Administration Reform' (has started)
Canton of Zürich: City of Winterthur'	'Results-Oriented Public Management WOV' (has started)
Canton of Zürich: City of Dübendorf	'NPM Project Dübendorf' (in preparation)
Canton of Zürich: City of Uster	Authorities and Administration Reform 'Optimus' (has started)

Projects with NPM elements

Projects that do not or cannot satisfy the comprehensive requirements of NPM but aim to move in the same direction are numerous today. This reveals a difficulty with NPM: its definition is not unequivocal. Is it NPM, for instance, if a canton abolishes the status of 'public servant' and introduces flexible employment conditions instead? From what degree of realization onwards may we speak of NPM? Even projects which are being conducted under the NPM label partially refrain from a full realization of the philosophy because they are afraid of excessive resistance from trade unions or from political bodies. The following section will show what projects with NPM elements are now running in the various polities.

At *federal level*, two general thrusts can be observed:

- the review of various special acts in the field of administration law and
- concerted measures in respect of certain institutions in public administration.

Table 8.4.   Further Projects with NPM Elements at Federal Level (selection)

Confederation in general	Personnel and Organisation Development (Guidelines 1990 and Legislation Plan 1991–1995) * Preparation of administrative structures and culture for coming modernisation drives
Confederation in general	Partial review (1995) and total review (in preparation) of the Civil Service Act * Increased harmonization with private labour law
Confederation in general	Partial review of the Financial Audit Act (1994) * Modernisation of audits, including value-for-money audits
Confederation in general	'Management Accounting in Federal Administration' (since 1991) * Creations of increased transparency as a management instrument
Federal Institutes of Technology	Review of parliamentary participation in and supervision of the Federal Institutes of Technology (in preparation) * Introduction of output-oriented information and control in federal universities and research institutes
Post and Telecommunications	Holding-company organisation of the PTT Group with the corporate divisions Post and Telecom (in preparation)
Swiss Federal Railways	Operative and corporate reforms (in preparation) * Separation between operations and infrastructure is being discussed
Institute for Intellectual Property	New legal form of the former Federal Office for Intellectual Property (since 1996) * Corporatisation of an administrative unit with functions partially involving national sovereignty

In connection with the review of special acts, a significant project is going on that has a bearing on the Civil Service Act. A partial review was already decided upon, which introduced a far-reaching flexibilisation of working hours, of pay policy instruments and, in particular, an increased performance-orientation in the pay system. A total review is now being worked on, which is meant to provide completely new regulations, particularly as regards the status of 'public servant', and which will also move closer to private labour law in all the other questions. At the same time, the Federal Personnel Office is launching an offensive for the introduction of systematic personnel and organisation development.

A partial review of the Financial Audit Act provided the basis for the Federal Financial Audit Office to make more frequent use of value-for-money audits. At the same time, its independence was reinforced, even though the creation of an independent audit institution was again deliberately not envisaged. Methodically, the new act is modelled on the directives of the International Organisation of Supreme Audit Institutions (INTOSAI) regarding efficiency and effectiveness audits.

Institutionally, the two conspicuous projects are the large-scale reforms of the railways and of the postal services. The organisational separation between postal and telecommunications services has increasingly given rise to voices demanding a complete privatization of Telecom. However, it still looks as if a state-owned holding company might be the preferred solution.

At *cantonal level*, it is above all the hospitals which have been active for some time: they have been testing new forms of control by means of globalised budgets and performance agreements. Various attempts have also been made to work with diagnosis related groups (DRGs); however, there are hardly any data available in this respect. A further element of NPM which is becoming more and more widespread is quality management. In this context, a certification according to ISO 9001, primarily in production-oriented units (for example civil engineering departments) initiates a process that should lead to systematic quality management. Although certification according to ISO 900+ is becoming increasingly attractive, it has again invited criticism, particularly in connection with public administration: an exact determination and fixation of processes does indeed involve a danger of conditional thinking becoming predominant again. Instead of encouraging flexibility in the sense of customer-orientation, it is feared that ISO 9000 will result in a new rigidity of processes if the culture of public administration cannot be radically changed in advance.

Further elements of NPM are also being introduced at local level; however, the number of communities precludes the presentation of a detailed list. Basically it may be said that medium-sized cities (50,000 to 150,000 inhabitants) have managed to find, or are still looking for, some quite innovative solutions for parts of their administrations, whereas in small and very small communities, it is not so much NPM in the sense of decentralization that is of topical significance, but a tendency towards achieving an economical minimum size by means of cooperation. This reveals a further gap to be filled by research: as a rule, examples from other countries refer to major cities and frequently clearly defined functions. Switzerland, however, is characterized by a great number of small communities (100 to 1000 inhabitants), which nonetheless have to offer an enormous range of services. They are active in social welfare, schools, civil protection, planning permission, and all the infrastructural functions such as streets, sewage system, waste disposal, to name but a few. In this contest, the supporters of NPM will have to develop creative solutions to satisfy these specific requirements.

Table 8.5.   Further Projects with NPM Elements at Cantonal Level (selection)

Canton of Appenzell-Ausserrhoden	One-line budgets/performance agreements for hospitals (ongoing) New Budget Act (1996)
Canton of Basel-Landschaft	New Budget Act (in preparation) * Creation of a possibility for one-line budgets
Canton of Basel-Stadt	'Redimensioning of Cantonal Functions in the Canton of Basel-Stadt' (REKABAS) (1994) * Cost-cutting programme with contracting and privatisation
Canton of Berne	Outsourcing of information technology services to BEDAG (since 1990) * Corporatisation of the Office for Information Technology 'New Financing Systems in the Health Service' (trials in 13 hospitals, since 1993) * Various financing alternatives are compared in practical tests
Canton of Fribourg	Quality Management in the Office of Civil Engineering (1995) * ISO 9001 certification as a starting point
Canton of the Grisons	Performance agreements and one-line budgets for hospitals (in preparation)
Canton of Lucerne	'Results-Oriented Hospitals LOS' (since 1994)
Canton of St. Gallen	One-line budgets in hospitals (3 pilot hospitals, since 1995) * 'Customer-Orientation in the Office of Environmental Protection' (1995)
Canton of Schwyz	Review of functions (has started)
Canton of Thurgau	'Integrated Budgeting in Hospitals' (performance agreements and one-line budgets, since 1993) Quality Management System in the Office of Civil Engineering (since 1995) * ISO 9001 certification as a starting point
Cantons of Vaud and Valais	Outsourcing of the waste incineration of 54 communities to SATOM SA, Monthey/VS (since 1972)

Project Assessment

This section will examine the introductory strategies pursued by the various projects. A distinction can be made between various dimensions of implementation strategies.

Universal Reform Versus Single-case Reform

Reforms can be implemented directly universally, or gradually by means of single cases (pilot projects). In the context of NPM, many aspects call for implementation through single cases. In this manner, the risk can be limited to clearly demarcated organisational units to begin with. Moreover, learning effects can be used for a later extension of the reforms; this precludes the risk of the same mistake being made universally. Finally, it is easier in terms of organisation psychology to implement a universal reform if successful examples can already be found in one's own organisation.

An introduction of NPM, however, does not only affect the organisational unit concerned but soon has a certain wider effect. Cost/performance accounting, for instance, cannot function without the participation of the internal performance suppliers and purchasers: the building surveyor's office must report, for example, how high the rents for the office space will have to be. Experience shows that this requirement causes the building surveyor's office to think along different lines, although this office is not actually involved in this introductory or trial stage. As it is a typical cross-section office, which is in contact with all other administrative units, it spreads the new way of thinking and thus supports a process which then begins to become universal. The question as to whether an NPM reform should be conducted by means of pilot projects or introduced universally can therefore not be answered conclusively.

Practice shows a clear picture: only those projects where NPM proper has been preceded by another reform are universal: the Canton of Solothurn reorganised its structures completely, and the Canton of Valais opted for an initial overhead cost analysis before switching to NPM in a second stage.

The vast majority of polities come to organisation development through an experimentation stage with a few pilot projects. As a rule, the first step is a conceptual stage in which the major cornerstones of the trial are established. In this context, there is increasing cooperation among the various polities characterized by a far-reaching openness. In the meantime, this has developed to a degree where experts from advanced cantons are hired as consultants for newcomers so that a quasi-automatic alignment is taking place.

Virtually all the projects have been devised in such a manner that in the case of failure, full reversibility will be guaranteed. However, this restricts the creative freedom of the trials in major areas. Thus there is no possibility, for instance, of working with completely different human resources; by the same token, no pilot has so far been freed from the traditional pay scales. Also, the interfaces with internal service suppliers (personnel department, office for information technology, office material stores, and so on) are reluctant to switch to genuine customer/ supplier relations. Finally, internal performance agreements continue to lack the fundamental elements of a contract, which hardly changes the legal position of the offices concerned in comparison with traditional public administration. Sanctions and rewards are thus limited to existing possibilities, which, however, have been extended by a considerable measure and have not been fully exhausted to date (for a list of these see Emery and Schedler 1994, p. 219).

Direct Implementation Versus Trial Stage

Zürich is the only canton to implement NPM without the detour of an experimentation stage. All the other known projects have been or are being preceded by a trial stage to test the new instruments and to prepare politics and public administration for a possible definitive reform.

Within the scope of a Zürich project entitled 'Results-Led Public Management WIF)', selected areas of public administration are being prepared to make the transition to operations according to NPM principles. However, this requires Zürich to create the legal basis suitable for a definitive implementation – the experimentation clauses of other projects are not applicable here. Moreover, this concept makes significantly greater demands on the political support of the project. Whereas in cantons such as Berne and Lucerne, the possibility of returning to the old system has been explicitly laid down, the Canton of Zürich will not be able to avail itself of this option.

5.   Conclusion

From a theoretical point of view it must be said that so far, no project in Switzerland has changed the political/administrative system to such an extent that the postulates of NPM have been fulfilled. Researchers are engaged in an intensive dispute about the desirability of such a change, and cooperation across the borders of individual disciplines would appear to have started. The entry of lawyers and political scientists into the academic discussion has resulted in a marked enrichment of the debate while extending the range of questions triggered off by the implementation of NPM. Management theory is called upon to work with its neighbouring disciplines to find answers to the questions that are still open in order to reinforce its newly defined position within management theory and in order to make a contribution towards fruitful further developments in this field.

From a practical perspective, the current reform projects represent a great opportunity to counter the growing danger of lethargy in the public sector caused by rising budget deficits and a permanent pressure to cut costs, and to act rather than react. Discussions with the public administration managers concerned have shown that NPM is giving rise to high, but realistic, hopes. It has also been revealed that even in the preparatory stage of the reform, intellectual and cultural changes have been achieved which were not expected to such an extent and in such a short time.

To sum up, it may be said that NPM can also be an important element of comprehensive state reform in Switzerland and, as Mastronardi (1995) emphasizes, is rather more political in a time of general change than it wants to appear.

Notes

1. Schwarz (1990, p. 4) regards the recruitment moratorium ordered by individual parliaments as an institutionalisation of the (political) pressure to reform.
2. It must be pointed out, however, that this compulsory legal referendum represents a rather unusual measure of direct democracy. Various other cantons have been able to create the same prerequisites through the government itself or at least through parliament.

References

Buschor, E., 1993. *Wirkungsorientierte Verwaltungsführung, Wirtschaftliche Publikationen, Heft 52*. Zürcher Handelskammer, Zürich.
Buschor, E. and K. Schedler (eds), 1994. *Perspectives on performance measurement and public sector accounting*. Paul Haupt, Bern/Stuttgart/Wien.
Emery, Y. and K. Schedler, 1994. 'Darstellung der Kantone'. In: Y. Emery (ed.), *Leistungslohn im öffentlichen Dienst, Schriftenreihe der Schweizerischen Gesellschaft für Verwaltungswissenschaften*, vol. 27, SGVW, Bern, pp. 219–70.
Finger, M., 1995. 'New public management – un débat manqué'. *Swiss Political Science Review*, vol. 1(1), pp. 138–43.
Frey, R.L., 1995. 'New public management und Finanzausgleich'. In: P. Hablützel *et al.*, *Umbruch in Politik und Verwaltung*, Paul Haupt, Bern/Stuttgart/Wien, pp. 425–438.
Germann, R.E., 1994. *Staatsreform: der Übergang zur Konkurrenzdemokratie*. Paul Haupt, Bern/Stuttgart/Wien.
Hablützel, P., T. Haldemann, K. Schedler and K. Schwaar (eds), 1995. *Umbruch in Politik und Verwaltung: Ansichten und Erfahrungen zum New Public Management in der Schweiz*. Paul Haupt, Bern/Stuttgart/Wien.
Haldemann, T., 1995a. 'New Public Management: Ein neues Konzept für die Verwaltungsführung des Bundes?' *Schriftenreihe des Eidgenössischen Personalamtes*, vol. 1, EDMZ, Bern.
Haldemann, T., 1995b. 'Gefährdet New Public Management das politische System und die Verwaltungskultur der Schweiz?'. *Swiss Political Science Review*, vol. 1(1), pp. 144–8.
Klöti, U., 1995. 'Auswirkungen des New Public Managements auf den Föderalismus'. In: P. Hablützel *et al.*, *Umbruch in Politik und Verwaltung*, Paul Haupt, Bern/Stuttgart/Wien, pp. 411–24.
Knoepfel, P., 1995. 'New Public Management: Vorprogrammierte Enttäuschungen oder politische Flurschäden – eine Kritik aus der Sicht der Politikanalyse'. In: P. Hablützel *et al.*, *Umbruch in Politik und Verwaltung*, Paul Haupt, Bern/Stuttgart/Wien, pp. 453–70.

Mader, L., 1995. 'Responsive Gesetzgebung – Für eine bessere gesellschaftliche Adäquanz gesetzgeberischen Handelns'. In: D. Berchtold and A. Hofmeister (eds), *Die öffentliche Verwaltung im Spannungsfeld zwischen Legalität und Funktionsfähigkeit*, SGVW, Bern, pp. 158–75.

Mastronardi, P., 1995. 'Staatsrecht und Verwaltungsorganisation. Reflexionen am Beispiel des New Public Managements'. *Aktuelle Juristische Praxis*, vol. 12, pp. 1541–53.

Müller, B. and P. Tschanz, 1995. 'Neue Stadtverwaltung Bern: Vorgehen und Bedeutung der weichen Faktoren'. In: P. Hablützel *et al.*, *Umbruch in Politik und Verwaltung*, Paul Haupt, Bern/Stuttgart/Wien, pp. 223–41.

Müller, G., 1995. 'Funktionen des Legalitätsprinzips im Organisationsrecht'. In: D. Berchtold, A. Hofmeister (eds), *Die öffentliche Verwaltung im Spannungsfeld zwischen Legalität und Funktionsfähigkeit*, SGVW, Bern, pp. 15–25.

Reichard, Chr., 1992. 'Auf dem Wege zu einem neuen Verwaltungsmanagement'. In: J. Goller, H. Maack und B.W. Müller-Hedrich, *Verwaltungsmanagement*, Raabe (Loseblatt), Stuttgart, nr B 1.1.

Schwarz, P., 1990. *Organisationsentwicklung als Strategie der Verwaltungsreform, Schriftenreihe der Schweizerischen Gesellschaft für Verwaltungswissenschaften, Band 14*. SGVW, Bern.

Schweizer, R.J., 1995. 'Staatsrechtliche Voraussetzungen und Schranken einer dezentralen Ergebnissteuerung in der öffentlichen Verwaltung'. In: D. Berchtold and A. Hofmeister (eds), *Die öffentliche Verwaltung im Spannungsfeld zwischen Legalität und Funktionsfähigkeit*, SGVW, Bern, pp. 146–57.

CHAPTER NINE

The Administrative Modernisation Policy in France

Luc Rouban
Centre de Recherches Administratives, Paris

1. Introduction

The administrative modernisation policy in France has been a governmental priority since the early 1980s. This policy has been implemented very irregularly due to various political conditions but also to the rather different ideas that each government has about the word 'modernisation'. At first sight it would appear that modernisation policies were responsible for the numerous technical reforms that have regularly appeared in French administration history since the Revolution. Administrative modernisation implies, however, a global administrative transformation that exceeds the boundaries of classical technical reform aiming, for example, at simplifying administrative procedures or offering users new ways of action to oppose administrative decisions. Modernisation, in its French meaning, implies both the development of public management techniques and the preservation of the social balance that prevails within the ranks of public administration. The modernisation process is a search for a third way between neo-liberalism and administrative conservatism. In 1994–95, the word 'modernisation' was replaced in the government literature by the broader concept of 'State reform'. This is not just paying lip-service to some political science flavoured concept. This change indicates the ambition of the projected change as well as the political risks of the modernisation. In order to appreciate the extent of the transformations that are underway, it is necessary to take into account the specificity of the French case.

The question of the State has always occupied a central place in the French political culture and the public services are at the heart of the economy. In December 1995, strikes in the railway and bus transportation systems have clearly demonstrated that the social meaning of the 'public service' concept was alive and prevented the government from entailing neo-liberal changes. The very notion of public management is therefore closely conditioned both by this historical inheritance and by the strategic game the various actors of the reform can play. The result of such an interrelated process is that there is not one modernisation policy but many. Priorities have changed with time and the reform has always oscillated between the introduction of new management techniques, the cultural change of the civil service, and the transformation of ministerial structures. Successive governments have alternately used different tools without knowing how to combine them. The impact of the modernisation policies is therefore difficult to evaluate. Notably, the Balladur government in 1993 gave up the project of a global evaluation of the modernisation process. Change within public administration is an undeniable fact, but this is far from demonstrating that deep social structures have really changed. New rules of the game have been implemented piece by piece and only a few organisations have been really concerned. The public service culture has undoubtedly evolved more rapidly at the senior managers' level than at the level of intermediate rank civil servants or clerical staff (Rouban, 1995a). The results of the modernisation process in France are somewhat confused and potentially conflictory.

2.   The Search for a New Public Management

Traditional concepts of public management have never had in France the force that they may have in Britain or in the United States. French public administration has been historically built around administrative law. The development of management concepts did not occur before the 1960s (with the exception of some theoretical controversies raised in the 1930s) when the Ministry of Finance experimented with an emulation of the well-known PPBS (Planning, programming, budgetary system), the RCB (*Rationalisation des choix budgétaires*). At this time, public management was viewed as a centralising mechanism designed to satisfy the strategic interest of the Treasury Department. Furthermore, until the 1990s, most schools of professional training, such as the ENA (Ecole nationale d'administration), have paid little attention to public management teaching. The very idea of 'management', with its Anglo-American sound, has never seduced higher civil servants (especially those coming from the administrative *grands corps*) who thought that such systems of integrated information would better serve politicians than civil servants and that they would help more to renew political control over public administration than to rationalise day-to-day administrative action. Public management was culturally unknown, did not meet their intellectual sensitivity and appealed only to economists. Public management has only developed within big public enterprises, such as EDF (Electricité de France) or the SNCF (Société nationale des chemins de fer français), because it fitted well in the professional culture of civil servants coming from the ranks of technical *grands corps* (Polytechnique, Mines, Ponts-et-Chaussées). So, public management has been historically related to a particular public policy style: those of big infrastructure or industrial programmes, planned on the long term, requiring a global and top-down commitment from the State.

Another characteristic of public management in France is that it has not included the civil service policy and was largely defined outside its realm as a correction and compensation mechanism. The civil service policy has always been defined along the lines of a parallel and closed procedure, where labour unions and government representatives met around three great strategic questions: the civil servants' purchasing power, the extension of professional rights by the civil service status, and the numerical increase of the personnel in some sectors. Civil service questions, financial management and organisational design have never been part of a global and systematic 'public management' process. For many years, the search for new management techniques has been made through limited experiments and with restricted objectives: the limitation of running costs or the following-up of some brand-new equipment (notably data-processing). The policy of modernisation is an attempt to articulate personnel management and the development of public management. This evolution is linked to three factors that have changed the nature of public action.

The Welfare State Crisis

Administrative modernisation can be regarded as a response to the Welfare State crisis. The nature of this crisis determines the kind of administrative tools the various governments choose in order to foster their legitimacy.

One factor is related to the opening up of the decision-making systems. One of the main characteristics of the Welfare State in France was that it was based upon professional corporatisms. Each administration and sometimes *bureau* had its preferred corporate 'representatives' with whom they established an institutionalised debate. The regulation of the Welfare State rested therefore on the decision making process closing. With decentralisation and European integration, administrations have had to transform their modes of action. The very principle of a State-centred, top-down, decision-making process is vanishing while various forms of a partnership with locally elected leaders, business firms and authorities of Brussels are flourishing. The growing number of actors being able to interfere with public policies management has favoured the multiplication of interministerial arbitration procedures. The classic vertical framework of the administrative action associates henceforth with horizontal procedures and network management.

Furthermore, new forms of collective action have appeared (associations, public interest groups, ad hoc committees, and so on) that discredit political parties or labour unions and push forward demands for an immediate efficiency (Perrineau, 1994). The mediation offered by politicians is less prized today than direct contact with public services. Correspondingly, a new interest has been shown for a regular evaluation of public action, of its efficiency as well as of its effectiveness (*Revue française d'administration publique*, 1993).

A second factor is related to the struggle against public deficits so as to respect the criteria of financial convergence that conditions the creation of the European unique currency (the deficit does not have to exceed 3 percent the GNP while it was about 5 percent in 1995). The civil service accounts for 40 percent of the State's annual running costs, approximatively 580 billion FF a year. This financial factor is really crucial. Most recent reforms were motivated by the need to cut down public expenditure without severely limiting the users' service. Nevertheless, it rapidly appeared that policies of staff reduction were very difficult to implement: between 1986 and 1988 the liberal government has been able, at best, to stop the expansion of the civil service but not to reduce it significantly. It is socially unthinkable to decide on real reductions in staff while social policies (the struggle against unemployment, revival of urban centres, integration of immigrants, and so on) constitute priorities for successive governments. Public management appears therefore as a substitute for more radical measures of budget-cutting. By 'putting the pressure' on the civil servants and asking them to find new savings, public management allows politicians to avoid difficult choices between opposing policies, or to escape their responsibility *vis-à-vis* the electorate.

This political mutation is all the more sensitive within the civil service ranks and has caused many critical periods in recent years.

Civil Service Troubles

The State has also confronted challenges of internal order (Bodiguel and Rouban, 1991). The search for new tools of management has become necessary since the model offered by the higher civil servant of the 1960s (the 'social moderniser') has been found outdated, as was the case for the integrative procedures of the planning process or for global industrial policies. Although public administration procedures and the legal framework have adapted somewhat to the new social environment during the two last decades, the rules of the game have not really changed for civil servants.

The modernisation policy is therefore as much a conceptual change than a set of new organisational 'rules of thumb'. It is largely a mixture of pragmatic considerations (most politicians come from the civil service ranks and clearly know what they may do effectively) and more implicit assumptions about a new kind of governance departing from the classical decision-making process. Initiatives launched in the middle of the 1980s by the *Direction générale de l'administration et de la fonction publique* (the main department within the civil service ministry) constitute an attempt to associate, from the perspective of participation, reform needs and the preservation of the social peace, which has been undermined by several tensions.

One tension is due to the declining purchasing power of civil servants, especially that of the higher civil servants. This is a highly debated point because global figures are not very explicit and could feed a never-ending controversy between the unions and the government. As a matter of fact, the purchasing power of higher civil servants has dropped by 14 percent between 1982 and 1992 while that of employees climbed by 3 percent during the same period (Rouban, 1996). Higher civil servants have felt all the more the erosion of their social status in that their working environment (staff, running budget) has suffered from budgetary restrictions, while they were asked at the same time to increase their personal productivity or to be more responsive to political demands. Moreover, this phase of stagnation or decline has followed a long period (beginning in the 1950s), during which the growth of public sector earnings had been superior to the increase of the private sector average earnings, a growth that put the civil service on a quasi-equality with the other socioprofessional categories. The result of this long term evolution is that public administration, noticeably in technical sectors, is confronted with more competitive job offers coming from the private sector and is no longer able to retain its best managers. One can observe that the usual mechanism of the *pantouflage* (implying that a public manager can quit his position for a better paid position in the private sector after many years of duty) has singularly evolved. Departures to the private sector are no longer occasional but constitute today a real choice of career. For example, the number of Inspectors of Finance leaving in *pantouflage* rose from an average of 6 per year at the beginning of the 1980s to 9 in 1988 and to 12 in 1989 (while the *corps* recruits only 6 inspectors per year). At the same time, the average age of those leaving was about 30 in the 1990s, while it was about 40 ten years earlier. It was very rare before 1980 to find a *pantoufleur* under 35. One notices finally that the sectors which the civil servants are joining are no longer limited to the traditional banks and insurance companies but have widened to industrial enterprises.

A second crisis factor is related to the fact that inner circles of the decision-making process (that is to say higher ranks of management in ministries) have been submitted to a growing politicisation since the presidency of Giscard d'Estaing (Lacam, 1994; Mény, 1987; Rouban, 1995b). This politicisation is due to two interrelated changes: a new governmental style implying that the President as well as his Prime Minister have to commit themselves to precise programmes in order to fulfil their electoral campaign promises, and the four successive political changes between the left and the right in twelve years. This has fostered systematic interventions from members of ministerial *cabinets* in the daily administrative management (Quermonne, 1994), while implying an active participation of the higher managers in the governmental option implementation. The speed and the range of this politicisation vary considerably from one sector to another and from one government to another, according to those sectors or interests most defended (for instance, in 1981, the most rapid changes occurred at the National Education, Justice and Culture ministries). Some global data are, however, significant. The population of ministries' departments heads (*directeurs d'administration centrale*) was almost entirely renewed in 1986–87, when the conservative government of Jacques Chirac came to power, when there were 132 departures (from an average annual population of 160 directors). The 1988 *alternance* (political change), when the Socialist candidate won the presidential election, was more moderate since departures in 1988–89 did not exceed 73. This figure climbed to 89 for the 1993–94 period when the Gaullists came back. Beyond figures, one has to underline the fact that most public policies in France today are submitted to more political debate, media scrutiny and controversies. The time is past when civil servants, representing an all-mighty State, could steer most actors in public life and could impose their choice without too much difficulty. Moreover, the classic political game has been changed. Controversies are no longer built along the lines of ideological frontiers but involve technical arguments that often cross the political parties' boundaries. The majority of senior civil servants we interviewed underlined this point: politicisation has been emphasised but can be explained more by the intensification of controversies than by the political radicalisation of some governments (Rouban, 1995b). Thus, politicisation involves the specialisation of controversies that could blur the frontiers that have until now separated the administrative world from the political world.

A third source of tension is due to the fact that civil service careers no longer assume their traditional function of social promotion. The administrative *grands corps* has been put under growing pressure for social selection. Access to the higher ranks of the civil service has not been democratised. Between 1962 and 1985, the share of the ENA (Ecole nationale d'administration) students coming from upper social categories (liberal professions, private or public sector managers, big business) has climbed from 39 percent up to 65 percent while the share of students coming from the lower class (blue-collar workers) has declined from 5 percent to 3.6 percent (as an average of external and internal competitions). Between 1981 and 1990, the average of recruitment through the external competition system was 79.8 percent for children of higher managers and 1.4 percent for children of blue-collar workers (respectively 47 percent and 9.3 percent for the internal competition system which offers civil servants upper positions in the hierarchy). Similarly, recruitment to the inferior ranks is very competitive, with candidates having generally many more degrees that these positions would normally require. For instance, 40 percent to 50 percent of candidates competing for category B positions have a university master although these intermediate rank competitions are open to candidates with a bachelor degree. Most competitions have a coefficient of selection superior to 20 (that is to say that there is an average of 20 candidates for one position). This situation creates frustration. The perspective of a real career associated with the concepts of professional merit and seniority is gradually vanishing and the public service tends to organise on a dual basis. The level of entry into the public service increasingly determines the professional future. The civil service becomes a shelter for average classes while upper classes tend to flee to the private sector.

A fourth crisis factor is due to the organisations' architecture and rationale. The introduction of new technologies, notably data-processing and micro-computers, as well as the necessity to adapt to diversified demands have generated two phenomena. Public sector professions have evolved very rapidly and the culture of civil servants has been transformed. Public sector agents define themselves less as 'multi-purpose all-doers' and increasingly as specialists having the mastery of a particular know-how. Careers paths as well as administrative organisations have not adapted to this new situation. There is now a gap between the day-to-day professional activity and self-representation on the one hand and the organisation of careers on the other hand. Professions no longer offer frameworks for long-term socialisation and neither allow nor define standardised behaviour or a legitimate social hierarchy. This factor is coupled to a second phenomenon, the dualisation of organisations. The necessity to be responsive in a short time leads public as well as private organisations to distinguish *and* to relate to directly those who supervise the strategy from those who are in charge of the execution, skipping the intermediate levels. The organisation charts tend to flatten, putting an end to the idea of a regular progression in the career. Strikes in 1986–87 as well as in 1995 have highlighted this problem. Protest movements are not so much concerned with pecuniary demands than with questions related to the civil servants' social status. Most strikers and labour unions claim that the new social game, linked with the EC integration process, could destroy the public service.

3.   Contrasted Policies

The policy of modernisation has not developed in a regular manner but has undergone mutations according to political conditions. One can distinguish four major periods that indicate the progressive end of the French specificity.

1984–86: The End of the Socialist Illusions

In 1984, when Laurent Fabius became Prime Minister, a deep political change occurred because the economic crisis and the need for low inflation rates had destroyed the Socialists' illusions. The new government then began to fully measure the economic weight of the important increase in the civil service population between 1981 and 1983 (+ 6.8 percent). It was a real U turn. The Socialist government repudiated its 1981 promises when it proposed to stop the public service degradation through massive hiring and new funding of major ministerial areas. After 1983–84, modernisation was essentially dedicated to strengthening the judicial and legal background of the public service (new laws were voted to organise the local civil service and careers in public hospitals) and to develop computerisation of public administration. For the first time, the 'modernisation policy' was separated from the civil service policy and appeared on the governmental agenda as a new political priority. First of all, one notices that the creation of new civil service positions was severely reduced after 1985. Then, new initiatives were taken to improve the public service's day-to-day relationship with users. Quality circles were implemented in technical services (the Postal service, the Infrastructures ministry and some services within the Treasury Department). Nevertheless, these modest innovations take on an important meaning: that quality is more precious than quantity, and that the improvement of public action is the business of each civil servant without it being necessary to adopt ambitious reform plans. A top-down logic is succeeded by a bottom-up logic. The Finance ministry as well as the Civil Service ministry, open to the experiences in the private sector, have encouraged reform in such a way that it has appeared not too costly and practical in a period of budget restriction. This inflection in the policy of modernisation has found its clearest expression in the report that the minister of the civil service released to Parliament in November 1985. Human resources management became a central preoccupation. It is supposed to outreach the obsolete framework of the civil service policy whose global cost is always growing because no one can really control its implementation (many categorial measures are taken to satisfy the interests of some *corps*).

1986–88: A Tentative Neo-liberal Policy

The Right came back to power in 1986 and developed explicitly a neo-liberal programme with a systematic comparative approach, trying to emulate what was happening in Britain or in the United States. Of course, this led to a drastic change in the government speech. The civil service became the target of many criticisms, both for its alleged global cost as well as for its culture which appears archaic. From being a model of social success, the civil servant became an awful figure, the pure representation of waste and incompetence. But the intellectual infatuation for neo-liberalism that developed from 1982–83 did not match public opinion, which was, of course, looking for improved public services but not for their dismantlement. At the very moment when the Jacques Chirac government was thinking of launching a large privatisation programme, public opinion polls showed a passive but real defence of major public services (national education, research, postal service and telecommunications) that forbade all real remodelling of the public service system. Finally, the only effect of the neo-liberal rhetoric was to reduce the number of students allowed to enter the ENA each year and to change some structures within central administrations. For the main part, the modernisation policy pursued the experiences started in 1985. Quality circles and 'total quality groups' multiplied and were referred to as the 'new management' which is spreading over the business world. The Japanese model is regarded by most private and public sector consulting groups as a stimulating system because it seems to base productivity on the opening out of the hierarchy.

1988–92: The 'Public Service Renewal'

The return of the Left to power in 1988, and the nomination of Michel Rocard as Prime Minister, opened a decisive era for the administrative modernisation policy. The global objectives that had been assigned to modernisation from several years before were still at the heart of the government decisions. But the administrative modernisation process, henceforth called 'the public service renewal', was transformed into a real public policy. The circular signed by Michel Rocard on February 23, 1989 offered a real charter by fixing the objectives as well as the philosophy of the modernisation: innovations had to be negotiated within each service and they were not accompanied by any threat to the civil servants' status. The main goal was to mobilise the personnel through participatory management techniques, to specify programmes and targets for each service and to establish efficiency and result indicators. The modernisation policy was not supposed to be a legal reform but a cultural reform.

In eighteen months, three government top-level seminaries (in September 1989, June 1990 and April 1991) met, bringing together representatives of each ministry, in order to mobilize the whole public administration apparatus on the modernisation theme. The experimental method used since 1985 was continued: 'quality' operations and efforts for improving internal or external communication were encouraged, notably within field offices. These methods were gradually completed by the development of 'strategic plans' (*projets de service*) and 'budgeting centres' (*centres de responsabilité*) based upon internal contracts (and contracts with the Budget ministry and the Civil Service ministry) specifying operational objectives, ways of implementation and evaluation criteria. The modernisation rationale was still to favour innovations generated by the services themselves especially those with a direct contact with users (most experiences were launched in préfectures, social assistance, police and Treasury services). Furthermore, human resources management was given a new priority in order to stimulate agents.

The social and financial room to manoeuvre was relatively narrow. Indeed, the country's good economic health allowed the government to sign a global salary agreement with labour unions in 1988; another agreement on professional training was signed in 1989. But social conflicts multiplied and lasted: in the penitentiary administration, air traffic control, tax administration and the postal service sectors, conflicts were tough and there were sporadic strikes. Moreover, the nature of these conflicts changed in a singular manner. Unions could not control their members who created spontaneous organisations (*coordinations*) which no longer obeyed the instructions coming from the official leaders. These *coordinations* defended pure sectoral claims related to their own working conditions and specific career paths. Weakened unions could not really oppose the public service renewal because they could hardly control their troops and because this policy may improve the civil servants daily work on practical grounds.

Public service modernisation was therefore a compromise between the very progressive introduction of public management and the preservation of the traditional public legal and financial framework. Some structural reforms were pushed forward to ease day-to-day management. The empowerment of agents, and especially of senior managers, required a devolution of the budget decision-making process, especially for those running expenditures that could be decided upon without referring to the upper levels of the hierarchy. Services managers were also empowered to launch personnel performance appraisal systems for the clerical staff.

The public service renewal policy was accompanied by broader measures aiming at improving the career paths and working conditions of civil servants: the salary grid was reformed after some new career paths had been enlarged (*accords Durafour*, February 1990); the professional training budget was connected with the salary mass according to the 1989 and 1992 agreements with labour unions; personnel performance evaluation systems were initiated to complete the traditional procedure of professional notation; and human resources management was systematically developed in some sectors (especially the postal service) in order to counterbalance the negative effects of new businesslike methods.

When the Prime Minister changed, in 1991, most priorities set by the previous government remained on the government agenda. Salary bargaining resumed with the unions. Nevertheless, during the next two years, the policy of modernisation was uncertain, because the spirit of the renewal tended to be short of breath. Civil servants who had been mobilised because of their service performances, or who were engaged in strategic planning, were disappointed when they observed that the renewal was unable to improve their salaries. Budgetary restrictions made internal contracts more difficult to be signed. The Treasury Department partly took control of the situation.

1993–95: Towards the State Reform

The new political change of 1993 was characterised by a 'frozen' situation. The government of Prime Minister Edouard Balladur tried successfully to avoid the ideological pitfalls of the 1986–88 period. The new civil service minister, André Rossinot, urged an overview of the modernisation outcomes. Many evaluations were made in order to assess the devolution of administrative authority to field offices; the concrete impact of the controversial *délocalisation* policy (aiming at displacing some authorities and public services from Paris to the regions in order to balance the administrative network); and the global results of the administrative 'strategic planning' procedures, which finally proved to be rather satisfactory (Fraisse and Serieyx, 1995). More attention was devoted to users, as a 'minimum' modernist stance. The modernisation policy then departed from its previous participatory flavour and entered classical administrative reform questions: the organisational chart of ministries, ethics in the civil service and the professional training of senior managers. Reports by Prada (1993) and Picq (1994) offer illustrations of such a reflection. Beyond this very classical stance, new questions arose about the global role of the State as the European integration was under way and the economic struggle called for more privatisation. The modernisation policy aims were displaced: they were no longer a means to avoid a social crisis within the civil service but a new organisational deal dedicated to change the Welfare State rules of the game. The members of the *grands corps* themselves felt suddenly concerned as the stakes of the reform were higher. The whole French model was put under scrutiny. Notably, the Picq report referred to major transformations of structures and managerial methods used elsewhere in Europe. The Picq report proposals led to a clearer separation between decision and evaluation functions on the one hand, attributed to central offices in ministries and policy implementation and management on the other hand, attributed to 'empowered' field offices. Other proposals shared the same managerial flavour: a new interest in policy evaluation, regarded as a major component of any 'modernist' administration, a plan to rationalise the geographical service organisation of the territory, and final considerations about the need to better separate administration from politics in limiting the size of the ministerial *cabinets*. A *'commissariat* for the State reform' was created in 1995 and the Prime Minister Alain Juppé signed a new circular in July defining the goals of this new modernisation.

4. A Mixed Result

One cannot underestimate the effects of the modernisation policy. More than 600 *projets de service* and 200 *centres de responsabilité* have been set up since 1989: professional schools, such as the ENA, have reformed their programmes in order to allow room for more public management; policy evaluation is at least partially regarded by public managers as useful and a pedagogical effort has been made by the Civil Service ministry to diffuse new practices and methods throughout the various ministries and to incite them to emulate successful experiments. The cultural change is one of the most positive results. Innovative behaviour may be viewed now as a resource for a bright career. 'Strategic planning' has often broken the routine and changed the perception that the various categories of agents had of their own role. 'Budget centres' allow the expenditure process to be eased without changing the organisational structures. Internal contracting has focused higher managers on their steering role.

Civil servants have been relatively receptive to the modernisation process. Up to 80 percent of senior managers have been committed to operations of modernisation and up to 70 percent estimate that this policy has at least improved the situation slightly. The modernisation process has partly fulfilled their aspirations, because they strongly desire more managerial autonomy. Category C agents (employees and clerical staff) have benefited from measures of salary improvements and from

Table 9.1.   Results of Modernisation Operations by Type of Administration as Analysed by Higher Civil Servants in 1991 (%)

	Administrative grands corps	Ministries	Field Offices
Work productivity			
Improvement	72.2	65.6	74.9
No improvement	11.1	14.1	9.3
Do not know, no answer	16.7	20.2	15.9
Users' service			
Improvement	70.4	62.6	81.2
No improvement	7.4	13.1	7.4
Do not know, no answer	22.2	24.2	11.5
Administrative coordination			
Improvement	62.9	60.7	53.7
No improvement	18.5	20.2	33.0
Do not know, no answer	18.5	19.2	13.3

N = 500.
Source: Rouban, 1994.

professional training. Hesitation and reluctance is more frequent among category B agents (intermediate level) because they have generally poor career prospects and because the modernisation process tends to destroy the uncertainty of resources on which they base their organisational power. If the modernisation has changed the spirit and the culture of a large proportion of civil servants, one must not ignore the obstacles.

First of all, modernisation is not an homogeneous phenomenon. Managers in field offices are generally more favourable to the modernisation policy than managers working in central administrations or members of the administrative *grands corps*. They share specific socio-political characteristics. Their sociology, their training and their socio-professional heredity separates them from the other categories of senior managers (Rouban, 1993, 1994). Working in a competitive environment, where arrangements are inevitable, they are confronted by the need for getting results. Modernisation has been much more difficult to implement in ministerial central services because these staff administrations are confronted with pressing political demands, while field offices can play the card of 'expertise' to defend their autonomy *vis-à-vis* the prefects as well as the local elected leaders and their own services.

The second obstacle is due to the fact that the modernisation process cannot lean on a real managerial culture. The modernisation policy has been welcomed especially in sectors systematically developing a business-type activity (the Infrastructures ministry, France Telecom, the postal service) confronted with a competitive market and whose civil servants share an homogeneous culture diffused in technical *grandes écoles*. The interest for public management in purely administrative sectors is obviously less because civil servants do not see what advantage they could gain from it. Moreover, it is difficult to change the mentalities of experienced civil servants who have been trained twenty years ago. One cannot imagine that professional training could change habits acquired during their initial training and deeply integrated in their career prospects.

A third obstacle comes from the fact that it is particularly difficult to assess the whole process of modernisation and the various governments may wonder whether the benefits are worth the social costs. Paradoxically, the modernisation policy has not always been able to satisfy users because traditional bureaucratic rules have not been upset. New quality criteria have been set up but they cannot satisfy an ever-growing demand and an ever-dissatisfied user. In the eyes of users as well as in those of civil servants, modernisation is the last step before privatisation, a transitional phase which cannot offer more legitimacy to public administrations. In some

Table 9.2.   The Civil Servants' Professional Concerns in the 1990s (%)
(Question: in your current position, do you benefit from ?)

	'Yes, a lot' and 'yes, a little'	'Not much' and 'not at all'
A good salary	26	74
A stimulating job	85	15
A position that allows you to use your personal know-how	72	27
Sufficient responsibilities	72	28
The opportunity to be rewarded for your merit	50	49
Professional opportunities (of advancement)	29	70
A good professional atmosphere	85	15
A good relationship with your immediate superior	87	11

N = 7 400 (all civil service categories).
Source: SOFRES, 1990.

cases, the modernisation policy may produce perverse effects. Many civil servants have perceived modernisation as a means to blame them for political choices that have not been decided at the top level; as a tricky game whose winners are always the politicians who can get rid of embarrassing responsibilities in a time of budget cuts and, simultaneously, of high defensive corporatism. For users, classic pitfalls of the public service (delays, paperwork, legal constraints) have become more intolerable than ever because they cannot understand why the modernisation did not go further. Surveys have shown in the early 1990s that civil servants were relatively satisfied with the traditional administrative model.

Finally, innovations concerning mechanisms of decision-making have been difficult to implement. The policy of administrative devolution has been a governmental priority since the beginning of the 1990s (law of February 6, 1992, decree of July 1, 1992). Its goal is to transfer to the local level most tasks of day-to-day management. Devolution is an institutional policy dedicated to balance the effects of the decentralisation, but also of the European construction that allows regions to receive European funding directly (notably through the Leader programmes). Each ministry has appointed a committee in charge of elaborating proposals of devolution. The central administrations of the various ministries have been, however, rather reticent to be committed in this way. If running costs have been largely delegated to field offices, it seems that this devolution is slower concerning equipment costs. Other factors impede the devolution policy: personnel management is still highly centralised, the distribution of competence between the State and local governments is still to be clarified, and rivalries and competition between *corps* and ministries call for many negotiations.

A complete institutional machine was created in 1990 close to the Prime Minister so as to launch systematic policy evaluations. Evaluation is indeed considered as the cornerstone of any managerial reform of the State, linking the clarity of information to its rational utilisation by decision makers. The Rocard circular as well as the Juppé circular grant it considerable importance along the lines of many official reports and academic works. Unfortunately, the difficulties of implementation have multiplied. First, because nobody really agrees on the definition of evaluation. For the administrative officials, evaluation means simply auditing, while it means a sociological analysis of public action for the experts, and the necessity to strengthen checks and controls for the citizens. Second, because the information feedback to public managers has proved to be poor or useless. On the one hand, this information is paradoxically too complex to be integrated timely in the decision-making process. On the other hand, evaluation tools are largely in the hands of the executive and Parliament has not been able to use them in order to contest decisions or governmental policies. Parliament members themselves are very reluctant to create new evaluation agencies that they consider as a threat to their political power. Finally, evaluation procedures, to be efficient, would include a general reorganisation concerning higher civil service training as much as the organisation of the budgetary debate or a long-term policy programme which is still lacking. Under these conditions, one can understand why evaluation has been especially used for consensual or, at least, non-controversial policies such as acid rain, the computerisation of public administration or the social minimum wage follow-up.

5. Conclusion

A global statement on the modernisation policy in France is not an easy task. Until December 1995, one would have thought that an implicit consensus existed within the ranks of civil servants to develop public management. In fact, this consensus is only spreading among politicians. When Juppé's government tried to reform the special retirement regime of civil servants (who contribute 37.5 years as compared to 40 years for the private sector wage-earners), the union reaction was particularly strong, generating a three weeks strike in major transportation systems. The development of management implies structural reforms that appear hardly acceptable for civil servants and their unions (reduction of the number of *corps*, systematic evaluation of individual performances, management autonomy). On the other hand, the modernisation policy changed the culture and allowed more attention to be devoted to practical users' needs and demands. This policy was indispensable but it has remained peripheral and has not touched the heart of the State. The administrative *grands corps*, which concentrate the expertise and the power to check the administrative apparatus, have not really engaged in the modernisation policy. Members of these *corps* are not hostile to public management. They regard it as useful but they do not feel concerned. The modernisation policy has arrived at a threshold where more global reforms are needed, but any ambitious change would hurt the social and historical structures of the public service. One question for the future is related to the political capacity of any government, be it from the Right or the Left, to impose changes that are largely regarded as inevitable but are strongly opposed by civil servants. The fact that most politicians are former civil servants does not simplify the solution. Another question is knowing whether the government will play the card of the European construction, which pushes for deregulation of the main public services, or will choose to defend the French specificity.

References

Bodiguel J.-L. and L. Rouban, 1991. *Le fonctionnaire détrôné?* Presses de la Fondation nationale des sciences politiques, Paris.

Fraisse R. and H. Serieyx (eds), 1995. *L'Etat dans tous ses projets*. La Documentation française, Paris.

Lacam J.-P., 1994. 'Haute fonction publique et politique'. *Regards sur l'Actualité*, vol. 204, September–October, pp. 25–44.

Mény Y., 1987. 'A la jonction du politique et de l'administratif: les hauts fonctionnaires'. *Pouvoirs*, vol. 40, pp. 5–24.

Picq J., 1994. *L'Etat en France. Servir une nation ouverte sur le monde*. Rapport au Premier Ministre, La Documentation française, Paris.

Perrineau P. (ed.), 1994. *L'engagement politique: déclin ou mutation?*. Presses de la Fondation nationale des sciences politiques, Paris.

Prada J., 1993. 'Rapport sur l'encadrement supérieur de l'Etat, Rapport au Premier Ministre', partially published in *La Revue Administrative*, vol. 280, July–August, pp. 335–60.

Quermonne J.-L., 1994. 'La mise en examen des cabinets ministériels'. *Pouvoirs*, vol. 68, pp. 61–75.

Revue Française d'Administration Publique, 1993, vol. 66, April–June, special issue 'L'évaluation en question'.

Rouban L., 1993. 'France in search of a new administrative order', *International Political Science Review*, vol. 14 (4), pp. 403–18.

Rouban L., 1994. *Les cadres supérieurs de la fonction publique et la politique de modernisation administrative*. La Documentation française, Paris.

Rouban L., 1995a. 'The civil service culture and administrative reform'. In: B.G. Peters and D. Savoie (eds), *Governance in Changing Environment*, McGill-Queen's University Press, Montréal-Kingston, pp. 23–54.

Rouban L., 1995b. 'Civil service politicization in France: the new rule of the game'. Paper presented at the *91st Annual Meeting of the American Political Science Association Chicago*, August 31–September 3, French Conference Group Panel 3.

Rouban L., 1996. *La fonction publique*. La Découverte, Paris, collection 'Repères'.

SOFRES, 1990. *L'appréciation des conditions de travail dans la fonction publique (survey)*. Mimeo, Paris.

CHAPTER TEN

Shifting Frames of Reference in Dutch Autonomisation Reforms

Frans O.M. Verhaak
Erasmus University Rotterdam

1. Introduction

The organisation of Dutch central government is in transformation. Since 1981, divisions of departmental organisations are being autonomised based on government policy. Autonomisation can be defined as the granting of a form of independence to an executive public service. Examples of organisations which have received greater independence are Dutch Rail, the Central Agency for Road Traffic, the Land Registry, the Information Management Group, the General Civic Pension Fund, the National Computer Centre, the State Lottery, the Tax Agency, the Immigration and Naturalisation Agency, the Superintendent of Public Health and the Superintendent of Social Insurance. In this contribution to the Yearbook, we discuss the autonomisation policy of the Netherlands with a focus on two central themes:

- the frame of reference for the Dutch autonomisation policy;
- the relationship between the Dutch autonomisation policy and Dutch administrative science.

Frames of Reference

Policy is often characterised by its dynamism, and the Dutch autonomisation policy is no exception. It served several purposes in the course of its time. In order to do the policy justice, the analysis should concentrate on its dynamic nature. For this reason, the frame of reference concept is used in this chapter. We define a frame of reference as the collection of concepts and theories about policy for which consensus exists in the policy community. A policy community consists of actors who share an interest in a functional policy area (de Vries, 1995).

157

The dynamics of policy with respect to purposes has been mentioned above, but other dynamic aspects can also be highlighted by analysing Dutch autonomisation policy with a focus on frames of reference. It will become clear that various types of autonomisation have been used in the course of time to serve various purposes. The analysis will also demonstrate that the policy community possessing the most interest in a specific functional policy area changes over time or is supplemented.

Relations Between Policy and Administrative Science

Kickert has pointed to the relationship between academia and practitioners of public administration in the Netherlands, 'In comparison to surrounding countries such as France, Germany and Great Britain, in the Netherlands the relationship with and the influence upon administrative practice by administrative scientists with a political science orientation is notably strong' (Kickert and Verhaak, 1995). If the bond between academia and the practice of public administration can be analysed on the basis of such concepts as frame of reference and policy community, it is worthwhile to determine whether this characteristic of Dutch public administration is also apparent in Dutch autonomisation policy.

If a bond exists between academics and practitioners, administrative scientists will maintain some form of contact with policy makers. One important indication of this bond is participation in a policy community, however, mere participation in a policy community says little about possible influence. In order to discuss influence, more conditions must be met. For example, the concepts used by administrative scientists will have to be part of the vocabulary and the frame of reference of the policy community.

When it appears that administrative scientists participate in a policy community promoting autonomisation and that the concepts introduced by these scholars are used in the policy community, we have an important indication that the relation between academics and practitioners is strong and that academics have substantial influence on practice with respect to autonomisation.

In order to map Dutch autonomisation policy and the influence of the administrative scientists' privatisation policy, we first need to outline this policy. Section Two presents a process description of the policy before moving on to specifics about the two themes mentioned above. The process description is done in such a manner that it does justice to the dynamic nature of the privatisation policy. In other words, using the process description we should be able to draw conclusions about the frames of reference and the policy communities.

2.   Process Description of Dutch Autonomisation Policy

The process description is based on memos and notes which are supplemented with data from supporting research about the policy community. Since a series of memos and notes may encompass a long period, it might be that another series of memos and notes finds its origin in that period as well. As a result, the process description is not entirely chronological.

The process description is also selective. Matters which do not directly contribute to knowledge about the frames of reference and the policy communities of autonomisation will not be described. Furthermore, the discussion is limited to the autonomisation policy of Dutch central government with respect to ministerial departments. The relation and influence of administrative scientists will be described from this perspective.

The Reconsideration Operation

In 1981, the Van Agt Cabinet (centre-right) started a so-called reconsideration operation (in Dutch *heroverweging* comparable to the British *scrutinies*). In retrospect, this is the starting point of the Dutch autonomisation policy. In order to maintain the welfare state in the light of a dwindling budget, regular testing of the efficiency of public services was deemed necessary. Difficult choices could no longer be avoided (Postma, 1982). The reconsideration basically concerned two joint issues: is government doing the right thing and are these activities properly executed? (Boorsma, 1986).

The review was shaped by a large number of interdepartmental working groups under the supervision of the Ministerial Commission of Reconsideration, a cabinet commission consisting of the Prime Minister, the Vice-Prime Minister and the Minister of Finance. The Ministry of Finance, specifically the Inspectorate of Central Finances (part of the Directorate General of the Government Budget), was the most important actor in this operation. The Inspectorate was responsible to the Secretariat of the Civil Service Commission for Reconsideration. This secretariat prepared inventories of subjects that could be reviewed, monitored the progress of reviews and assessed the results of reviews. Furthermore, the associates of the Secretariat of the Civil Service Commission also handled the working groups secretariats (van Nispen, 1993).

Profit Principle and Privatisation

In the first two budget years of 1981 and 1982, a total of 48 areas were subject to reconsiderations (30 in the first year and 18 in the second year) (van Nispen, 1993). Both in 1981 and 1982, a large number of distinct policy areas across the range of the public sector were reviewed. A number of general topics were also studied such as the application of the profit principle, privatisation, deregulation and decentralisation (Boorsma, 1986).

The application of the profit principle and privatisation was examined in the first year (Tweede Kamer 16 625, nr. 8). It was an interdepartmental issue of concern. In spite of the fact that the interdepartmental working group acknowledged a clear path from the profit principle to privatisation (according to the Commission, the concepts are related), both issues were addressed separately in this report. The major portion of the report was devoted to the application of the profit principle, also called the privatisation of demand.

According to the interdepartmental working group, the application of the profit principle meant that users of a service could be asked a (higher) direct price if that service was currently offered at a rate below cost- or market price (Tweede Kamer 16 625, nr. 8). The application of the profit principle was thus motivated by:

- allocation considerations (optimal allocation of available means);
- distribution considerations (better tuning of costs and benefits to one another and reducing the possibilities of hiving-off collective burdens); and
- budgetary consideration (shifting the financing burden from government to the consumer so that the budgetary problem of government is reduced).

In addition, the review report also addressed privatisation which was interpreted broadly by the following definition: privatisation consists of all types of autonomisation in which tasks performed by government are partially or entirely removed from direct government influence (Tweede Kamer 16 625, nr. 8). The privatisation of sections of an organisation, contracting out and abolishment of tasks were all viewed as privatisation (Boorsma, 1986).

Two clusters of arguments in the reconsideration report on the application of the profit principle and privatisation were used to substantiate privatisation:

- the Economic argument (more efficient and effective policy); and
- the Administrative argument (reduction of governments' task load).

The Reconsideration on Privatisation

A second round of reconsiderations occurred in 1982 and for the second time privatisation was subject to investigation. In this review, the application of the profit principle was no longer mentioned.

As with the first reconsideration in 1981, the 1982 working group for privatisation was interdepartmental and the secretariat rested with the associates of the Secretariat for the Civil Service Commission. External experts were brought in by the working group on privatisation. In the first phase of this research, Professors Boorsma and Nentjes and engineer Knipscheer were invited to provide comments and remarks on the theoretical part of the working group's report. Part of its report was based on Boorsma's report *Streamlining in the Public Sector* (Boorsma, 1981).

The working group on privatisation defined privatisation in the same manner as its predecessor, thus the vagueness about types of privatisation remained. While new arguments in favour of privatisation were added to the economic and administrative arguments, the emphasis on the economic argument remained the overarching rationale of all reviews:

- the Innovative argument (the market offers better opportunities for development, innovation and export) and
- the Macro-economic argument (economic recovery through substantial growth of the private sector).

Large Operations

With the inauguration of the Cabinet, privatisation became the core of cabinet policy. It corresponded to the free-market ideology of this centre-right cabinet. The reconsideration policy was placed in a larger framework. In 1982, under the heading of 'Large Operations', several initiatives were aimed at reducing both the Dutch budget deficit and collective expenditures. A large number of these operations was not new. With the inauguration of the Lubbers Cabinet, decentralisation attained the status of a large operation. The same can be said for the reorganisation of central government. In 1982, it was also decided to remove deregulation and privatisation from the reconsiderations and to combine them into a separate institutional framework (van Nispen and Noordhoek, 1986). This separation of other large operations from the reconsiderations emphasises the importance of the latter for the former. It is for this reason that Postma stated that reconsiderations were the mother of all large operations (Postma, 1986). In addition to the large operations already mentioned (privatisation, reconsiderations, decentralisation, reorganisation of central government and deregulation), personnel reduction was the only new operation.

The Large Operation on Privatisation

As a consequence of the decision to place privatisation under a separate heading, the Interdepartmental Supervisory Group for Privatisation was created in December 1982. This group, with its secretariat at the Ministry of Finance (the Inspectorate) was given a stimulating, coordinating and advising role in the pursuit of privatisation. Its task was to select subjects which would be suitable for concrete privatisation research, which could then be used for political decision making. In principle, all public services and activities had to be considered for privatisation (Tweede Kamer 17 938, nr. 1).

This group used the privatisation definition from the first reconsideration report (Tweede Kamer 17 938, nr. 1) (see above) and the four motives from the first report. Emphasis was placed on the fact that the motives for privatisation corresponded with general cabinet policy aimed at reducing government shortages, limiting the collective burden and strengthening the market sector (Tweede Kamer 17 938, nr. 1).

One new aspect was the explicit distinction of three main types of privatisation:

- a situation of complete removal of a public service: the clearest type of privatisation in which the private sector both determines the size of the service as well as the production and the financing;
- a situation in which government will keep determining the size of a service through planning, but the production will be contracted out to a private company; and
- a situation in which tasks are transferred to somewhat autonomous organisations with indirect government supervision (Tweede Kamer 17 938, nr. 1).

Table 10.1.   Numbers and Personnel Size of Privatisation Projects in the 1986–1991 Period

	Number of Projects		Size of Personnel		Excluding State Companies		
	Absolute	(%)	Absolute	%	Absolute	(%)	Civil Servants (%)
Projects	50	100	119 647	100	17 972	100	11
of which: Autonomisation	23	46	115 545	97	13 854	77	9
Privatisation	10	20	900	1	825	5	1
Contracting out	17	34	3 293	3	3 293	18	2
of which: State Companies*	4	8	101 675	85			

* These include Post, Telegraph and Telephone, State Printing and Publishing Company, Postbank and the State Fishing Harbour Agency.

Source: Boneschansker and De Haan.

Some Empirical Facts

In order to get a perspective on the distribution of privatisation proposals according to these distinguished types, Boneschansker and De Haan conducted an evaluation in 1991. Fifty privatisation projects in the 1986–91 period were evaluated (see Table 10.1).

Based on these figures by Boneschansker and De Haan, it appears that complete removal is the variant most used, both in terms of the number of projects as well as in the number of employees involved. Privatisations in the 1986–91 period involved some 100 000 employees from state companies and some 18 000 civil servants.

To get an impression of the nature of the organisations which were considered for privatisation, Boneschansker and De Haan divided the privatisation projects among the following three categories:

- state companies: the Postbank, PTT Telecom, State Fisher Harbour Agency and the Royal Mint;
- larger government services: the State Purchasing Office, the State Psychiatric Asylums, the Radio and Television Office, the State Automobile Centre and the Pilot Service; and
- smaller supporting government services: departmental accountants, organisation consultants, security services and printing offices (Boneschansker and De Haan, 1991).

The Large Operation on Privatisation (sequel)

In order to make the experience with privatisation available to government departments, the Civil Service Commission for Collective Experience with Privatisation was created at the end of 1988. With the assistance of external experts, this commission wrote the handbook on privatisation that was to serve as a guideline for the execution of privatisation projects (*Handboek Privatisering 1990*). For the working group on juridical aspects of privatisation, Professor De Ru was the external expert.

In the Handbook, the Commission concluded that the arguments in support of privatisation policy have evolved over time. While the budgetary motive remained primary, the administrative and economic motives gained in importance (*Handboek 1990*).

The Reconsiderations on Self-Management

The institutional decoupling of privatisation from the reconsideration operation did not mean the end of reconsiderations. As mentioned, reconsiderations became a large operation after 1982 and the institutional framework for the reconsiderations was maintained.

In 1983 an interdepartmental working group was created to consider improvements in the management of government with Boorsma as an external advisor, since he had been an advisor to the reconsideration working group in 1982. Also Professor Mol, of the public administration faculty of Twente University, became a member.

The Cabinet assigned this working group with the task of researching the possibilities of developing better systems of cost management within the public sector (Ministerie van Financiën, 1983). This task description appears to be based on the idea that different management systems would result in savings in the longer run. The working group considered it possible to achieve structural improvement of public management by introducing a different management concept, self-management, with which the private sector had had favourable experience. Self-management was defined as 'the execution of the authority within an agency to regulate and steer production without direct interference from outside' (Ministerie van Financiën, 1983). Contract management became the vehicle for self-management and an annual contract was to be concluded between individual sections and the head of the department which obliged all parties to execute activities and make the necessary means available (Ministerie van Financiën, 1983).

Compass for Self-Management

In 1985, the final report of the Interdepartmental Working Group on Self-Management was published under the title 'Compass for Self-Management: A New Course for Management in Central Government'. Although self-management was no longer a part of the reconsideration process, the structure of the reconsideration operation was maintained; it remained an interdepartmental activity which could be supplemented by external experts. Mol was also now a member.

This report suggested that self-management was in vogue and a new report to indicate further developments in self-management was written. In this report, self-management was further operationalised and projects were selected and prepared (Ministerie van Financiën, 1985). Ultimately, the self-management experiments worked out differently than envisaged by the working group.

Self-management experiments were initiated in various departments by the end of the 1980s, but they were not positively evaluated. The Ministries of Finance and of Home Affairs did not apply the frameworks developed for self-management in a flexible manner even though they had been requested to do so. In practice, the autonomy was limited to personnel and finance and sensitive subjects were excluded from the evaluations. Furthermore, the autonomy was not to have structural consequences for the period after the management contract.

In 1991, in spite of these evaluations, a new reconsideration operation was initiated with virtually the same subject: the differentiation of (financial) management rules (Ministerie van Financiën, 1991). In this report the concept of agencies was introduced which had a great influence upon the Dutch privatisation policy.

Functional Decentralisation

The Ministry of Home Affairs was 'home base' for the discussion on functional decentralisation which began in 1988. In principle, this was not connected to the discussions at the Ministry of Finance about the profit principle, privatisation and self-management, but we will see how these two discussions came together in 1992.

The independent public bodies were central to the discussion about functional decentralisation. These had been defined as public bodies of central government empowered to execute public tasks without hierarchical subordination to the minister (Scheltema, 1974). Although the term 'independent public body' is rather recent, the parliament had created these as early as the 19th century.

Several memos were written on this topic and external research was frequently referenced. The most important research in this respect was that of Boxum, De Ridder and Scheltema. Their report, which investigated several independent public bodies, was written at the request of Home Affairs (Boxum, *et al.*, 1989). In their report, the authors distinguished the following reasons as important for the creation of independent public bodies:

- getting experts involved (an independent public body offers the opportunity to delegate decision making to those experts necessary for performing a task);
- objective task execution (an independent public body offers the opportunity to fulfil public tasks independently from government);
- participation of interest groups (an independent public body offers the opportunity to share responsibility with societal organisations).

In the Cabinet report, *Functional Decentralisation, Why and How?*, conclusions and recommendations were drawn from the Boxum research (Tweede Kamer 21 042, nr. 4). The Cabinet accepted the three motives mentioned above and added a fourth:

- improving/rationalising central government (an independent public body provides the opportunity to downsize bureaucracy into smaller units) (Tweede Kamer 21 042, nr. 4).

Given the close relationship between functional decentralisation policy and the reorganisation of central government, a subcommittee of the Advisory Committee for Central Government was created, chaired by Professor Oele, to advise on aspects of effectiveness and administration.

Reconsideration of Management Regulations (Agencies)

As will become clear, the change of government in 1989 had a substantial impact on Dutch privatisation policy. The liberals in the second Lubbers Cabinet were replaced by social democrats. It also gave new impetus to the reorganisation of central government, as is illustrated by the following quote from the cabinet agreement:

The main issue will be to increase efficiency and effectiveness and to assess policy contents in relation to societal developments and problems that central government should fulfil. This will be based on the idea that the major policy functions should remain with the central government, while the execution can be delegated to other governmental units or to independent public bodies and independent agencies.

The Lubbers cabinet commenced several activities in order to achieve the desired reorganisation of central government. As a consequence, the Inquiry Committee of the Second Chamber was created in which renewed attention was given to privatisation and management.

The reconsideration concept was again used with respect to the renewed attention for management and in 1990 the Working Group on the Reconsideration of Management Regulations was created. It was hoped that their research would lead to renewed discussion about the desirability of differentiating management rules – especially in the field of public finance – in the short term, and would lead to practical solutions (Ministerie van Financiën, 1991).

That practical solution was found in another management regime: the agency. This was inspired by developments in the United Kingdom. Agencies were believed to have greater independence than the existing departmental (deconcentrated) services (Ministerie van Financiën, 1991). Some advantages of an agency, such as a flexible year-end budget, reserve possibilities and flexible working conditions, were viewed as further steps toward self-management.

In addition to the introduction of agencies, a distinction was made in this reorganisation report between internal and external privatisation. The following types were distinguished by this working group (Ministerie van Financiën, 1991):

- internal privatisation in which privatisation takes place within a department (agencies);
- external privatisation through functional decentralisation (independent public bodies); and
- external privatisation by the creation of companies which operate under market conditions and according to the profit principle (privatisation).

Table 10.2.   Agencies

Created January 1994	*Created January 1995*	*Proposed January 1996*
Computer Centre	Royal Meterological Institute	Central Judicial Collection Agency
Plant Health Office	Office for Judicial Institutes	State Archive Office
*Senter	Civil Service Information Office	School Financing Centre
Immigration and Naturalisation Office		Military Building, Works and Area Office
		Operational Affairs Telecom and Post
		Medicines Evaluation

Source: Ministry of Finance (1995).

In a short time, the internal type of privatisation became popular. From 1994 to 1996, 13 agencies were created and many organisations are about to become an agency (see Table 10.2).

Autonomisation and Privatisation

Since 1981, autonomisation had been defined in terms of privatisation and privatisation included all types of autonomisation in which government diminished or eliminated their influence over certain tasks (Tweede Kamer 16 625, nr. 8). This changed in 1991 starting with the reconsideration report on management. In this report privatisation was considered a type of external autonomisation achieved through the creation of companies operating under market conditions.

When Kok, a social democrat, became Minister of Finance in 1991, the memos changed as well and autonomisation became the central concept as evidenced by a memo entitled 'Autonomisation and Privatisation'. Privatisation referred to the complete abolition of a public task or the contracting-out of tasks. The motives also changed during this period. Both autonomisation and privatisation served:

- to enhance the effectiveness so that budgetary cutbacks can be realised; and
- to encourage administrative streamlining so that the quality of government could be improved (Tweede Kamer 21 632, nr. 1).

The integration of autonomisation and privatisation appears to be a fact given the change in concepts and motives. Nevertheless, the processes undertaken by departments in order to realise either of the two types still exhibited signs of the former distinctions. Both the Advisory Committee for Central Government as well as the Interdepartmental Supervisory Group on Privatisation fulfilled a stimulating, supervisory and advisory role. This situation ended in 1995. A team of civil servants from the Ministries of Home Affairs and of Finance was created to serve as the knowledge, service and coordination centre (Tweede Kamer 21 042, nr. 15).

In order to prevent conceptual ambiguity, Table 10.3 presents the situation of autonomisation in 1991.

Table 10.3.   Forms of Autonomisation

	Organisational	*Juridical*
Privatisation	external	private
Independent Administrative Body	external	public
Special Regime Agency	internal	public
Self-Administration	internal	public

Source: Kickert, (1991).

Core Departments

The last development in the field of autonomisation did not occur at the level of the autonomous agencies but at the departmental level. This shifting of attention in autonomisation towards departments is a consequence of the emerging discussion in the 1990s regarding the distinction between policy and execution. The agreement of the Kok Cabinet of 1994 stated that autonomous organisations were to focus on execution and departments were to focus on their core business. Departments would be smaller and therefore more efficient and effective. This idea of core departments is now central in the discussion on autonomisation. The 1993 Wiegel Commission defined core departments as small, flexible, high quality departments focused on strategic policy making and the main issues of policy.

Several commissions were influential in developing the idea of core departments. The Wiegel Commission, the Scheltema Commission and the College of Secretary-Generals are the most important (all in 1993). The Wiegel and the Scheltema Commissions reported as part of the Inquiry Committee of the Second Chamber and they used a substantial number of external advisors. Professor In 't Veld was a member of the Wiegel Commission and Professor Scheltema was chairman of the commission named after him. Secretaries of both commissions were recruited from academia: van Twist was the secretary to the Wiegel Commission and De Ridder to the Scheltema Commission.

Although notes of criticism can be heard lately, the general consensus about the desired development of central government appears to be in favour of the core departments. How these should be created, however, remains a subject of debate. A difference of opinion between the Wiegel Commission and the secretaries-general exists regarding internal autonomisation. The former considers internal autonomisation as a possibility to realise the desired separation of policy and execution (van Twist, Bagchus and Verhaak, 1996). Since the publication of a highly critical report on independent public bodies by the Chamber of Accounts, the Cabinet has also developed the opinion that internal autonomisation is preferred above the external variety (Tweede Kamer 24 130, nr. 3). The primacy of politics, an important item for the Kok Cabinet, is closely linked to the preference for internal autonomisation.

3.   Shifting Frames of Reference

The process description of Dutch autonomisation policy allows us to suggest some conclusions about the dynamic nature of this policy. To this end, we introduced the concept of frames of reference, defined as the collection of concepts and theories about a policy which meets with consensus in the policy community. Policy community has been defined as the group of actors who have an interest in a functional policy area.

The following dynamic aspects can be distinguished in Dutch autonomisation policy:

- the dynamics with respect to the goals of autonomisation,
- the dynamics with respect to the different types of autonomisation and
- the dynamics with respect to the policy communities.

By examining various forms of autonomisation over time and linking these with the stated goals and the institutional frameworks in which they were voiced, we can draw conclusions about the dynamic nature of Dutch autonomisation policy in terms of frames of reference. Before defining these frames of reference, we summarise autonomisation policy per (dynamic) aspect.

Goals of Autonomisation

Various goals of autonomisation policy can be distinguished over the years. In the beginning, privatisation referred primarily to budgetary aspects. In the course of time, budgetary aspects became less important, most notably when Kok became Minister of Finance. Memos written under his leadership were no longer entitled 'privatisation' but more neutrally 'autonomisation and privatisation'. Ideas about more efficient and effective management were replaced by discussions regarding the need to enhance effectiveness so that – after an initial phase – budgetary cutbacks could be realised (Tweede Kamer 21 632, nr. 1).

Since 1990, reconsiderations that coincide with the improvement of the organisation of central government are increasingly emphasised in Dutch autonomisation policy. In his report, Scheltema proposed to use core departments as a starting point (Scheltema Commission, 1993).

In the next section, the goals of Dutch autonomisation policy and the types of autonomisation will be summarised.

Types of Autonomisation

In the Netherlands, autonomisation has long been a container concept for the various ways in which organisational tasks could be exempted from the existing departments (de Vries and Korsten, 1992). An examination of the various memos reveals that (implicitly or not) a particular type of autonomisation was always emphasised. Functional decentralisation, for instance, was about independent public bodies and privatisation concerned companies working under market conditions. By distinguishing between internal and external autonomisation in 1991, the various types could be related to one another.

We have seen that the fragmented nature of Dutch autonomisation policy led to different motives for autonomisation. This fragmentation also resulted in an emphasis on different types of autonomisation. These are summarised in Table 10.4.

Table 10.4.   Types and Motives of Autonomisation in Various Periods

Period	Type	Motive
1981–82	profit principle	– optimal allocation of available means – more direct and precise tuning of costs and benefits – shift of financial burden from government to consumer
1981–91	privatisation	– efficient and effective management – downsizing government tasks – improved opportunities for development, innovation and export – substantial enlargement of the private sector
1983–present	self-management	– effective management – cost control
1988–present	independent public body	– improvement/rationalisation of central government – involvement of experts – objective task fulfilment – participation of interest groups
1990–present	privatisation	– enlargement of effectiveness – administrative streamlining
1991–present	agency	– strengthening effective management

The motives for the separation of policy from execution and of core departments are not mentioned here since they do not concern a specific type of autonomisation.

Policy Communities

As is clear from the process description of Dutch autonomisation policy, the membership of the policy community was in constant flux, as indicated by the situation between 1990–94 when two different commissions existed to supervise autonomisation processes. Both the Oele Commission and the Interdepartmental Commission on Privatisation maintained a supervisory role. Oele operated on behalf of Home Affairs while the Interdepartmental Commission was based in the Ministerie van Financiën. Currently, the supervision is in the hands of a team in which civil servants from both ministries are involved. The various subjects and actors are summarised in Table 10.5.

An examination of the various types of autonomisation over time linked with the motives used and the institutional frameworks in which they were initiated leads us to conclude that clear changes have occurred in Dutch autonomisation policy. In terms of frames of reference, one could say that an economic frame of reference was dominant in the first period of privatisation and self-management. In the course

Table 10.5.   Subjects and Policy Communities in Dutch Autonomisation Policy

Subject	Policy Community
Application of the profit principle and privatisation; Privatisation	Interdepartmental Reconsideration Working Group; secretariat at the Ministerie van Financiën
Privatisation	Interdepartmental Supervisory Group on Privatisation and the Commission for Collective Experience with Privatisation
Self-management	Interdepartmental Reconsideration Working Group; secretariat at the Ministry of Finance
Functional decentralisation	Ministry of Home Affairs
Agencies	Interdepartmental Reconsideration Working Group; secretariat at the Ministry of Finance

of time, the juridical framework emerged as a result of the attention for independent public bodies. The shift to agencies (1991) and later to core departments (1993) brought, respectively, a managerial frame of reference and a policy frame of reference to the forefront. The emphasis on the managerial and the policy frames of reference results in decreasing importance for the economic and juridical frames of reference. This does not mean, however, that these have disappeared completely. The various frames of reference are summarised below.

Figure 10.1.   Shifting Frames of Reference

```
Economic (1981)

      I
      I
      I
      I          Juridical (1988)
      I
      I               I
      I               I
      I               I
      I               I

   Managerial (1991)

         I
         I

   Policy (1993)
```

4. The Relation Between Dutch Autonomisation Policy and Administrative Science

Kickert identifies the close relationship between academia and practice in the Netherlands as a goal of public administration. Unlike the natural sciences, public administration not only has the descriptive–analytical goal of providing theoretical explanations from empirical explanations, but also the prescriptive goal of improving the functioning of government (Kickert, 1996).

The close relationship between academia and practice is, according to Kickert, also apparent in the fact that professors often come from the world of practice and *vice versa*. Furthermore, administrative scientists often hold memberships on permanent or temporary advisory bodies and they are often contracted to undertake research for public bodies (Kickert 1996).

In this section, we investigate whether the close relationship between academia and practice is evident in Dutch autonomisation policy by using the concept of policy community. When administrative scientists are part of the autonomisation policy community and when their concepts are adopted in that policy area, we have

Table 10.6. Autonomisation Policy Communities and Administrative Scientists

Policy Community	*Administrative Scientist*
Interdepartmental Reconsideration Working Group on the Profit Principle and Privatisation	–
Interdepartmental Reconsideration Working Group on Privatisation	Boorsma Nentjes Knipscheer
Interdepartmental Supervisory Group on Privatisation and Commission for Collective Experience with Privatisation	De Ru
Interdepartmental Reconsideration Working Group on Self-management	Boorsma Mol
Home Affairs	Boxum De Ridder Scheltema Oele
Interdepartmental Reconsideration Working Group on Management Regulations	–
Inquiry Committee on Core Departments	In 't Veld Van Twist Scheltema De Ridder

Table 10.7.   A Comparison of Text Fragments from Scholarly Work and Policy Documents

Text Fragments from Scholarly Work	Text Fragments from Policy Documents
Boorsma, *Cutbacks in the Collective Sector*, 1981	*Reconsideration Report on Privatisation*, 1982
Using three functions, namely production, financing and planning, we can distinguish four 'market' types: – the consolidated market, in which these three functions are exercised by the same actor; – the contract, in which the planning actor contracts production out; – the regulated market, in which the planning actor does not regulate production and financing; and – the *granted market*: the subsidised market, in which financing is not linked to decisions about the production	With respect to the degree and form of government intervention, the following elements can be distinguished: a. The functions that government exercises directly or indirectly with respect to a service. As main functions we can distinguish: planning or regulation (size of the service), financing and production. b. The degrees in which government intervention appears with respect to these functions can be subdivided into the following market types: – the consolidated market, in which the three functions are exercised by the same actor (government); – the contract, where government finances, regulates and distributes, but contracts out the production; – the 'granted market', the subsidised market in which government partially finances and the private sector plans, produces and distributes; – the regulated market, in which the private sector distributes, produces and finances, while government holds the competence to intervene through regulations; and – the 'free market' without any government intervention
Boxum, De Ridder and Scheltema, *Autonomous Public Bodies*, 1989	*Cabinet Report on Functional Decentralisation, 1990*
An independent public body offers the opportunity to: – give decision making authority to experts needed for the execution of a task; – execute tasks independent from government; – realise co-responsibility of societal organisations	Several motives and goals can form the foundation of the desire to realise functional decentralisation: – Improvement of central government – Involvement of experts or experienced administrators – Co-responsibility of societal organisations
Twist and In 't Veld, *On Core Departments*, May 1993	Wiegel Commission, *Core Departments*, June 1993
Core departments, a preliminary definition: We define core departments as small, flexible, highly qualified departments that focus on strategic policy making and the main issues of policy	A core department is a small organisation (several hundred to a maximum of one-thousand people), primarily aimed at policy development. A core department consists of highly-qualified civil servants who are sensitive to societal issues and have a well developed political instinct. Characteristic for a core department is its outward orientation. The size of core departments may differ, but size depends primarily on the number of tasks or policy areas under the jurisdiction of a minister

an important indication of the existence of a relationship between academia and practice.

Administrative scientists have frequently been mentioned as members of a policy community. In Table 10.6, these individuals are listed according to the policy community.

The inclusion of administrative scientists in a policy community is not evidence of their influence in that community. In order to discuss influence, the concepts used by administrative scientists must be imitated by the policy community and used in their frames of reference. This too was the case. For example, part of the reconsideration report on privatisation was based on Boorsma's report *Cutbacks in the Public Sector*. Likewise, the cabinet memo entitled *Functional Decentralisation, Why and How?* used conclusions and recommendations from the Boxum *et al.* research. Ideas from In 't Veld are clearly evident in the report of the Wiegel Commission (*Core Departments*), and ideas of Scheltema are evident in the Scheltema Commission Report (*Relevant Ministries*).

Fragments of texts from publications by Boorsma, Scheltema and In 't Veld are compared in Table 10.7 to text fragments from policy documents. This table serves to illustrate that concepts were introduced by academics, copied into the policy community and accepted into the frames of reference of that policy community.

5.   Postmodern Public Administration

While it is clear from the excerpts presented in Table 10.7 that ideas and concepts developed by scholars have been imitated and used in the frames of reference of the policy community, not all academics who have researched autonomisation are participants in the autonomisation policy community. Professor Frissen, inspired by post modernism, is an example.

Although Frissen, like Scheltema, has researched autonomisation processes on assignment from Home Affairs, his ideas have not been accepted into the policy community (Frissen *et al.*, 1992). Moreover, the current emphasis of the Kok Cabinet on the primacy of politics runs counter to Frissen's ideas.

In *Autonomisation of Government*, Frissen describes two ideal-typical configurations of autonomisation based on the characteristics of that policy process (Frissen *et al.*, 1992). In the case of sequential policy, policy must meet the following conditions:

- policy goals are set by a central actor;
- the policy is relatively complete, that is, the goals and means of the policy are established and noncontroversial;
- the conditions under which the policy is executed are highly stable;
- the policy enjoys a clear goal-means structure.

If the policy process has these characteristics, it is possible for parts of an organisation to autonomise. This type of autonomisation usually concerns policy execution which meets with little controversy. When a specific policy area possesses strong interdependencies:

- the goals of policy are established by various actors and often through conflict;
- the policy is often incomplete and controversial both in terms of goals and means;
- the environment in which the policy is executed is dynamic and conditions for execution are unstable;
- there is no clear goal-means structure to policy.

According to Frissen, it is possible to autonomise even if a policy process possesses these characteristics. Moreover, Frissen believes that the necessity to autonomise in this situation is even greater. Autonomisation of this type concerns the entire policy cycle. A more encompassing responsibility for all policy phases is delegated as a result (Frissen, 1996).

These latter autonomisations advocated by Frissen have consequences which are contrary to the ideas of the Kok Cabinet. The Kok Cabinet wants to strengthen political decision making while Frissen would like to see function left to autonomised organisations. Since Frissen's ideas do concur with those of the cabinet, they are not found in the frame of reference. Whether this will be the case in the future remains to be seen.

References

Boneschansker, E. and J. de Haan, 1991. 'Privatisering'. In: C.A. de Kam and J. de Haan (eds), *Terugtredende overheid realiteit of retoriek?, een evaluatie van de grote operaties*, Academic Service, Schoonhoven.

Boorsma, P.B., 1981. *Sanering in de collectieve sector*. T.H. Twente, Enschede.

Boorsma, P.B., 1986. 'Privatisering'. In: F.K.M. van Nispen and D.P. Noordhoek, *De grote operaties: de overheid onder het mes of het snijden in eigen vlees*, Kluwer, Deventer.

Boxum, J.L, J. de Ridder and M. Scheltema, 1989. *Zelfstandige bestuursorganen in soorten*, Kluwer, Deventer.

Commissie Scheltema, 1993. *Steekhoudend ministerschap, betekenissen toepassing van de ministeriële verantwoordelijkheid*, 's-Gravenhage.

Commissie Wiegel, 1993. *Naar kerndepartementen, kiezen voor een hoogwaardige en flexibele rijksdienst*, 's-Gravenhage.

Frissen, P.H.A., 1996. *De virtuele staat, politie, bestuur, technologie: een postmodern verhaal*. Academic Service, Schoonhoven.

Frissen, P.H.A., P. Albers, V.J.J.M. Bekkers, J. Huigen, K. Schmitt, M. Thaens and B. de Zwaan, (1992). *Verzelfstandiging in het openbaar bestuur, een bestuurskundige verkenning van verzelfstandiging, verbindingen en informatisering*. 's-Gravenhage.

Kabinet Kok, 1994. 'De regeringsverklaring'. *Staatscourant*, 17 augustus 1994.

Kickert, W.J.M., 1991. 'Verzelfstandiging in het openbaar bestuur'. *Bestuurswetenschappen*, vol. 6, pp. 406–19. Groningen.

Kickert, W.J.M., 1996. 'Beleids- en bestuurswetenschappen in Nederland: Ontstaan, ontwikkeling en stand van zaken'. *Bestuurswetenschappen*, vol. 1, pp. 34–61. Groningen.

Kickert, W.J.M. and F.O.M. Verhaak, 1995. 'Autonomizing executive tasks in Dutch central government'. *International Review of Administrative Sciences*. Vol. 61, Sage, London.

Ministerie van Financiën, 1983. *Zelfbeheer*. 's-Gravenhage.

Ministerie van Financiën, 1985. *Kompas voor zelfbeheer*. 's-Gravenhage.

Ministerie van Financiën, 1991. *Verder bouwen aan beheer*. 's-Gravenhage.

Nispen, F.K.M. van, 1993. *Het dossier heroverweging*. Eburon, Delft.

Nispen, F.K.M. van, and D.P. Noordhoek, 1986. *De grote operaties, de overheid onder het mes of snijden in het eigen vlees*. Kluwer, Deventer.

Postma, J.K.T., 1982. 'Heroverweging en privatisering'. *Economische Statistische Berichten*, pp. 852–7.

Postma, J.K.T., 1986. 'Heroverweging van overheidsuitgaven essentieel voor doelmatig beleid'. In: F.K.M. van Nispen and D.P. Noordhoek, *De grote operaties: de overheid onder het mes of het snijden in eigen vlees*. Deventer.

Scheltema M., 1974. *Zelfstandige bestuursorganen*. Tjeenk Willink, Groningen.

Secretarissen Generaal, 1993. *De organisatie en de werkwijze van de rijksdienst*. 's-Gravenhage.

Tweede Kamer der Staten Generaal, 1982–1983, 17 938, nr.1, *Privatisering*, Brief van de minister van Financiën.

Tweede Kamer der Staten Generaal, 1989–1990, 21 632, nr.1, *Verzelfstandiging en privatisering*, Brief van de minister van Financiën.

Tweede Kamer der Staten Generaal, 1990–1991, 21 042, nr.4, *Functionele decentralisatie, waarom en hoe?*, Regeringsstandpunt.

Tweede Kamer der Staten Generaal, 1994–1995, 21 042, nr.15, *Functionele decentralisatie*, Brief van de minister van Binnenlandse Zaken en Financiën.

Tweede Kamer der Staten Generaal, 1994–1995, 23 171, nr.3, *Agentschappen*, Brief van de minister van Financiën.

Tweede Kamer der Staten Generaal, 1994–1995, 24 130, nr.3, *Verslag van Algemene Rekenkamer over 1994*.

Twist, M.J.W. van, and R.J. in 't Veld (eds), 1993. *Over kerndepartementen, een vergelijkend onderzoek naar departementale veranderingsprocessen in Groot Brittannië, Zweden, Noorwegen en Denemarken*. VUGA, 's-Gravenhage.

Twist, M.J.W. van, R. Bagchus and F.O.M. Verhaak (eds), 1996. *Kerndepartementen op afstand?, een vergelijkend onderzoek naar departementale veranderingsprocessen binnen de Nederlandse Rijksoverheid*. Eburon, Delft.

Vries, J. de, 1995. 'De dynamiek der departementen: Een overzicht van de ontwikkelingen bij de rijksoverheid'. *Beleid en Maatschappij*, 1995/6, pp. 355–64. Groningen.

Vries, J. de and A.F.A. Korsten, 1992. 'Verzelfstandiging: panacee of placebo? Een introductie'. *Bestuurskunde*, vol. 1, pp. 4–7. Boom, Amsterdam.

CHAPTER ELEVEN

Modernising Spanish Public Administration: Old Inertias and New Challenges

Carlos Alba
Autonomous University, Madrid

1. Historical Introduction

Politicisation and Bureaucratic Power

The Spanish bureaucracy suffers from a lack of deep historic roots. As professor Garcia de Enterria (1964) has shown, the history of Spanish administration has been nothing more than a continuous effort to recreate *ex nihilo* an homogeneous public service at the European level. The modern history of Spanish administration starts in the middle of the nineteenth century, taking the Napoleonic model as a pattern. Our theorists and politicians understood that the Napoleonic pattern offered the best solution to give the country a highly professionalised administration which could become the instrument of a powerful and centralised government. The Spanish tradition of instability, of permanent conflict between political factions, of the selling of public jobs and, finally, our typical 'spoil system', were not the best foundations for the establishment of a professional modern civil service.

On the other hand, the public employees affected by the spoils system were always a group interested in the fall of the government, which had been the cause of their spoil retirement, and this situation certainly did not contribute to political stability. Favouritism and patronage were the principal means of recruiting and organising the civil service and political class. Two attempts have been made in recent history to try to put an end to the pathologies of our administration: the reform project of Bravo Murillo in 1852 and the Statute of 1918. These two foundation stones of the legal reform of public administration tried to put an end to clientelist patronage under which the public employees lost their jobs according to the changes of the party in power. It was the beginning of the idea of the merit system as an alternative to the spoil-patronage one.

Until 1918 the spoils system was effective and its purpose was to politicise the public administration. In these circumstances of instability and protectionism some civil servants monopolised the exercise of the authority of the state, including fundamental public tasks such as the budget, tax policy or public works. This situation of monopoly was intimately connected with the knowledge and experience that only these public officials had which enabled them to enjoy stability against the instability of the other public officials and also to achieve an *ius singulare* as a legal base of their situation. This circumstance made it possible for certain groups of public officials, due to their professional competence, their political affiliations, the importance of their functions and their group solidarity, to create *special corps*, from which some became powerful members of the political class, crystallising into an elite structure which has remained until now. Either by substituting politicians, or by filling up empty spaces of power or creating a specific techno-structure, they became the main actors in the political decision processes, in the implementation of those decisions and even in political life itself, taking up positions in parties and parliament.

In contrast with other corps of public officials, the administrative–political elite throughout many different historical situations always maintained its well established privileged position. Even in situations of rapid changes such as the Second Republic (1931–36), they occupied almost 60 percent of all the political positions in the government. Contrary to other administrative corps which were seriously affected by the Civil War (1936–39), some special corps did not find it a serious obstacle. These special corps have been the cause that the (always blurred) demarcation line between the political and administrative spheres in the Spanish case is almost inexistent.

At the beginning of this century some ministries created general corps (technical and auxiliary) and the administration began to organise itself in a structure of professionalised corps, but the political positions already occupied by the powerful corps of the administrative elite were still in their hands. Due to these circumstances many political fights are in fact at the very same time corps' fights.

Primo de Rivera's dictatorship, with its modernisation and development through a technocratic formula, reinforced the ascending tendency of the elite corps, especially those connected with the Finance Ministry (Ministerio de Hacienda), which turned into the most vigorous structure of political domination in the state's apparatus.

These public officials were not going to restrict themselves to monopolising certain state sectors under the authority of the political leaders and to accept the mere role of implementing the decisions of the politicians. It can rather be said that they became politicians: the government consisted mainly of high civil servants, the parliamentary assemblies, always weak, were supported by a high percentage of public officials and the state itself had become a bureaucratic–authoritarian system. The rest of the public officials formed a group which was noted for its politic apathy, inefficiency, hostility towards political change and deeply conservative tendencies. The politic class and its ideology always considered this mass of public officials as a mere instrument and never bothered to reform it. The ideology said that government and its leaders saw to the ends (politics) and not the means (the administration). But they forgot that those non-elite public officials were powerful enough to be able to stop or distort the implementation of their decisions.

Failed Reforms

The Second Republic's (1931–36) politics concerning the public administration went through two serious attempts at reform which turned out to be failures. Once the Republic was unveiled, a phase of revolutionary euphoria arose that was centred on two goals: the revision and criticism of the dictatorship's politics (Primo de Rivera, 1923–30) and a profound and thorough reform of the republic's bureaucracy. These impulses hardly reached two years of life, from then onwards the mechanisms of the bureaucracy itself managed to paralyse any progress towards reform.

Because of the bureaucracy's attitude of rejection to reform, the only solution seems to be to impose the reform from the political field and this has certainly been tried on several occasions in Spain. Usually the only result has been the politicians' inability to understand the public function's complex world and even more acute, the lack of independence of the politicians in their relation to the high civil servants who monopolise the experience and knowledge. Once these high public officials and their corps have become the most important support of the politicians in power and became the link that enables the state to control the administrative apparatus, one can imagine the result of the conflicts between politicians and high public officials. The support of the higher civil servants is obtained by the politicians, in exchange for maintaining their bureaucratic privileges. During the republican period, governments ended up getting used to the interests of the grand corps and by 1934 the air of reform had evaporated.

The second important moment in the Republic's politics concerning the bureaucracy came with the surgical measures of Chapaprieta in 1935 from the Ministry of Finance and inside the conservative government.

Despite the obstacles of *de facto* and bureaucratic powers, Parliament approved the law, but it was of no use. Not only did Chapaprieta fall with the change of government, but also the possibilities of the law's implementation would have been really difficult. The *Frente Popular* (Popular Front), in a rushed move to recreate the atmosphere of the year 1931, tried to start the administrative reform again, but the civil war put an end to all the potential reforms.

In the words of Professor Chapaprieta in 1935: 'The reform requires, in order to be beneficious, a deep and thoughtful study and enough time, that is to say, security of remaining in power, sufficient authority, without a single obstacle, a propitious parliament and above all, a quiet political and social atmosphere. On the contrary, expecting to try it in a few months, with unsuspected urgency, particularly for a government which was almost without presidential confidence and a parliament which was about to be dissolved, only led to aggravating the disagreement and disorganisation which has been felt since ages in the Spanish public administration.'

Special Corps in Spanish Administration

Undoubtedly, its organisation into 'corps' is one of the most highlighted elements of the Spanish public administration. This event involves a high degree of bureaucratisation of the professions, a peculiar use of corporatist theory (not as a form of linking the state and the civil society, but as the corporatisation of certain groups inside the state) and an irrational compartmentalisation of administrative cadres. The corps is defined as 'a group of public officials of homogenous specialisation, recruited by a common procedure and formed to occupy, at different moments of their career, a series of positions related with the kind of preparation they require to enter the corps' (de la Oliva, 1968b).

However, in fact the corps keep together due to several common interests: economic, professional, status, promotion and so on. The candidates who pass the different selective tests during a process of concourse organised by each corps, go directly into the service of a particular corps, not into the administration's service. They display loyalty to the corps and are socialised according to the moral code of their own corps so that they can distinguish between their own 'territory' and the foreign one, between comrades and strangers. There is insufficient knowledge of the origins of these corps and their bureaucratic and political functions through the years. The few studies show that the incentives of these corps have been the particularist interests of a group of citizens in achieving a certain status which would consolidate the prebends which they enjoyed; a peculiar mixture of patrimonialism and corporatism of the public functions which has been going on and has increased till the present moment. In a certain sense, these corps sprang up in a juridical vacuum. Regulations of their role do not exist and the limits of their particularism depend on the other corps' particularism. This could probably explain the hegemony of these 'Grand Corps' which, as they were originally constituted, were not limited at all in their search for power. When the state tried to stop this irrationality by imposing a legislation to create an administrative general corps, either it was never accepted or it was never applied to the Grand Corps. The important power struggles have been the ones between the general corps and the 'special' or Grand Corps. Those corps, heirs of the state's organisation which arose in the French Ancient Regime's *corps d'officiers* and was consolidated by the Napoleonic model, are in Spain a result of a very complex historic process by which many tendencies have been revealed: security, the appropriation of a sector inside the state's apparatus, the control of the recruiting processes for new candidates, the obtaining of patrimonial power and the use of an *ius singulari* as a source of all kinds of privileges. All these tendencies have been permitted in extreme forms since 1939 in the 'new state'. The interesting fact is that the corps' pressures have been realised in practice inside the state's apparatus and by the occupation of political spheres, thus being the source of the legislation and the policies which regulate their own privileges. Having a corps meant a defence against the *cesantias* (typical name for the Spanish spoil system) which was usual in Spain at least till 1918. Once this aim was achieved, the control of the cooption process and the maintenance of the corps' small size became especially important for its power privileges to last. The obtaining of earning sources which do not figure in the state's budget and which are not publicly known, has been a factor which has probably contributed more to the difference.[1] The para-fiscal and extra-budgetary incomes have constituted the distinct basis for the corps and formed a new element which became somehow 'autonomous' inside the state apparatus. The oligarchic politico–bureaucratic class which is recruited in these corps, with plenty of power inside the government and against it, is privileged, due to the fact that it has exerted its functions in an authoritarian regime, without political parties, without political pluralism or fundamental freedoms, and its position has been maintained till almost the present time.

The main elements of the Spanish Grand Corps were:

1. The control and self-government of the corps in having sufficient control over the recruiting of new members and promotions, the right to be consulted about the dispositions that affect their interests, in having a 'chief' in the corps who strives for its interests, not as some kind of institutional authority inside the corps but as a personal and corporatist leader.

2. During Franco's regime, in the absence of democratic structures, of freedom of speech, of free expressions of political opinions and of adequate participation channels, those corps behaved as singular pressure groups inside the state, very often by the occupation of political positions.

3. Their political and administrative roles are completely overlapping and their participation in politics far exceeds the limits of the distinctions made by Chapman when speaking of the public officials as policy makers.

4. The 'leave of absence' plays an important role. They are relieved from their administrative functions to serve in political positions. Quite frequently, this absent rule measure becomes permanent, so that a member can spend most of his life outside the corps, 'at the state's service' (the corps acts as if it lends staff to the state), but remaining linked to the corps as a participant member and sharing important incomes that the corps distributes periodically. Some of the people who have leave of absence have the responsibility for a policy that affects or might affect the corps. For instance the state's lawyers' corps, consisting of 200 members, has provided 15 ministers and 49 general directors between 1939 and 1970. A further great number of its members work in public companies, in the public banks, or in other local and regional political positions. Probably, in the history of these 200 members' lives more than half of

them have always been outside the corps. A member of this corps and also a general director, publicly declared: 'My political intervention was originated by an intimate link with the professional formation and leaving aside previous activities, my vocation was decided the day I went into the State's Lawyer corps. For the profession implies, and I apologise for my lack of humbleness, having a capacity, a sense of responsibility, an objectivity and a dedication, all of them very important features for a politician. And last but not least, it is also very important that our political leave of absence permissions are never doubted by the people who grant it, because our returning to the corps is always guaranteed.'

5. The place that the corps have inside the state apparatus shows a sort of incongruency between the specialty of the members of each corps and the department that they control, through the 'colonisation activities' in other departments.

6. Not only are the corps interministerial, they also have complete control over their own organic department and, in some particular cases, over departments not linked with their corps. Obviously, if a corps has all its members in its own organic department, it doesn't have the power to penetrate other sectors. If a corps is spread over all the departments there is no chance of being in control anywhere. The best case indeed is that of a corps which is in control of its own department and over various others. This colonisation of the state by the Grand Corps restricts the freedom of recruitment of new directors, since the positions are reserved for particular corps.

7. The polyvalence of certain corps has two important consequences. Firstly, the ministerial decisions to choose 'directors' are influenced by the fact that if the Minister recruits from only one corps, it gets to be isolated (even more if this particular corps is not very polyvalent). Secondly, the close correspondence between the corps and the ministries can only be overcome through those administrative corps that have been successful in their capacity to penetrate. The paradox is that on the one hand it is better to have a director member of a polyvalent corps, but that on the other hand this forms an obstacle for surpassing the pathologies that the philosopher Ortega y Gasset referred to as the 'uncommunicated compartments' in his *Espana Invertebrada* ('Invertebrate Spain').[2]

2. Francoism and Bureaucracy: Technocratic Reform

The administration underwent many changes during the civil war and the post-war years. Violent deaths, political purges and several repressions decimated the number of public officials. New recruitments and the meritocratic system gave way to political compensations, to the bureaucracy's (civil bureaucracy and party bureaucracy) duplication. The apparatus quickly took over its newly bureaucratised role and saw itself involved in routine paperwork. Those public officials who had no clear political goal were dominated by the elite corps which had the necessary knowledge and experience to reorientate the state's administrative machine. It is true that the elite corps greatly supported the new regime and made them pay for those services. The result was the maintenance of old privileges and the creation of new ones: important earnings, the control over their own bureaucratic body and over others and, above all, the appropriation of certain sectors and political positions.

These mandarins and their reproducing mechanisms created during Franco's regime a situation of profound overlap between political leaders and high civil servants. Both groups obtained their legitimacy in a bureaucratic way. To make a career within the administration was the only way to make a political career in a system which had outlawed political parties. There was no politic–democratic life that would permit other ways of leadership. The policy and the political struggle was fought inside the bureaucracy and administrative reform was nothing more than a disguise for a struggle for power which would later be abandoned for more promising platforms. The public official's Law of 1964 was an expression of those political struggles, it was approved when no one needed it once it had lost its political virulence.

The legal reforms, affecting the central administration, the civil servants, the budgeting process and the economic planning, were the first attempt to modernise the administration, introducing new techniques derived from the private sector and creating many of the institutions that have continued until the present moment, when a new wave of administrative reforms are looming on the horizon (Lopez Rodo, 1956; Carro Martinez, 1960). Spain has never had, nor has, a modern administration comparable with its European neighbours. This non-modernity of the administrative machine can be observed in various respects: the regulation of incompatibilities, the absence of an administrative career, the lack of distinction between politics and administration, the lack of a general outline of retributions impregnated with at least a minimum degree of rationality, the jungle of regulations and legal dispositions and so on ...

3. Democratic Transition and Administrative Reform

The transformations in the Spanish public administration have occurred as a side-effect of the deep political changes within a general democratising framework. They were not a result of a clear policy based on a rigorous analysis of the factual situation and on clear targets to be achieved (Prats, 1982).

After Franco's death in 1975 Spain experienced a most profound and successful transition to democracy. Through a consensual model, which accommodated the light Francoist reformist and the rupturist democratic forces, the country substituted the old principles and structures for new ones, drafted a new constitution, inaugurated democratic electoral processes and changed the very centralised political system into an asymmetrical quasi-federal one. At the same time, it had to manage a deep economic crisis. All those elements revealed the inadequacies of the old bureaucratic structure for the new scenario.

Elimination of Fascist Elements

The political covenant forced the new political class to eliminate the more salient fascist elements of the Spanish public administration. The dismantling of the Francoist ministerial trade union organisation, the *Movimiento* and the 'mass media' structures, the repressive interior ministry, the propaganda and censorship departments and so on, was followed by new legal procedures and the establishment of regulations granting the right to strike and the freedom to form unions among civil servants.

Public administration was not one of the important issues on the overloaded agenda of the political transition craftsmanship and no one was ready to open such an uncertain and potentially dangerous window. Although the main changes occurred during this period (1976–82) they affected mainly the basic Francoist institutions: the official trade union and the *National Movement*. The intention was to dissolve these structures into the regular civil bureaucracy. In October 1976 the Institutional Administration of Socio-Professional Services (AISS) was created as a frame for the official Francoist trade union bureaucracy. Under the pressure of the new democratic trade unions (socialists and communists) this new institution was integrated into several ministerial departments and finally abolished.

A similar process, although a slow-moving one because the democratic union's pressures were absent, was applied to the *Secretaria General del Movimiento* which was abolished in April 1977. The minister in charge of this department became minister without portfolio in the new democratic cabinet. The civil servants and the material resources belonging to the *Movimiento* were also integrated into the regular civil bureaucracy.

The political transition did not produce substantial changes inside the civil service. The logic of the process of political accommodation, the pactist culture and the consensual approach, prevented any kind of political prosecution or political purges. In fact the total system of the public administration was, to some extent, outside the political battles. The administrative machinery was in a severe crisis, practically paralysed and the bureaucratic elites were not clearly aware of the political transition and its political consequences. Only those civil servants especially linked with the most repressive side of the Francoist administration silently faded away.

A total of about 30 000 public employees, coming from the Francoist administrative structures, were reconverted into regular civil servants and integrated in the regular public administration. This reform was almost costless in political terms, but in administrative and financial respects it was a heavy burden. The technical difficulties of this invasion were badly managed and enhanced the already existing syndrome of parasitism, lack of motivation and imbalanced structures. This process was not rationally planned, nothing was done as regards recycling or training in the jobs of the new incumbents, the distribution of this large group was more a sponta-neous and improvised system with no logic whatsoever. It had a severe impact on the state's regular administration, it introduced a group with a different back-ground, dissimilar training and recruiting processes and those facts added an ele-ment of distortion in a not very coherent universe.

Little Political Support for Administrative Reform

The political changes and the new constitution established a new framework for the administration. The new features of the administration were as follows: a relative autonomy of the administration with respect to the government, the idea of profes-sionalism within the public service, the government's command of the administra-tion (art. 97), the administration serves with objectivity the general interest and behaves according to the principles of efficacy (an 'indifferent efficacy' political neutrality), hierarchy, decentralisation, deconcentration and coordination ... (art. 103). The access to the civil service would be according to the meritocratic system and, finally, a regulation of the incompatibilities for the civil servants was enacted. Those formal provisions ran parallel to a structural situation of an unmotivated personnel, probably inflated in quantitative terms, with all kinds of rigidities in the functioning mechanisms, segmented along the administrative corp's lines, severely affected in their salaries and with a lack of bargaining power. The Spanish civil service, in this situation, was confronted with dramatic changes in the state struc-ture (the process of devolution and the creation of 17 new regional governments and correspondent administrations), new democratic rules of the game, internation-alisation of the country and so on (Moderne, 1983).

In terms of governmental policies, the balance was a mixture of lack of interest, incompetence and political instability. In 1979 the Ministry of the Presidency was in charge of administrative reform. In 1980 the government presented a bill on *Government, Administration and Civil Service*, but a delay in parliament ended up with the government deciding to withdraw it. In 1981 new legal regulations were proposed on the civil service statute and on the rights and freedoms of the civil servants. Both were abandoned following the parliament's dissolution. The parlia-ment (neither the Congress or the Senate) did not pay much attention to administra-tive reform.

The main political parties agreed more on the diagnosis of the situation and less on a model for the reform and much less on the implementation of any measures (incompatibilities, role of the 'special corps', role of the trade unions, relations centre-periphery, reward system, politicisation versus neutrality ...).

Probably, the non-reform of the administration during the transition years was a price that was paid in exchange for political consensus on the salient issues of the political agenda. But the unwanted effects were very serious on the central administration, on the new regional governments (*Comunidades Autónomas*) that lacked the means for developing *ex novo* their own public administrations, and also at the local level.

4.   Reforms under the Socialist Government

In 1980 a most respected scholar wrote an important article entitled 'The dark night of the public service' in which he precisely reflected the situation when the socialist party came to power in 1982. The political transition did not directly affect the administrative organisation but indirectly produced deep changes. The problems and tensions latent for many years came to the surface. The absence of any channelling mechanism led to a progressively deteriorating situation. Old problems arose in the new democratic arena with special virulence (Nieto, 1980). The principal ones were: the reward system and the 'bronze law' (civil servants accommodate their efforts to their perceived salaries; if they think it is 50 percent of what it should be, they will work half as hard), the backdoor entrance in the administration as a provisional civil servant (normally lasting for ever) or under labour contract, avoiding the regular system of corp's recruitment, promotion as an arbitrary mechanism related to all kinds of clientelism, the narrow margins for bargaining within the administration, the lack of discipline and the impunity of the civil servants and the deeply rooted corruption of all kinds. Furthermore, there were specific problems caused by the democratic change: firstly the impact of the political parties and trade unions in building a family network within the administration which affected recruiting and promoting; secondly the new regional governments produced the transfer of civil servants and services from the centre to the periphery, with the potential danger of bureaucratic duplication through the devolution and the necessary reorientation of the remaining structures and personnel at the central level.

How did the civil servants themselves perceive the situation? In 1983, one year after the socialist party came to power, the Centre for Sociological Studies conducted a survey among the civil servants (Beltran, 1987) and almost 95 percent of the respondents considered the reform 'necessary' or 'very necessary'. Not every one had in mind the same type of reform (44 percent thought in terms of efficacy and efficiency and 40 percent related the reform to professional benefits). The survey revealed that only 57 percent thought that the (socialist) government was seriously interested in its implementation, or that it had the political will to do it.

Further Politicisation

The very first policy of the new socialist government was the publication of a decree in December 1982 on *Urgent measures of administrative reform* with an ambitious title but poor content. It only announced small changes in the number and names of the several levels below the minister (state-secretaries, undersecretaries and general directors), the cabinets of the President and ministers and, finally, it contained a rhetoric declaration on clear-cut distinctions between politicians and civil servants. Immediately the new authorities implemented clock timing control of the administrative offices and the incompatibility regulations. The climate in the country was very favourable to the reforms but the political practices progressively destroyed the great expectations. The government started what has probably been the most dramatic and radical spoil system; 'being one of ours' was the rule and, as a consequence, many of the most qualified leaders, managers and top level technicians migrated to the private sector and many of the ones who decided to stay were moved to secondary jobs in what was known in the bureaucratic jargon as 'elephant cemeteries'.

The year 1984 saw the most important regulation affecting the civil service (commonly known as 'Ley 30/84'). For the first time the government accepted that an overarching reform was impossible and the new policy was to develop concrete measures leading eventually to civil service reform. The objective needs of the country (adjusting the administration to the new democratic system, to the new European realities and to the new quasi-federal government) were postponed indefinitely. One of the main purposes of the 'measures for the reform of the civil service' was to destroy the long lasting structure based on corps and to create a new one based on a job system common for all the administration (central, regional and local). In fact they made a serious mistake in confusing the corporatism pathologies with the actual functions of the administrative corps. They produced disenchantment, destroyed the very logic of the compatibility between specialities and administrative positions, marginalised the professional careers and left room for politicisation, clientelism, *amiguismo* and, in fact, a growing process of deprofessionalisation (Gutierrez Renon, 1987, 1990).

The implementation of these measures has produced uncertainty and unpredictability in the administrative machinery, a profound politicisation of the administration under the political control of the government, the abuse of the mechanism of 'free designation' (sometimes covered under a formal concurs and merit system) and consequently an incoherent and inefficient public policy-making system.

If we add to this scenery the legal reinforcing position of the so called 'most representative trade unions' (UGT and CCOO) in the centres for collective bargaining and policy making inside the administration, together with the regulation of the 'personal degree'[3] and the regulations to facilitate the functional and geographical mobility, the negative conclusion is that a historical opportunity was lost and the administration was damaged, in fact and potentially.

5.   The Plan of 1989: From Legalism to Management

In 1986 the Socialist Party again won the general elections with an absolute majority. For the first time in our history a Ministry of Public Administration was created to evaluate the past failures and to prepare the necessary changes in the administration. The new minister was also empowered to coordinate the jungle of relations among central and regional administrations. Three years later the ministry produced a report on *Reflections on Modernising the State Administration* (MAP, 1989) and the new minister, Almunia, pointed out that this report should be publicly discussed and subsequently be used as a guide for 'the administrative reform still pending' (Almunia, 1986, 1990a, 1990b).

Change of Culture: From Legalism to Management

The report consisted of: a careful empirical study of the heterogeneity of the Spanish administration, acknowledging that the functioning of the administrative machinery was unsatisfactory for the challenges of the country (adaptation to the European Union, coordination of the several levels of government, especially the new Comunidades Autónomas, delivering the services to the citizens in a more efficient manner and so on). The innovation was of a non-legal character (breaking the very long-lasting legalistic tradition) and included the introduction of 'new management techniques'. In the words of the Minister of Public Administration 'Spain was changing from a culture based on the legality principle to one more concerned with results, with the outcomes ... The services should be delivered according to the principles of efficacy and efficiency' (Almunia, 1990b; MAP, 1989). This requires: firstly, to draw a precise boundary between the political and the administrative spheres and to determine what should be the decision making powers of each one; and secondly, once the place and the role of the administration has been clarified, the modernisation plan should have a full perspective including organisational, functional and personnel approaches. The proposed method was to proceed from the particular to the general, to modernise piece by piece with the idea of filling up the whole puzzle.

The reform should not be reduced to technical criteria, the main target should be to change the administrative culture from the present values of legalism, formalism, juridical emphasis and very little attention for efficiency and managerial resources, to an administrative culture characterised by efficacy, efficiency within the limits of legality, considering the citizens as regular customers, a division of labour between politicians as strategic decision makers and civil servants as implementers, flexible organisations open to external innovations and attention to human resources.

Main Aspects of Reform

The three main areas of modernisation are:

Organisational aspects

−   From the traditional ministerial structure to new administrative modules that can handle the new complexities of a three-tier government. The process of devolution has implied the transfer of a large volume of services and civil servants. These new units should be self-sufficient in budgetary, manpower and authority terms and operate in a decentralised way.
−   From an overlap between politics and administration to a clear structural distinction.
−   From an administration in the old provinces (today self-governing communities) which used to represent the central one, to a new model that should take into account the new regional governments and their own administrative structures.[4]

Procedural and functional aspects
Today the Spanish administrative model does not promote the responsibility of the managers for several reasons: undefined field of jurisdiction, insufficient autonomy for decision making, too many *ex ante* legal controls and, finally, lack of personnel trained in the managerial skills. The modernisation in those aspects will imply an integrated managerial system based on defined targets, a new decentralised network of organisations, simplification and rationalisation of the formal procedures and the introduction of new technologies.

Human Resources
The ministerial authorities suffer from an absence of an efficient management of the human resources: artificial classification of personnel categories (not only of the statute civil servants but also of the ones under labour contract), artificial homogeneity of the public employees and their legal status, lack of motivation, a non-competitive and irrational reward system, scarcity of good administrative cadres, lack of a real administrative–professional career, difficulties in recruiting good candidates, and so on. According to this diagnosis, the solutions would consist of: professionalisation of the public administration, reforms of the reward and recruitment systems, specific legal status for the different sectors of the administration (teaching, health, justice, police, foreign service and so on), training and specialisation and a clear map with a detailed description of the public posts.

The purpose of the Ministry of Public Administration with the publication of the Report was to mobilise the civil servants, public opinion, mass media, experts and so on, to create a potential climate for future action. Qualitative studies – using the Delphi method – were conducted among higher civil servants to facilitate their involvement and, eventually, to reach a consensus about the modernising strategies. An *Inspeccion General de Servicios* (IGSAP) was created to control the consulting activities required by the different administrative units, leading to the practical implementation of debureaucratisation and more efficient working methods.

Finally, a very important development is to try and find a new balance between public and private, between state and market. Some public companies have been privatised, mostly in juridical terms, new 'quangos' (parastatal organisations) arose as hybrids with both public and private legal status (Agencia Estatal de Administración Tributaria, Consejero de Seguridad Nuclear, Consejo Económico y Social, Instituto Cervantes, Agencia de Protección de Datos and so on). The business public sector increased by the creation of new public firms. Likewise regional governments and local authorities built up their own business public sector.

6.   The Plan of 1992: Micromanagement of Reform

After six years Minister Almunia had left the administration with a diagnosis and with a general formulation of modernising strategies, but with very few significant changes of any kind. Various obstacles can explain this failure: a mixture of reluctance and scepticism among the civil servants, the resistance of the trade unions, the weakness of the socialist party in power and so on.

In 1991 the former Minister of Industry took charge of the Ministry of Public Administration and in April 1992 he presented parliament with a *Plan of Modernisation of the State Administration* (MAP, 1992). It supposed a change from the macro management strategies to the micro management ones. In some ways it remembers the technocratic reforms of the 1960s. The Plan contained 204 projects distributed over the several ministries with the intention to specifically improve:

– the information and communication with the citizens as customers (better phones, publicness of activities, labelling, opening times and so on);
– the quality of the services (for example, the free choice of a family doctor, the procedures for getting a retirement pension and so on);
– the introduction of new techniques such as evaluation, cost-benefit analysis, efficiency indicators, auditing and so on.

The authorities admitted that the administration could not be changed by decree and could not be transformed overnight. Modernisation should be understood as a gradual and never-ending process which implies constancy and perseverance. Modernisation is oriented to change the administrative culture and focused upon producing results and balancing costs and benefits.

Although the authorities explained that the Plan was a zero-budget one, about 1500 higher civil servants had actually been involved in several teams, commissions and committees and it is unthinkable that all this involvement would have cost nothing. All the projects were presented with specific objectives and deadlines.

Although it is probably too early to make up a balance of the results,[5] the first impressions are:

- the new reformers are confusing formal regulations with factual impact and change;
- the majority of the measures are trivial or irrelevant in terms of the modernising challenges of the Spanish administration;
- the secrecy of the whole process, even for the analysts, is not a good indication of the fluid information and communication principles on which the Plan is based;
- they are misleading the public opinion in selling those minor changes as the modernisation of the administration.

7.   Conclusion: Lost Historical Opportunity

Since 1976 everybody has understood the profound reasons for modernising the public administration (consolidate the new democracy, face the European challenge, adjust the old structures to new values – management, efficiency, cost-benefit – *governare la fraamentazione*, using the title of Dente's book and so on). Moreover, Spain experienced a fast growth in public expenditure from 25 percent to 45 percent of the BNP as a consequence of being a latecomer in the development of a welfare state. The public expenditures have been strongly decentralised. In 1975 the central administration (including the health system) expended 90 percent, today central expenditures are less than 60 percent. This fundamentally new situation was not paralleled by fundamental changes in the administration. Moreover the paradoxical situation is that the same people who proclaim a smaller public sector are, at the same time, in favour of more and better public services.

In the new language of administrative reforms across Europe we are probably importing the formal labels and building up meanings and references which have little or no relationship with their original contents. Recently a Spanish public management expert wrote: 'public management is, in practical terms and in the majority of the cases, only bureaucratic management and the public manager is an expert in the legal and procedural labyrinth ... There is a conflict between legalist control and the fight against discretionality, on the one side, and management flexibility, on the other' (Ortun, 1993).

Spanish administration has missed a historic opportunity and challenge. The historical circumstances provided an optimal basis for administrative reform. It was desired by the civil servants and by society as a whole, so it is hard to understand why successive governments failed. Probably they followed the advice of a minister, who during the political transition has said 'no more bulls in the ring and especially not one so dangerous as the civil servants and their organisations'. Not only did the centrist and socialist governments fail to take advantage of the favourable political climate of democratisation, they also lost the good old times of economic growth. Today the two main objectives are the reduction of the public deficit and the fight against political corruption. The latter is again reinforcing the *ex ante* juridical control over the administrative actions.[6]

Tables

Table 11.1.   **Administrative modernisation in Spain (1852–1995) I**

Reforms	Causes	Strategies	Actors	Obstacles	Coordination	Reforms
1852	Attempt to abandon spoils system	none	Prime Minister	–	no	yes
1918	Profession-alism/legal statute	none	Prime Minister	–	no	yes
1964	Technical adjustment to a more dynamic economy under authoritarian regime	Yes. Long Term	Ministry of the Precidency	Special Corps. Falangist families within the regime	Yes. Adm. Reform + Economic Planning	yes
1976–1982	Dismantling francoist adm structures/free trade unions + strike rights	none	Govern-ment	Finance Ministry. Corps Fights	no	no
1982–1986 Socialist I	Break the power of the elite corps/adjust-ments to the new Autonomous Communities and the E.U.	Political domination and control	Ministry of the Presidency	Skepticism of civil servant the trade unions and lack of political will	Very little	yes
1986–1991 Socialist II	Negative diag-nosis. Efficiency vs legality	Long term proposal	Ministry for Public Adm.	Finance Ministry. Lack of political support	no	no
1991– Socialist III	Micromanage-ment in some ad. units. Budget constrains	Piecemeal pragmatic reforms	Ministry for Public Adm.	Finance Ministry Civil Ser-vant etc.	no	no

Table 11.2.   Administrative modernisation in Spain (1852–1995) II

Reforms	Structures	Tools	Role Private Sector	Political Reforms	Degree of politization	Policy evaluation
1852	no	–	none	Polit.	–	yes
1918	no	Legal norms	none	Polit.	–	yes
1964	yes	Efficiency indicators Public surveys	Yes, Management tools	Polit. +	yes	yes
1976–1982	no	–	no	Polit. +	no	no
1982–1986 Socialist I	some	Legal norms + control	no	Polit. ++	no	yes
1986–1991 Socialist II	Yes, proposed	Efficiency indicators + management	yes	Polit. ++	yes	no
1991– Socialist III	no	Micro-management	yes	Polit. ++	yes ++	no

Table 11.3.   Administrative Modernisation in Spain (1852–1995) III

Reforms	Achievements	Negative Aspects
1852	None	Not a real reform
1918	End of the *spoils system*, inauguration of statutary system for civil servants	Maintenance of the old administrative structures
1964	Legal and Structural changes. Real modernization	Limited the Reform to a more technocratic modernization without questioning the political system
1976–1982	None	They missed a historical opportunity
1982–1991 Socialist I	Mobilization of expectations, incompatibilities …	Displacement of the real and important objectives.
1986–1991 Socialist II	Good analysis of the situation and a quite progressive plan	To be limited to a theoretical exercise
1991– Socialist III	Unknown. It looks as if the outputs are confused with the outcomes	???

Notes

1. Those extra-budgetary incomes were abolished with the technocratic reforms of 1964.
2. In the period from 1938 till 1975 some 57 percent of the directors came from these 'Grands Corps'.
3. The Royal-Decree 28/90 established that a civil servant who occupies a position at certain level during two consecutive years, will consolidate his 'personal degree' and cannot move down more than two levels below the one he has got. The consequence is twofold: firstly, it stabilises the politically promoted civil servants, and secondly, produces a big distortion in the administration for ever as the politically promoted civil servants do not possess the expertise required for the job.
4. The government is preparing a new bill on *Organising and Functioning of the General Administration of the State* (LOFAGE) regulating the new role of the remaining central administration (as a consequence of the intense process of the devolution of functions and services), and the new role of the central services in the periphery, especially the new role of the Civil Governor.
5. According to the official documents, in 1994 the balance for the first two years was: from the 177 projects of the original 204 (87 percent), 143 had already been implemented, 34 projects (17 percent) were being implemented at the moment and 27 projects (13 percent) had been cancelled for economic reasons. (See the report of the cabinet of the State Secretary for Public Administration, January 1994. *Balance Bienio 1992–93*).

6. The specific situation of the public administration in the Comunidades Autónomas and the way in which the reform policies in the central administration affected them could not be included in this chapter. A recent analysis of administrative modernisation in the 'Comunidades Autónomas' can be found in the journal *Autonomies*, no.18, July 1994 (Barcelona).

References

Almunia, J., 1986. *Comparecencia del Ministro de Administraciones Pœblicas para informar sobre la politica de su departamento.* Debate (pp. 526–70). No. congreso de los diputados. Comisiones.

Almunia, J., 1990a. *Comparecencia del Sr. Ministro para las Administraciones Pœblicas....* (Informe sobre la politica que desarrollara el nuevo Gobierno No. Diario de Sesiones, IV Legislatura, num.22). Congreso de los deputados. Comision.

Almunia, J., 1990b. Entrevista. *MUFACE*, March, 1990.

Beltran, M., 1987. *Nuevos Enfoques sobre la Reforma de las Administraciones.* Pœblicas No. Universidad Autõnoma de Madrid.

Carro Martinez, A., 1960. 'ÀQuõ es la reforma administrativa?' *Documentación Administrativa*, vol. 27.

Garcia de Enterria, E., 1964. *La Administración Espanola.* Instituto de Estudios Politicos, Madrid.

Gutierrez Renon, A., 1987. 'La carrera administrativa en Espana: evolución histõrica y perspectivas'. *Documentación Administrativa* (210–11), pp. 29–70.

Gutierrez Renon, A., 1990. 'Función del Cuerpo en un Sistema de Carrera'. *Rev. Vasca de Administración Pœblica*, vol. 26.

Lopez Rodo, L., 1956. 'La reforma administrativa del Estado'. *Nuestro Tiempo*, 27 (September 1956).

MAP, 1989. *Reflexiones para la Modernización de la Administración.* MAP, Madrid.

MAP, 1992. *Plan de Modernización de la Administración del Estado.* INAP, Madrid.

Moderne, F., 1983. 'L'Administration dans le debat politique en Espagne'. In: C. Debbasch (ed.), *Administration et Politique en Europe*, CNRS, Paris, pp. 177–99.

Nieto, A., 1980. 'La noche oscura de la Función Pœblica'. *Cuadernos Econõmicos de ICE*, vol. 13, pp. 9–18.

Oliva de la, A.Y.G.R.A., 1968a. 'Los Cuerpos de Funcionarios'. *Documentación Administrativa*, vol. 124.

Oliva, de la, A., 1968b. 'Los Cuerpos de funcionarios'. In: Varios (eds), *Sociologia de la Administración Pœblica Espanola*, Centro de Estudios Sociales, Madrid.

Ortun, V., 1993. *Gestion Publica.* No. Fundacion BBV. Centro de Estudios sobre Economia del sector Publico. Bilbao.

Prats, J., 1982. 'Administración Pœblica y Transición Democratica'. *Pensamiento Iberoamericano*, 5 b, pp. 445–62.

Part Three

**Management, Rechtsstaat
and Democracy**

CHAPTER TWELVE

Public Management between Legality and Efficiency: The Case of Belgian Public Administration

Rudolf Maes
Catholic University Leuven

1. Problem Definition

The objectives of the public sector differ from the objectives of the private sector. The difference originates mainly from the government's mission to guarantee the exercise of authority and general welfare to society. As a consequence, different values, legal rules and principles apply to public sector organisations, actors and activities. Because of the democratic and the *Rechtsstaat* prerequisites of legitimacy, government faces liabilities which do not exist in the private sector. Because of the government's mission to pursue the general interest, government equally enjoys certain rights which are not compatible with legal acts ruled by private law. Thus, administrative law encompasses the authoritative rules governing the organisation of the public sector, interactions between government and citizens and between public authorities together. This, however, does not entail a *summa divisio*, implying that only administrative law should apply to the public sector. It has never been questioned that public authorities take part in legal transactions or conduct policies using the rules applying to the private sector. However, this has never been unconditional.

The rules and principles applying to the public sector are not established once and for all. They themselves are subject to continuous changes. Administrative law, the ultimate goal of which is to establish the *Rechtsstaat*, reflects insights which existed in the field of public management at the time the legal rules were established. Some authors, therefore, have referred to administrative law as the 'deep-freeze' of the science of administration (van Poelje, 1986, p. 352). This automatically implies that rules will be challenged if changes of climate occur within the field of public management. This is currently the case, for a multitude of reasons. Government is developing new forms of steering and is in search of a new legitimacy. New methods of management, often originating from the private sector, are introduced.

Increased autonomy, more flexibility, responsibility and purposiveness have become key concepts.

The dominant value in contemporary public management is of an economic nature: it promotes 'value for money' and 'economy, efficiency and effectiveness' (Metcalfe and Richards, 1990). This may give rise to a potential conflict with the traditional value of the *Rechtsstaat*, which claims first and foremost that public administration is ruled by the principle of legality. The question arises whether the new public management is not caught in the middle between efficiency on the one hand and legality on the other hand (Bouckaert *et al.*, 1994, p. 57).

This chapter does not aim for a conclusive answer to this question. Rather, we would like to illustrate the existing tensions between current views of public management and administrative rules and examine how these tensions are dealt with. Recent evolutions and renovations in Belgian public administration should clarify the matter. The objective is not to be exhaustive; a selection is made of several items which might be valuable also from a comparative perspective. The following topics will be dealt with:

-   the extended interpretation of the principle of legality;
-   the refinement of the prerequisite of legitimacy;
-   the improvement of legal protection and the protection of interests;
-   the principles of the public service and the decline of certain public privileges;
-   the shifting boundaries between the private and the public sector;
-   enhanced autonomy.

It may cause surprise that deregulation does not feature in this list of topics. Over the past 25 years the Belgian unitary state has been transformed into a federal state. This has brought about an abundance of regulation. Deregulation, however, has up to now not been a priority on the political agenda in Belgium.

2.   The Extended Interpretation of the Principle of Legality

The principle of legality is of importance whenever the government interferes with the rights, the properties or the estates of citizens in the context of what is called *Eingriffsverwaltung*. In order to do so, a formal authorisation must exist by law or in accordance with the law. The principle of legality is equally important for the internal organisation of public administration, for instance when dealing with the rights and obligations of civil servants, as well as in intergovernmental relations. The hierarchy of norms to be respected eventually leads back to rules adopted by democratically elected constitutional or legislative assemblies. From these rules government and public administration ultimately derive their legitimacy.

Competencies must always be exercised within the limits of the mission for which they were accorded by law – this is referred to as the principle of speciality – and both the postulate of formality and exclusiveness apply. Formally a legal title, accorded by or on behalf of the assembly, must be available. Furthermore, action can only be taken in accordance with the authorisation (Oostenbrink, 1978). The transition of the state of authority to the welfare state and the rise of the *Leistungsverwaltung* next to the traditional *Eingriffsverwaltung* entailed that the postulates mentioned above were gradually given a different interpretation. Public action which is not positively admitted by the legislature, but which is neither explicitly forbidden, is now considered permissible – at least in view of the *Leistungsverwaltung*. The condition remains, however, that such actions must always be justified by a concrete mission of general interest.

This extended interpretation of public authorities' full powers to act is still the object of controversy. For instance, it is not clear whether this allows public authorities to participate in the creation of corporate bodies, or to conclude policy agreements without any clear legal authorisation. The key question here is whether public authorities are allowed to use the law on contracts, the private law on non-profit associations or the law on trading companies to mould their cooperation with other public authorities or private companies (d'Hooge and Peeters, 1994, p. 75).

Policy Agreements

The subject matter of policy agreements is in full evolution; it has not yet settled down to a clear doctrine. A policy agreement is understood as any agreement that involves the elaboration or the execution of public policy (d'Hooge, 1995). Policy agreements or covenants have mainly been turned to for the implementation of environmental policies. Central government concludes policy agreements or covenants both with the private sector as well as with local governments.

Policy agreements are tied to a different view of steering. The authoritative way of steering, in which public authorities are hierarchically situated above third parties, is replaced by a more voluntary way of steering. Increasingly, government aims for the self-imposed cooperation of other actors in a certain policy area, who are equally made responsible for policy. If this is not possible under public law arrangements, only the private law on contracts remains to shape this. The majority view in Belgian legal doctrine allows for a contractual procedure on the following conditions (van Gerven, 1985; van Gerven and Wijckaert, 1987).

Firstly, the use of the private law on contracts ought not to conflict with absolute rules of statutory law nor with general principles of law. This conflict would occur if policy agreements violated absolute rules of procedure, such as allowing the participation of third parties, or if they violated the principle of equality.

Secondly, the contractual arrangements should not involve a transfer of powers of the authority concerned nor ought it to involve repudiation of the powers of other public authorities.

Finally, the policy agreements should not affect the competencies and the freedom of assessment of the public authority involved. Contractual stipulations which prevent or constrain the public authority from using its unilateral power to regulate, are definitely problematic in this respect. Such conditions are only possible if it is stipulated clearly in the contract that the principle of changeableness prevails for the public authorities (d'Hooge, op. cit., p. 87).

Apart from this, it is generally accepted that policy agreements are of a less absolute nature than ordinary public contracts (d'Hooge, op. cit., p. 77). Indeed, if, for instance, public financial support is granted to a company on the condition it creates a certain number of jobs, it is difficult to see how this commitment, which also depends on the general economic conjuncture, is to be sanctioned (Favresse *et al.*, 1976).

The Use of Private Law Constructions

The question of whether or not public authorities may create new corporate bodies using private law constructions is even more controversial. Legal doctrine is affirmative, if at least similar conditions as apply to policy agreements are respected. First, *ratione materiae* the decision to be taken must belong to the field of competence of the authority concerned. Second, the creation of such corporate bodies should not result in a transfer of powers or to shifting off responsibilities (Lewalle, 1985; Maes, 1984).

It should be pointed out, however, that although jurisprudence in this field is rare and not well-established, it remains rather negative.[1] The ambiguity existing between legal doctrine and jurisprudence has contributed to a situation where more than once the legislator has interfered a posteriori to clarify the options which are open to public authorities, for example in the case of the Flemish government which had joined about a dozen non-profit associations established by private law. At the request of the Court of Auditors the Flemish Parliament has legislated to explicitly regularise this situation, by a decree of 23 March 1993. Another example is provided by the fact that the legislator has very recently detailed the options open to local government in this respect.[2]

3.   Refining the Prerequisite of Legitimacy

Legitimacy cannot be reduced to the mere application of the principle of legality. A democratic polity is characterised by, amongst others, a bilateral principal–agent relationship (Lane, 1993, p. 114; Stiglitz, 1987). Additional arrangements for information, communication and control are therefore required. The concept of the principal–agent relation originates from the private sector. More or less independently acting agents are obliged by contract to take the interests of the management of the company, the principal, into account. The contract also indicates how this is to be controlled.

In a democratic political system a similar relationship exists between the population, the citizens or the electorate, the 'principal', on the one hand and the elected political 'agents' on the other hand. Here also the agents should act in the interests of the principal. An analogous relationship is to be found in the relation between the politically elected bodies, playing the part of the principal and the bureaucratic organisations, acting as agents. To prevent the agents from protecting their own interests rather than those of the principal, more is called for than regular elections alone – elections often focus on a few eye-catching topics only and this mostly in slogans. Referenda do limit the margins for decision making for the political agents, but they cannot be organised at every moment. Moreover, the Belgian constitution does not allow for decisive referenda. Yet, the legislator recently has created the possibility for consultative referenda to be organised on the local scale.

Because of the limited possibilities for direct intervention of the principal additional instruments are indispensable in order to exercise control over political decision makers and to hold them accountable. The same holds true for the relation between political decision makers and administrative services. Strict requirements for output should be set for the latter. De-bureaucratisation should lead to a reduction of hierarchical layers. The monitoring of output is to be taken seriously. Incentives are introduced to improve the motivation of civil servants and to promote permanent training. Important in this respect is the introduction of functional careers and regular assessments in the Flemish Community civil servants' statute. The scale seniority obtained by civil servants results from annual assessments. If a civil servant functions satisfactorily he passes through his career at normal speed and scale seniority is identical to actual seniority. This speed may vary, reflecting the quality of performances; in this way the performances taken into account may count for twice or only for half of their real value. In case the performance over the year is assessed as insufficient it may even be disregarded. If a civil servant's performance is insufficient for two subsequent years, he is definitely qualified as unfit for service for professional reasons.

In the context of the contract with citizens special priorities are, for instance, openness, transparency and the notion of public administration as an 'open house'.[3] Other administrative reforms aim for the empowerment of the citizens as electors, but also as persons directly affected by public action or as users of public services. Examples of this are the explicit motivation of administrative actions, the organisation of citizens' participation, the elaboration of charters for the users of public services, and so on. Civil servants have acquired the freedom of speech, although for the time being this does not yet apply to public policies in the pipeline.

Very recently only, the problem of legitimacy has been articulated with regard to the many actual and complex ways of steering. In connection with policy networks or decisions taken in an interorganisational context questions arise regarding accountability (De Rynck, 1994). Indeed, the question remains which government body is to be held accountable for decisions made in a multi-actor and multi-level context or for decisions which possibly result from a public–private decision making process.

Actually, the views on accountability and legitimacy have transcended the requirements of a mere democratic functioning of the institutions. This follows from the current emphasis on values affirming the purposiveness and the effectiveness of public action. In this view legitimacy then mainly results from the conviction that government does the right thing and that it does it in the right way. Increasingly, policy papers supporting public actions are published. Financial budgets are abandoned in favour of programme budgeting, which emphasises outputs and cost-efficiency and subsequently provides more leeway for programme managers. The increased autonomy of several public services should allow for an improved control of their functioning, not only with respect to legality or regularity, but also with respect to quality and effectiveness. For the time being, these reforms are still in their initial stages, but it is to be expected that in the near future they will occupy a prominent place on the political agenda. All this should not cover up the existing tension between standards of democracy and effectiveness. The pursuit of legitimacy often will necessitate finding a subtle equilibrium between the two.

4. Improved Legal Protection and Protection of Citizens' Interests

Public action in the *Rechtsstaat* is moulded between rules and judges. Judicial review does not limit itself any longer to a mere formal control of legality. Judicial power thus acts as a counterweight to the ever growing freedom of assessment and the full powers to act encombing to or usurped by public authorities. On the other hand, citizens dispose of more extensive rights of complaint, transcending judicial review.

In the case of citizens' rights allocated by law, illegal public actions are subject to judicial review. But currently, public action is also measured by what are called 'principles of proper and just administration'. When the law leaves discretionary powers to the administration, judicial review will include in its considerations the carefulness and the reasonableness of a decision, the requirement of fair-play, the interdiction of confusion of interests, the necessity of contradictory procedures, and so on.

Specifically with regard to disputes about the civil service or the public personnel policy, the principles of proper and just administration play an important role in limiting the occurrence of arbitrary actions. In the future this may conflict with the pursuit of more flexibility in the public administration. At any rate, the Belgian Council of State requires a careful comparison between the merits of people considered for appointments or promotions and the explicit motivation of all decisions taken 'in the interest of the service'. The latter motive cannot be used to take disciplinary measures in a concealed way.

Judicial review has evolved from a mere control of legality to a control of legitimacy of public administration. In this evolution it is necessary to emphasise the exceptional importance of the principles of proper and just administration (Opdebeeck, ed., 1993; Daurmont and Baetsele, 1990, p. 262).

Also the increasingly more extensive interpretation of the notion of government's liability has contributed to this evolution.[4] Matters are different in cases where no legal rights are violated, but in which, nevertheless, unfair, unreasonable or improper public action may have taken place. Protection against such actions may be provided through mediation of an ombudsman. At the federal level of government the law of 22 March 1995 creates federal ombudsmen; earlier the decree of 23 October 1991 had established an ombudsman with the Flemish Community. Also in autonomous public companies such as the Post, Belgacom and the National Belgian Railway Company (NMBS) similar instances have been created to deal with consumers' complaints.

5. The Principles of the Public Service and the Decline of Some Public Privileges

Of all principles applicable to the public service, that of equality of access or the equal treatment of citizens has become more prominent than before. Any distinctions to be made between categories of legal subjects must find their origins in objective, reasonable and positive criteria; any difference in treatment must correspond to the principle of proportionality.[5]

It is true that the principle of the changeableness of the public service stands as such, but it only applies fully to unilateral public actions. Sometimes important caveats may apply to unilateral public action: for instance, consultation with the trade unions is a necessary condition to change the unilaterally laid down civil servants' statutes. The impact of the principle is more restrained in the case that unilateral public action has been replaced with contractual rights and obligations between public authorities and third parties. Public authorities may terminate such contracts unilaterally, but will generally refrain from doing so because of the obligation to compensate for any losses incurred by other parties.

Matters are different for the principle of the continuity of the public service. Certain goods belonging to the private property of public authorities may become subject to seizure, whereas before this was never possible. The condition remains, however, that their seizure must not affect the continuity of the public service; the latter is a matter for the judge to decide upon.[6] Also, it is now possible for the Council of State to suspend unilateral decisions against which serious legal grounds are put forward which might justify an eventual annulment, if the execution of the measure is likely to cause serious or irreparable detriments (Lewalle, 1993). The new regulation on the possibility to impose fines for delay in performance equally offers better legal protection. As regards the right of strike in the public service hardly any difference remains with companies in the private sector.

Together with the recently imposed obligations to explicitly motivate unilateral public actions and with the publicity of government, new definitions of the principles ruling the continuity of the public service clearly affect the government's traditionally privileged position.

6.   The Concepts of 'Public Authority', 'Public Service' and the Scope of the Public Sector

The application of administrative law and principles of the public service, the publicity of government and the competencies of the ombudsman requires, of course, knowledge of the precise scope of the public sector.

Answering this last question transcends the competencies of the Belgian Council of State, since the Council of State is still conceptualised as a judicial college which only judges administrative authorities to the extent that they perform unilateral legal acts. It does not interfere with disputes about contractual relations with public authorities, unless it is possible to isolate unilateral acts from the contract as such. Nevertheless, the rulings of the Council of State are important because they offer criteria which enable us to delineate the scope of the public sector.

According to rulings of the Council of State, the competence of the Council to nullify unilateral legal acts if contrary to the law – such as the establishment of a personnel statute and acts of personnel policy – extends to the following hypotheses:

– Acts of limited liability companies or corporate societies established by law or in accordance with the law, in which the government is a shareholder and of which the government ultimately is in charge of the management. The existence of private shareholders does not alter this, as long as government clearly retains a majority in the board, or government remains ultimately in charge through the administrative tutelage.[7]
– Acts of institutions created by private initiative, in so far as the bodies of these institutions are authorised by law or in accordance with the law to perform unilateral public actions. This is, for instance, the case when private universities grant diplomas, to the holders of which government in the general interest grants the right to exercise certain professions, or when private universities establish personnel statutes.[8]

In these categories one easily recognises the classical definition of the public service, either in the organic or the functional meaning of the word. However, government often participates in private companies in which it is ultimately in charge of the management or holds a majority of the shares, without having the intention to subject these companies to the rule of administrative law. Originally this took place in the context of the government granting direct financial support to enterprises in difficulties. Later this also resulted from indirect government intervention through public investment companies. This construction is also used for the creation of environmental holdings and companies or reconversion companies (Deom, 1990, p. 34).

The question at hand is broadened even more by referring to public actions based on private law procedures, which are dealt with above. Whether or not the administrative law procedures and principles apply to such cases is not clear and is the subject of controversies. Yet, the question whether this is not an all too easy way of circumventing certain administrative renovations, cannot be begged. Recent statements by policy makers seem to indicate that government thus provides an escape from the stricter prerequisite of legitimacy. This is definitely the case for companies or holdings operating with government funds. Even if government holds the majority of the shares, these companies are considered as private actors, which are subjected to private law rather than administrative law. From an economic point of view they belong to the public sector. Yet this is not the case from a legal point of view. Such enterprises may, as well as commercial companies, be adjudged bankrupt. This, however, would not justify the conclusion that none of the marginal conditions for public action would apply any longer. The question where to draw the exact dividing line between the public and the private sector is one of the current challenges to the legal system.

7. Enhanced Autonomy as a Problem of Reconciling Autonomy and Control

Functionally autonomous authorities are managed by separate boards, the members of which are usually appointed by government. They are not hierarchically subordinated to government, but government continues to exercise administrative tutelage. In the Belgian context, functionally decentralised institutions have grown more important than territorially decentralised authorities, for which direct elections are organised.

In 1954 an evolution started to strengthen control over the most important functionally decentralised authorities. A more uniform regime was to apply to the financial and personnel management. The minimal condition imposed upon these functionally decentralised authorities was a duty to inform the legislature about their financial management. Government was represented on the board by government commissioners. The commissioners disposed of the right to suspend all decisions taken by the board; it was up to the government to decide whether or not to uphold the decisions. Government's control over the financial and personnel management was systematically expanded (Deom, op. cit.). This evolution towards more control was motivated, amongst others, by the fact that ultimately the government was responsible for any budgetary deficits of these organisations.

From 1990 onwards, the evolution which started in 1954 has been countered. A new settlement has been introduced by the law of 21 March 1991 for four large state-controlled enterprises, namely the Railway Company, the Post Office, the Telecommunications Company and the Aviation Authority. On the one hand this was an operation of financial reform: it is legally established now that the state no longer carries the deficits of the companies concerned. A management contract is concluded between government and the companies, which clearly states which public services the companies should render and what will be the government's financial contribution to this effect. The legal value of such a contract, however, is uncertain.

On the other hand this operation was a form of privatisation-in-disguise. It is stipulated that the companies may develop other activities than those mentioned in the contract. If compatible with their original purposes, the companies may even establish branches. In this field, however, they must face competition and they do not enjoy government support. In case they cannot survive in the market, it is likely that they will have to give up such activities (Nuchelmans and Pagano, 1991).

Subsequently, the autonomous public companies are ruled by a dual legal regime depending upon the kind of activities they develop. The question arises whether the principles of proper and just government and the laws of public service still apply to the activities developed outside of the management contract.

The increased autonomy based on the management contracts has made redundant several mechanisms of control established by the 1954 law. More specifically control by parliament is reduced. Instead, new arrangements are put forward such as the new settlements for complaints' management or such as consultative committees in which the users of public services are represented.

New arrangements have been established also by the law of 17 June 1991 on the organisation of the public sector of finance and the harmonisation of the conditions for the control and the functioning of it. In the meantime, some of the public credit institutions have become involved in privatisations, the former state-owned shares being sold. These privatisations originate much more from budgetary motives, trying to find new sources of revenue, than from considerations regarding the management of these institutions.

Currently, proposals are under consideration to create agencies. These proposals originate from an explicit concern with the management of these services, with regard to the autonomy required, the necessary accountability and the control of output (Vermeulen, 1994, p. 443). Agencies would not necessarily be created outside of the traditional ministries. The amount of autonomy to be granted is founded in long-term agreements dealing with the financial management and the standards for output: they are part of an agency contract. The emphasis lies on the responsibility of the management and their freedom to act with regard to policy, personnel management and the management of inputs. This may be accompanied by the use of positive incentives as well as negative sanctions. Periodically accounts of conducted policies, both financially and substantially, must be rendered.

From the point of view of administrative law, questions arise about the delegation of competencies to civil servants in charge of agencies and about the enforceable nature of such agency contracts.

8. Conclusion

Public management is often inspired by private management. Equally, certain legal constructions in the public sector are increasingly mirrored by private law arrangements. The new interpretation of the principle of legality is based on a logic that is more typical of the private sector than of the public sector. Private parties are free to shape their legal relationship as they want, except where this goes against rules of law and order. Within this context everything which is not explicitly forbidden is deemed acceptable.

In this sphere in the public sector a distinction is still made between authoritative actions, to which the traditional interpretation of the principle of legality still applies, and public actions in the context of public policy and public services. The problem remains, however, that in practice this distinction is not always clear. Contract management, therefore, can never be seen in isolation from the prerogatives of government, based on the principle of changeableness. It is indeed generally accepted that policy agreements, management or agency contracts as they exist now, are not equal to private law contracts as regards their legal value and their enforceability. They constitute a new kind of administrative contracts, the scope of which is still the subject of controversies. Not surprisingly, the legislator sometimes is compelled to justify these practices a posteriori in explicit legal settlements.

In some cases, the recourse taken to private law might cause shifting boundaries between the public sector ruled by administrative law and the private sector ruled by private or commercial law. Certain examples of public action, such as participating in the creation of capital in industrial companies, create problems in this respect. Equally problematic from this point of view is the development of certain activities outside the law ruling public action, because this would be less appropriate or because the effectiveness and efficiency would be hindered by procedures considered superfluous or controls deemed a nuisance. An example of this is provided by the frequent recourse taken to private law constructions of non-profit associations to shape public action in the Belgian context. In this case a radical review of administrative law would be called for. But here, as often is the case, the law trails the facts.

On the other side, an evolution is visible limiting the freedom of action of public authorities because of the prerequisite of legitimacy and the legal protection and the protection of interests. This is achieved by introducing more checks and by increased accountability. Also, the traditional prerogatives of government are clearly pushed back. The premise that public actors under all circumstances act in the general interest and always act properly and justly, is no longer self-evident, hence, the new limits set to public action. Here, administrative law has exercised an innovative and stimulating influence. This does not imply that the new legal rules are always very clear. They usually contain exceptions to the general rule, which are open to interpretation. This is specifically so for the new rules on the publicity of government.

The pursuit of more effectiveness and more efficiency on the one hand and the quest for a new kind of legitimacy on the other hand, has definitely put the law governing the public sector in motion. The challenge currently confronting administrative law is to find a new equilibrium between the newly defined *Rechtsstaat* prerequisite of legitimacy and between the freedom to act which is necessary to change the outlook of public management.

Notes

1. Belgian Council of State, decision no. 40 314, 15 September 1992, in the case Driessens; decision, n° 22 55, 19 October 1982, in the case 'v.z.w. Inspraak'. See also: d'Hooghe, D., op. cit., 93.
2. A new article 263bis is inserted in the Communal Law by law of 28 March 1995. The article deals with autonomous communal enterprises: they are allowed to participate in public or private law companies, associations or institutions on the condition that the autonomous communal enterprise holds the majority in the votes and assumes the presidency in the boards of branches.
3. The new article 32 of the Belgian Constitution states that: 'Everybody is entitled to consult all administrative documents and obtain a copy, except in the cases and on the conditions established by law, decree or ordnance'.
4. In the first instance the distinction between public actions *iure imperii* and *iure gestionis* has disappeared. Wrongful action, the negligence to act, taking unfit measures or omitting the carefulness which should rule ordinary legal transactions, may result in dammages.
5. The principle of equality does not apply to public administration only. The Court of Arbitration, established by the special law of 6 January 1989, has the competence to nullify laws, decrees and ordnances violating the principle of equality.
6. Law of 30 June 1994 inserting article 1412bis in the Judicial Code, *Moniteur Belge*, 21 July 1994.
7. Well established jurisprudence. In the decision of the Council of State n° 24 251, 29 June 1984, in the case S.P.R.L. Oswald Heck, it is accepted that in such companies or societies a distinction can be made between:
   - legal actions, undertaken by an administrative authority and therefore subjected to review by the Council of State;
   - private law actions, which cannot be considered as actions of a public authority.
8. Council of State, decision no. 19 776, 27 July 1979 in the case Scheuermann; no. 21 467, 16 October 1981 in the case Franssens; no. 26 712, 24 June 1986 in the case De Cree.

References

Bouckaert, G., 1994. 'De overheidsmanager: noodzakelijke of onvoldoende voorwaarde voor een goed bestuur en beleid'. In: G. Bouckaert, A. Hondeghem and R. Maes, *De overheidsmanager: nieuwe ontwikkelingen in het overheidsmanagement*, Vervolmakingscentrum voor Overheidsbeleid en Bestuur, Leuven, p. 57.

Daurmont, O. and D. Baetsele, 1990. '1985–1990: cinq années de jurisprudence du Conseil d'Etat relative aux principes généraux du droit administratif'. *Administration Publique*, p. 262.

Deom, D., 1990. *Le statut juridique des entreprises publiques*. E. Story-Scientia, Brussel.

Favresse, J.M., M.A. Flamme, A. Jacquemin, Ph. Maystadt, Ph. Michaux, P. Orianne and P. Verkaeren, 1976. *Aspects juridiques de l'intervention des pouvoirs publics dans la vie économique*. Bruylant, Brussel.

Gerven, W., van, 1985. 'Beleidsovereenkomsten'. *Academiae Analecta*, vol. 47.

Gerven, W., van and M. Wijkaert, 1987. 'Overeenkomsten met de overheid', *Tijdschrift voor Privaatrecht*, pp. 17–46.

Hooghe, D., d', 1995. 'De mogelijkheid voor openbare besturen om beleidsovereenkomsten te sluiten en deel te nemen aan de oprichting van rechtspersonen'. *Tijdschrift voor Gemeenterecht*, vol. 2, p. 75.

Hooghe, D., d' and B. Peeters, 1994. *Convenanten, in het bijzonder milieuconvenanten*. Tjeenk, Willink, Zwolle.

Lane, J.E., 1993. *The public sector. Concepts, models and approaches*. Sage, London.

Lewalle, P., 1985. 'Les A.S.B.L. moyen d'action des pouvoirs publics?'. In: *Les A.S.B.L. Evaluation critique d'un succès*. Story Scientia, Brussel.

Lewalle, P., 1993. *Le référé administratif*. Faculté de droit, Liège.

Maes, R., 1984. 'Overzicht van het instrumentarium en van de technieken voor het oprichten van overheidsinstellingen. Institutioneel kader'. In: Albrecht, D. and J. De Groof, *Versnippering van overheidsinstellingen: noodzaak of onmacht*, Kluwer, Antwerpen.

Metcalff, L. and S. Richards, 1990. *Improving Public Management*. Sage, London.

Nuchelmans, D. and G. Pagano, 1991. 'Les entreprises publiques autonomes'. *Courrier Hebdomadaire CRISP*, nrs 1321–22.

Oostenbrink, J.J., 1978. *Kanttekeningen bij de wetmatigheid van het bestuur (Observations on legality of government)*. Buijten en Schippersheijn, Amsterdam.

Opdebeeck, I. (ed.), 1993. *Algemene beginselen van behoorlijk bestuur*. Kluwer, Antwerpen.

Poelje, S.O., van, 1986. 'Bestuurswetenschappen, bestuursrecht en bestuurskunde'. *Bestuurswetenschappen*, vol. 6, pp. 352.

Rynck, F., De, 1994. *Streekontwikkeling in Vlaanderen. Bestuurskundig bekeken*. Afdeling Bestuurswetenschap, Leuven.

Stiglitz, J.E., 1987. 'Principal and agent'. In: J. Eatwell, M. Milgate and P. Newman (eds), *The new Palgrave dictionary of economics*. Macmillan, London.

Vermeulen, P., 1994. 'Overheidsmanagement en bestuursvernieuwing: autonomie à la carte, de agencies'. *Tijdschrift voor Bestuurswetenschappen en Publiekrecht*, pp. 443.

CHAPTER THIRTEEN

Entrepreneurial Management or Executive Administration: The Perspective of Classical Public Administration

Klaus König
Postgraduate School of Administrative Sciences, Speyer

1. Public Administration in perspective

New Public Management

Since the reform movements of the sixties and seventies, public administration in continental Europe has time and again been confronted with management models. Such models of 'Management by ...' – Objectives, Delegation or Exception and so on – have, in themselves, made little mark on the everyday administration business in many countries. Certainly, the underlying ideas such as a higher degree of delegation do actually find expression in the continental European administrations. Yet, so far, when administrative practitioners have adopted management rhetoric, there had to be doubts about whether this was having any essential effects (Laux, 1972). In this respect, a difference becomes apparent in comparison with public administration in the United States of America. It is true that managerialism may sometimes seem in the nature of a fashion here too. For instance, it strikes the observer that, in the past, the concept of public policy was resorted to in differentiation from a public administration school that was considered old-fashioned, whereas today, the tendency is to refer to public management (Newland, 1994). Yet, together with political and bureaucratic orientation, the idea of management has always been one of the US administration's intellectual traditions: beginning with Taylorism and extending to entrepreneurial management of the Reinventing Government type (Osborne and Gaebler, 1992).

However, the challenge faced today by continental Europeans in their confrontation with a New Public Management goes beyond the claim to an internal rationalisation of the public administration by means of good management. The new diction is the language of the market, of competition, of enterprises, services, customers and, in a nutshell, of entrepreneurial management symbolising the departure from the old administrative management. So, both the public administration and its social environment, civil servants as well as the community and the politicians, are all involved. In Great Britain, some even talk of a revolution, of a new model of the state (Ridley, 1995). Anyhow, the old Westminster public administration terminology appears to be superseded more and more by new modes of speaking, for example, by a contract management jargon. In the reports worked out by the Organisation for Economic Cooperation and Development (OECD) the industrialised countries are considered, at least implicitly, to be on the way to developing the New Public Management, changing over from the old welfare state to the slenderised state with well-functioning competitive markets. Associated with this are assessments of efficiency. A kind of idealised Anglo-Saxon model is presented as the most efficient way of modernising the public sector (OECD, 1993).

Public Administration's Performance

Both implications are without proof. The industrialised countries are quite plainly following different courses of development (Naschold, 1995, p. 39). This is even true within the Anglo-Saxon area with differences between Great Britain and Australia, the USA and Canada. Furthermore, there are comments even from New Public Management countries pointing to the more favourable economic situation in Japan and Germany, both of which are characterised by the persistence of the traditional bureaucratic patterns of control (Hood, 1991; Mascarenhas, 1992, p. 324). Some even hold that all countries exercising administrative control by way of fixed rules feature economic performance rates that are in almost all respects and dimensions clearly better than those in the countries under comparison (Naschold, 1995, p. 73). Now, it is already difficult to attribute different performances within one single administrative organisation to the various control mechanisms that may be applied. More problematical is the attempt to ascribe the social prosperity of a nation to the quality of its state and administration system.

On the other hand, one fact must be noted with regard to the New Public Management, namely, that in those countries where conceptions actually ended in implementations, there is a general lack of evaluations (König, 1995a, p. 354; Gray and Jenkins, 1995, p. 84). Even with advanced cases like Great Britain and New Zealand, it is difficult, at least for outsiders, to identify actual changes in the administrative culture and their effects on the public wealth. Anyhow, it is not sufficient, for instance, in an international competition of local authorities on the development stage of communal administration, to take the introduction of new control mechanisms as the standard of reference (Bertelsmann Stiftung, 1993). Information would be needed at least on local safety and order, on housing and industrial settlement, on health and old age, water and waste, on infrastructure and local transport, on culture and leisure-time facilities on the spot. In this situation of still insufficient experience it would appear expedient from the continental European point of view to compare the control mechanisms of entrepreneurial management with the system rationality of modern public administration in conjunction with basic realities. Experiments may be admissible in narrowly defined partial sectors of public affairs. But state and administration as such are no testing grounds. Where they have reached historical performance levels as in continental Europe, really compelling reasons would have to be brought forward before the patterns of control for the production and distribution of public goods and services may be altered generally.

A basic characteristic of modern societies is their functional differentiation into relatively independent subsystems and spheres of action together with the rationalisation of these fields in accordance with their respective principles (Luhmann, 1985). This includes the economic system which is governed by principles like private property, market and competition as well as the politico–administrative system with its principles of humanity, democracy and constitutional state order (König, 1982). The system rationality of public administration in modern times was characterised by Max Weber in his type of bureaucracy: the generally well-ordered levels of authority competencies, the hierarchical order of official positions, authority operation, adherence to rules and regulations, the system of permanently established civil servants, and so on (Mayntz, 1965). His aim was not simply to provide a prescriptive model. The experiences underlying this typification were taken from historic reality, in particular the Prussian administration. The public administration's performance system has proved to be strong enough to withstand strains in the course of time, although this does not preclude bureaucratism with dysfunctions such as formalism, schematism, impersonal attitudes, and so on.

Socialist Administration

Accordingly, Marxism–Leninism did not fight bureaucracy in terms of malfunctions but as an agency of the bourgeoisie (König, 1993a). Even in an administrative state as old as Germany, the bureaucratic institutions disintegrated and were replaced by a cadre administration of the practised socialism type, an administration which featured instrumental étatism in its functions and centralist rule in its organisation, which, in its proceedings, stood out for the transmission of the party will and whose staff were cadres (König, 1990a). Certainly, the cadres, after which that type of administration was named, were professional administrators, but with politically and ideologically defined qualifications. As a large-scale anti-modernisation test socialism in practice had to declare historical bankruptcy. Still, when some are talking of the 'market economy's victory' over the centrally planned economy, it must be noted that this is only part of the story. Highly differentiated social systems granting individual rights and standing for democracy, market economy, pluralist organised interests, state administration, and so on, have turned out to be superior to social conditions where individuals, society, economy, associations and state were collectivised in line with a party ideology.

The transformation of the socialist cadre administration (König, 1993a) swept a great variety of administrative expertise on to the consultancy market. Some are presenting rational models of management and administration claiming their universal applicability. Others point to administrative experiences in their western home country. And indeed – despite the globalisation of public problems and the increasingly international status of public organisations – public administration at the end of the 20th century continues to be seen primarily as a national state matter; that is, as French, American, Japanese and so on (König, 1993d). In addition, cooperation with developing countries in the administrative sector clearly illustrates the cultural purport of public administration *vis-à-vis* the universally applicable features of good management (König, 1986). Accordingly, it is difficult to make out an intermediate layer of common cultural features between a national state's administrative concept and a universal management conception. The distinction between civic culture administration and the classical administration system aims at marking out certain common characteristics in the Anglo-Saxon area and in continental Europe respectively, and then comparing them with one another (Heady, 1987). But contrary to the cadre type administration, this comparison is more a matter of rather gradual differences. Civic culture administration and the classical administration system both follow the same lines of bureaucratic tradition. Even in the US one would most likely have to talk of a bureaucratic managerialism. Yet in the course of numerous stages of modernisation many things have lost much of their former clear-cut image.

Continental European administrations like the French and German administrative systems may be termed as classical since the bureaucratic efficiency system established there in the modern age has been kept alive until today throughout all political instabilities and changes (König, 1992). They survived the various régimes of monarchy, republic, dictatorship and democracy and, in times of collapse, had to bear the burden of public action. In central Europe such a separate efficiency system has now proved successful again. Following the Marxist–Leninist rule and its cadre administration's bankruptcy in the GDR, the resulting consequences could be cushioned through the transfer of classical administrative institutions from West Germany. This was not a matter of colonisation on the lines of the Federal Republic. On the contrary, resort could be had to the traditions of the German and thus the classical continental European administrative and legal cultures in matters of public commitments and public property, federal and communal organisation, administrative law and public finance, civil service and human resources development. It was the public administration that enabled the new democratic policy on East German soil to function beyond the peaceful revolution. This became all the more necessary as the forces of the market did not develop the economic dynamism which had been expected of them, so that both the transformation and the unification process had to be implemented in state-centred procedures (König, 1995c).

Administration and Political Democracy

While bureaucracy in the classical administrative systems may be said to be older than democracy, the development of public bureaucracies in civic culture administration countries such as Great Britain and the United States was governed from the outset by the political régime, the historic continuity of which has been maintained up to the present day (Stillman, 1991, p. 19). These régimes admitted public administration services, defined their boundaries and strengthened their connection with the lasting democratic and participatory order of a civic culture, which does not mean that the public bureaucracies did not develop their own impetus. The American image of the 'iron triangle', a configuration of power in the hands of political representatives, lobbyists and members of the ministerial bureaucracies exemplifies this. Another example of this is the British TV visualisation 'Yes, Minister', where top bureaucrats thwart the political will. It goes without saying that civil servants endeavour to put forward bureaucratic values. However, instabilities during which the public administration would have had to continue working on its own account, so to speak, did not happen in the course of history. The party political constellations supporting the governments did change. But the political régime maintained control of public administration, however bureaucratic such administrative services may have been. The permanent dominance of politics over the public bureaucracies is in compliance with the concept of social values in a civic culture; continental Europeans, on the other hand, have had to learn by experience that, in certain historical situations, people may expect certain things from the administration which cannot be provided by the political sector such as, for instance, certain basic supplies in times of political confusion (Ellwein, 1981; Thieme, 1993).

The Idea of the State

The Anglo-American continuities, for the moment, have made the values of the political régime serve as identification patterns for the public bureaucracies. 'Servant of the crown' is a formula for this, that also appeals to people's feelings (Ridley, 1995, p. 574). In continental European countries, on the other hand, an idea reaching beyond the historical situation of monarchies, republics, dictatorships and democracies had to be found to give an identity to a continually functioning public administration. A regulative idea had to be established, in which the political system defines itself irrespective of the current political régime. That regulative idea is the 'state' and, concomitantly, officials are named the 'servants of the state'. That term is still not understood easily in the Anglo-American administrative culture although a discussion has meanwhile arisen in the US on the 'statelessness' of the US administrative concept (Stillman, 1991, p. 19).

For the moment, the state regulative is an idea that appears perfectly congenial to public bureaucracies. Civil servants in a civic culture administration equally look for identification patterns beyond the political régime. In retrospect, one may ask whether the British class society is reflected in the administrative class. One can be on the lookout in the present Anglo-Americanised world for the self-styled concept of a 'global professional technocracy' (Stillman, 1991, p. 77). Yet with a view to the regulative idea of state it must then be noted that this is not without risk. Abuse on the part of the state is abuse on the part of its servants. Beyond the dysfunction of bureaucratism it is also public administrations in continental Europe that have failed in the past. In Weimar Republic Germany, for instance, the administrative bureaucracy was not among the defenders of democracy.

Thus, the regulative idea of state needs to be supplemented protectively. That protection was found in the category of the 'constitutional state'. In the development of the constitutional state, continental Europe can again revert to pre-democratic experiences. Today, constitutional state order and democracy are closely linked. Constitutional state order does not only mean that there is a legal system with binding force for the public administration. There are certain definite principles which are guaranteed by the constitution and must be applied by the public administration service. Human rights have to be respected. The administration is bound by law and legal regulations. The administrative authorities must ensure that the means applied are in proportion to the purpose to be served. Legal protection is guaranteed against public administrative action and so forth. Going on from here, we could list further specific properties of continental European administration that are different from the civic culture administration: the highly differentiated administrative law, a particular legalism, an administrative jurisdiction system of its own, and so on. However, it has become sufficiently clear now that, in countries like France and Germany, the issue of New Public Management in the civil service meets with cultural premises that differ from those in Anglo-American countries. Therefore we will now endeavour to compare the control patterns of entrepreneurial management with those applied in the classical system of administration.

2.   Entrepreneurial Management

The intention underlying New Public Management is the internal economisation of public administration, ensuring an entrepreneurial spirit and entrepreneurial management for the administration proper (Mascarenhas, 1993; Reinermann, 1995). In this, it differs from external rationalisation approaches such as privatisation or deregulation (König, 1990b, 1995b). Certainly, this concerns the starting point only. As an open system, public administration, of course, is constituted not only by its inner system of order but through its social environment as well. The law, for example, has different impacts on administration: it means being subject internally to certain rules and regulations and it is a legal basis for external action. One cannot, internally, consider the political hierarchy superior to the force of law while living in a constitutional system of order. Accordingly, the control patterns of a

New Public Management must be compatible with the *res publica*. In this respect, the relatively indistinct nature of that reform movement has a problematical effect. In terms of its basic intellectual foundations, it is a popularised mixture of management theories, business motivation psychology and neo-liberal economy (Gray and Jenkins, 1995). In terms of subject matter, the mixture comprises both state-conformable reform proposals such as, for instance, decentral responsibility for resources and market-conformable ideas such as customer-oriented action. Sometimes, this ends in clichés, for example, when a municipal administration is referred to as a service group (Banner, 1993). True, this does not mean that the municipal authorities should act as groups of affiliated companies can under the pressure of rationalisation, namely sell affiliates, close down lines of production, shift certain locations and externalise costs, and so on (Laux, 1994).

Entrepreneur and Market Economy

Taking the concept of entrepreneurial management in public administration literally, one must point to the fact that the term entrepreneur is linked inseparably with a market economy system. The market economy is, as it were, personalised in the entrepreneur. He is the one who combines productive factors to produce goods and services for marketing at a profit. This interrelation with the market economy system still remains the same when property rights and risks are balanced out and salaried managers exercise entrepreneurial functions. Nor can such entrepreneurial management be regarded as fully developed, when certain service units in state and administration are termed as public enterprises, since they, on the one hand, are public property and, on the other, have certain scopes for independent action (Püttner, 1985). It is precisely for a lack of entrepreneurial spirit that such publicly-owned enterprises are constantly reproached, whether public railways or postal services, public broadcasting or transport corporations or communal supply and housing companies. Such reproaches are unfair to these organisations where orientation to profits as a standard of entrepreneurial success conflicts with the public purposes of the common weal and nonprofit activities (Dürr, 1995).

So, whoever demands entrepreneurial management in public administration must therefore create a compatible environment, that is, market conditions and competition. In this respect, the British administrative 'revolution' with its market testing, compulsory competitive tendering, and so on, has turned out to be the most uncompromising approach (Ridley, 1993; O'Toole and Grant, 1995). Two strategies are conceivable: entry into an actual competitive market or establishment of virtual organisational competition as the functional equivalent thereof. In the light of the modern society's functional differentiation, state and market are notable for their own characteristic strategies to control the supply of goods. The type, scope and distribution of private goods are decided on by harmonising the individual preferences within the market mechanism; decisions on the production of public goods, on the other hand, result from a collective, that is, politico–administrative, development of objectives. Economic theory has brought forth a wide variety of arguments about why the society's division of labour between state and market cannot be abandoned and the population needs to be supplied with public goods. Some of the characteristic causes for state activities are, for instance, the non-applicability of the exclusion principle – that is, utilisation cannot be made conditional on the payment of some remuneration – or non- rivalling consumption within capacity limits, which means consumption by one individual does not preclude consumption by others. Further reasons relate to external effects or rising returns to scale.

Market Failures and the State

This is why even economic liberalism does not query the state in itself. On the contrary, the state granting protection of legal rights is considered as a basic precondition for the establishment and development of a market economy. Moreover, the state is called for when the market fails to function. Both aspects have become evident in the historical phase of the socialist economic and social systems' transformation and particularly in the case of Germany. Even industrial circles praised the West German administration for its achievements in the protection of legal rights, a commitment that was formerly considered as a matter of course. In addition, the welfare state administration's achievements ensuring supplies for the East German population could well stand comparison with what market dynamism had accomplished there. But even in the view of New Public Management protagonists, this is, on principle, not a matter of entry into actual competitive markets, that is, of privatisation. This innovative strategy is so attractive to many administrative practitioners since – following Reaganism and Thatcherism – the fundamental demand is not for less public administration but for a better quality (Mascarenhas, 1993, p. 319). Thus, one can understand the viewpoints that are brought forward in continental Europe by social democrats and trade unions, rejecting the privatisation of public commitments but conceding that economy should be practised inside the public administration (Jann, 1994; Naschold, 1994; Naschold and Pröhl, 1994).

Virtual Competition

The conception of virtual organisational competition as a functional equivalent in the absence of market entry and privatisation is, for the moment, an intellectually attractive idea. In this context, attention should be drawn to the fact that in continental Europe, too, there is an – not so much prescriptive as rather empirically oriented – innovation movement, advocating the termination of legalist and hierarchical modes of control and replacing them by cooperative state action formulae, negotiations and contracts of both a formal and an informal nature (Benz, 1995). Here, the question may be asked whether this does not disregard the collective and authoritative background of administrative action and whether the 'soft' forms of administrative procedures are not actually backed inwardly by the tacit sovereignty of the state. Anyhow, the cooperation and contract movement is another manifestation of the intention to realise further innovations in public administration. The end that came about for the former antagonist on the European continent, the socialist state and its cadre-type administration, appears to have intensified modernisation pressure on the western state instead of relieving it (König, 1995d).

Here, it is the concept of competition that is considered really attractive by those who are sceptical about other ideas that are brought forward in the current modernisation debate: when inefficiency in the public sector cannot be remedied by means of the classical political control instruments but, on the contrary, is thereby aggravated, it is expedient, they say, to institutionalise a general set-up which rewards economical behaviour and penalises uneconomical attitudes. To reach this end, they say, there is nothing better than the competitive model, including competitive surrogates such as quasi-markets (Röber, 1995, p. 4). As a matter of fact, competition is a basic constellation of living together in society not only in the economic sphere but also in politics, sports, education and so on. Competition implies performance incentives which make it a basically desirable social relationship. Yet the important thing is the respective social system structure, not only because competition is 'perfect' but also, in view of market failure, mainly in the field of basic human needs (König, 1995d, p. 355).

Socialist Competition

An interesting étatist variant of artificial competition is the socialist competition as laid down in Leninism: socialism is considered not to suppress competition but, on the contrary, to be the first to create the possibility of truly applying it on a broad basis and on a mass scale. The ideological and organisational foundations of such competition included among other things social consciousness, harmony of interests, 'democratic centralism', the party monopoly in leadership and mass organisation, finally ending – due to socialist morals – not in a record performance on the part of individual persons or collectives but in an optimum overfulfilment of plans (König, 1990a). Principles apparently as harmless as publicity of competitions, comparison of results, repetition of the best achievements on a mass scale, intensification and rationalisation, recognition in moral and material terms took concrete shape in extremely problematical movements: the activist movement, socialist cooperative work, renewal movement, production propaganda, join-in contests, and so on, even extending to a contest for the title of *Bereich vorbildlicher Ordnung, Disziplin und Sicherheit*, the embodiment of exemplary order, discipline and security.

While this relativises the attractiveness of what Marx called *Wetteifer*, which means emulation, the difficulties faced by the state and administration in highly differentiated societies already begin with the dilemma of manoeuvring rivalry in a social system, the rationality of which follows other principles. In the classical public administration, it is not everybody's but only the responsible individual's business to take action. There is a firm system of competencies and, beyond this, the principle is applied that multiple competencies must be avoided. In case duplicate competencies should nevertheless arise, the rule says that action shall be taken by such authority as was first engaged in the matter. Accordingly, rules have been laid down for competency conflicts in such a way, for instance, that the supervisory authority determines who shall take responsibility. So, the control patterns of classical public administration are intended to prevent rivalries or to solve them by establishing applicable rules. When transferring that standard situation to a possible quasi-market system, there will be one single acting agency on the public goods supply side, which means a monopoly. The virtual organisational competition will not work. With local competencies as the basis, the result will be regional monopolies. What remains is a comparison of performances between, let's say, the registration of a motor vehicle by the municipal authorities of NW and those of SP, an absolutely helpful but unfortunately still insufficiently practised mode of procedure (Hill and Klages, 1992; Camp, 1994). Such a comparison of performances, however, is still not rivalry.

Single Public Authority

The idea of virtual organisational competition is no sufficient reason for the classical public administration to part with the principle of fixed orders of competencies and the prevention of multiple responsibilities. As far as concerns that sector of administration which interferes with the individual citizen's sphere of rights, this is clearly understandable without any further explanation. Citizens should have to deal with one single police authority, with one single building authority and with one single trade supervisory authority responsible for their affairs. Such a degree of certainty in legal matters is a must. Yet in wide ranges of benefits-providing civil services – social welfare office, housing office, or the local labour exchange – it is equally recommendable that competency should lie with one single authority, the more so as benefits and interventions can be very close to one another as, for example, in youth welfare matters (Pitschas, 1994). A welfare state like the Federal Republic of Germany with its social transfers cannot afford the duplication of work nor the potential duplication of payments which might result therefrom. Currently arising cases of abuse illustrate this time and again. Moreover, virtual organisational competition would mean that the entire organisational landscape would have to be rearranged. Yet such rearrangements will meet with their limits in particular in those spheres where decentralisation, federalism, regionalism and local self-administration are guaranteed by the constitution. Federal Länder, autonomous districts, self-governed municipalities and communes will hardly renunciate their regional monopolies (Laux, 1995).

There remains that field of public goods and commitments where the population can choose between various public services or where such options can be made available without damage to the organisational values of classical administration.

Such fields of policies and commitments may not be at the core of public administration, but there are many of them, for example, in the cultural sector: museums, theatres, libraries, and so on; in the field of education, they are concerned with universities, adult evening classes and also with secondary education institutions, while primary schools are subordinated to administrative districts; in the social welfare sector this also applies to old-age homes, kindergartens, social welfare centres, and so on. Certainly, difficulties will arise in this field, too. One should not underestimate the degree of specialisation of public goods. A modern teaching hospital, for instance, these days not only comprises a general surgery division but also sections for casualty surgery, urology, head surgery and many more. So, this is no homogenous production but a highly differentiated 'assortment'. One would hardly wish to give up such differentiation and reorganise all sections into general surgery divisions for the purpose of establishing perfect competitive conditions for virtual organisational competition (König, 1995b, p. 356).

Conditions for a Quasi-Market

But even if we assume that this kind of competition has been initiated, there would be further demands to be met for a quasi-market. Firstly, the greatest possible freedom in competitive conditions must be established to prevent excessively high barriers from hindering entry into and exit from the market. Secondly, it must be ensured that both parties in the market have easy access to information on costs and qualities. Thirdly, the cost of transactions implicit in market bartering – namely negotiations, contracts, accounting, system of payment, control, and so on – may not exceed the efficiency gains that result from such competitive behaviour. In the fourth place, suppliers must, at least to some extent, be granted financial incentives to react to price signals. And in the fifth place, it must be prevented in the interests of equal treatment that members of either the supply or the demand side simply 'cash in'. When we set these demands alongside public administration as experienced today, it becomes evident how difficult it will be to draw gains rationally from the utilisation of quasi-markets. Access to the administration is not easy – not just because of its bureaucratism but because of its complexity. Due to its high degree of social technicalities, the administration's transparency remains a problem. Every newly granted organisational independence causes high control costs (Püttner, 1989, p. 45), and financial self-interest meets with difficulties in budgetary and financial policy questions. Administrative services, too, like low-risk affairs, easy cases and solvent customers, and free-rider effects are not rare among beneficiary individuals or organisations.

Public and Private Service Delivery

A more favourable situation may be expected for rationality gains when market mechanisms are not planned in virtual organisational competition between administrative units but are put to use in a rivalry between the public supply of goods and privately offered goods. Such a dualism in the production and distribution of goods and services has a long tradition, for instance in banking, with a state-owned national central bank, local-government-owned savings banks, and so on, on the one hand, and private and cooperative banks and so on, on the other (König, 1990b). These days, with the overburdened welfare state, the political strategy to restrict commitments includes the approach to open up new markets where the step to substantive privatisation is not ventured upon. For example, private television and broadcasting were also admitted in continental Europe in addition to the traditional public broadcasting institutions. The coexistence of public supply and private offers does not yet create a perfect market as long as the public institution's losses are financed from tax revenues. Such an institution, from the outset, operates with public subsidies and has a safe budget from TV and radio licence fees, whereas the private company has to depend on profit-making, or when one party is obliged to adhere to nonprofit modes of supply while the other is, *sui generis*, free to orient itself to the profit maxim. But it is possible to institute at least quasi-markets as the party dependent upon the market must act as a rival and can thus be a challenge to the other market participant. Here again, the dual broadcasting system offers interesting illustrative material: when public broadcasting is not only financed from licence fees but also from advertising revenues, it is in a competitive situation and must fight for audience ratings that are the basis for advertising revenues. In the German case, this has triggered off an intensive discussion on rationalisation. This will not make the director of a public broadcasting institution an entrepreneur nor will it convert the broadcasting institution's administration into an entrepreneurial management. Yet partially entrepreneurial roles and partly entrepreneurial management functions will be inevitable. Accordingly, the cost of and benefits from dual systems of supply should be looked into even more thoroughly.

In the above, we have outlined the problems faced by the public sector on the supply side. However, state and administration also act both as self-suppliers and demanders. Except for the collection of taxes and public charges, the recruitment of young men liable to military service and some other public claims, social differentiation and the functioning money economy in modern times have had the effect that – other than under socialism in practice – demand on the part of public authorities is largely met by supplies from the market. But this is a separate topic. In view of the projected US 'Reinventing Government' reform, we shall confine ourselves to two observations regarding the procurement sector (Gore, 1993, p. 26). Firstly, continental European administrations are increasingly suffering from respective abuse. And secondly, the procurement sector holds promise of considerable rationalisation and economisation reserves.

3. On Executive Management

Rationality and Legality

In a state upholding the division of powers, the core of public administration lies in its executive function. Bound by the rule of legal regulations, it executes the laws passed by the democratic legislative body. In its hierarchical system of order it follows the instructions issued by the executive's political leaders. In the classical public administration, a certain degree of legalism is superimposed on public action, a fact that results from many historical reasons. This implies a normative character of law different, for example, from prejudice-based law. It is quite obvious that the number of lawyers, not only in the administrative élite but in the political élite too, always tends to be very high (Derlien, 1991). Yet, basically, this legalism has its origin in the claim of standing to reason. 'Rational state' and rational administrative law belong together. Civil servants rationalise public action by subsuming vital facts under legal standards. This attitude, in fact the civil servants' conception of themselves, is supported by far-reaching legal aid from the administrative courts (Sommermann, 1991). In hundreds and thousands of administrative court proceedings, the judges discuss legal issues with citizens and administrative authorities, trying to find the reasonable answer, the legally correct solution. A statement like the one made in a US administration manual, saying that 'Law is a barrier of rationality' is incompatible with this kind of administrative and legal culture.

Under continental European legalism, the conditional programming of administrative action by means of laws and legal regulations has been successfully transferred from the liberal state's regulative functions to the social welfare state's commitments and benefits. But as the social welfare state must provide more and more goods that cannot be specified in terms of individual beneficiaries, other forms of communication had to be developed in addition. Today, administrative action is no longer steered on the basis of legal facts and consequences alone but also by final programming, meaning that targets and means are defined as the premises for decision making (Thieme, 1995, p. 139): besides the Education Act there are education regulations, besides the Health Act there are hospital plans, and so on. This illustrates that Weber's bureaucracy in continental Europe has become somewhat one-sided. His view of bureaucratic administration was that each of its actions is backed by a context of rationally discussable reasons, namely either the subsumption under certain standards or the weighing of ends and means.

Continental European legalism has incorporated the means-and-ends-oriented rationalisation of public action into its reasoning contexts (König, 1970, p. 112). This reaches from the teleological interpretation of laws to the proportionality of means and ends in their implementation. Public plans and social transfer laws are tied up with the budget. The principles of thriftiness and economy must be observed. Audit offices supervise adherence to these standards of action. Administrative action may not disregard efficiency and effectiveness (Arnim and Lüder, 1993). However, in this regard everyday culture has not attained such socio-technological standards as were made possible by the genuine access to work on the law. Assessments of effects and successes, analyses of costs and benefits fall short of what legal argumentation is able to perform. In the German case, interesting illustrative material in this regard is offered by cabinet documentation, comprising descriptions of facts and assessments worked out by the civil servants in the central government to assist the head of government in the matters to be dealt with in cabinet meetings. It may be presumed that these documents manifest a high standard of legal considerations even if they have been prepared under the responsibility of a political economist. The civil servants are sufficiently sensitive when it is a question of the assessment of political criteria. Evaluations of the macroeconomic situation present no difficulty for them. But where effectiveness and efficiency of the administrative implementation procedures are concerned, assessments turn out to be poorer.

Public Management and Public Law

'That the study of administration should start from the base of management rather than the foundation of law' (White, 1955, p. XVI) is a viewpoint often heard with regard to the US public administration. Now, contrasts between managerial bureaucracy in the United States and legalist bureaucracy in continental Europe should not be overestimated. Meanwhile, there are both administrative scientists and practitioners on the European continent who are devoted supporters of public management. In the US it is precisely the reinventing government movement's focusing on the entrepreneurial spirit which has called those to the scene who stress the US administration's foundation on public law (Goodsell, 1993; Moe and Gilmour, 1995). And it is a fact that administration in the US is subject to the rule of law. However, with management-oriented attitudes – which politicians are demanding all the time from the civil service – the criteria of efficiency and effectiveness have gained a genuine access to the administration of public affairs and, with criticism and reform, they have advanced to a notable socio-technological standard (Bozeman, 1993).

Many a scientist or practitioner working in the field of public administration in continental Europe has difficulties with the category of management in the various languages. Some may make reservations purely on the grounds of linguistic aesthetics. Others may fear a managerialism that would appear inadequate with regard to public matters. Still, one must concede that management has become the term of a lingua franca in an increasingly internationalised administrative world. It signals that public administration implies planning and coordination, staff recruitment and development, personnel management and control, organisation, and so on, and that allowance must be made in all these respects for the scarcity of resources. One does not have to keep up with every management fashion. Analogous to the distinction between bureaucracy and bureaucratism, it is also possible to criticise the dysfunctions of management as managerialism (Hood, 1991).

Production of Public Goods

So, when we are talking of executive management here, this does not mean anything other than that the continental European administration must give more scope to effectiveness and efficiency on the socio-technological side without completely breaking with the values of the classical executive (Böhret, 1993). Strengthening these standards of action is peremptory for two reasons. Firstly, the 'cold star of scarcity' is gaining an ever greater influence on the public sector. When asking the three classical producer's questions – namely 'What is to be produced?', 'How is it to be produced?' and 'For whom is it to be produced?' – the answer to the first will refer to the primacy of politics. Accordingly, the definition of public commitments is in the hands of the legislature and of the executive's political leadership (König, 1995a). There remain certain autonomous spheres, above all in science and art. Yet it is neither the concern of a university administration nor of the administration of a museum to prescribe scientific or artistic subject matters respectively. Regarding the question of target groups, the normative reply will again refer the matter to politics, admitting, however, at the same time that, *de facto*, certain free scope will be left to the administration with regard to execution procedures. The administrative service can await applicants or, in a different approach, it can provide the people with relevant information. Whether quasi-markets might be helpful here may be doubted by those fearing that equality before the law might be replaced by equality before the dollar, the German mark or the yen.

There remains the question of *how* goods are to be produced. Here, it would be all too simple merely to distinguish between modes of procedure and substance. Frequently, modes of administrative procedure are prescribed with a view to specific subject matters, from budget implementation rules to administrative procedural law. Yet mass treatment, technicity, professionality, and so on, make the answer to this question a domain of public administration. We are here dealing with the range of secondary efficiency rates, that is, staff size, infrastructure, organisation, physical resources, and so on. Such secondary efficiency rates, not efficiency improvement by privatisation, are the main topic of approaches to modernise public administration in Europe. Differing from one country to the other, the relevant strategies all deal with results control, management by results, greater flexibility of civil servants, new personnel management, concentration on performance guarantee functions, contract management, decentralised responsibility for resources, new budget management and so on, also extending to the incorporation of market mechanisms into administrative action (OECD, 1993; Naschold, 1995).

Secondly, the apportionment of goods production between state and market remains ambivalent. There is no a priori concept according to which the insurance of individual rights, social welfare, humanity and quality of life works better when left to the market than to the state, or is better realised by the state than by the market. Legal, economic and social science theories each have their preferences. Pertinent ideologies are strong not only on the left but also on the right wing. The mercantilism of the 18th century was a prime mover in the socio-economic development in Europe; the party-ruled étatism in 20th century Eastern Europe in the end turned out to have exercised the opposite effect. State failure and market failure are both well-known. We have historical experience in this respect. As a matter of fact, it must be decided in every individual case whether state or market is to deal with a given historical situation. In modern rationalism, this needs to be substantiated. Here, the European welfare states – which, in the course of many historic struggles, have assumed more and more public commitments, thereby reaching government activity rates of almost 50 percent and some even more – will not find it easy to state convincing reasons for this. As a result, privatisation is the order of the day in many European countries. Yet on the other hand, there are many sectors – public banks, the health sector, postal services – where politicians do not give in even to plausible economic reasons. So, if the German municipal savings banks are not privatised, as politicians want to maintain them under the control of local self-administered authorities, the least that can be done is to establish a savings banks management fulfilling the criteria of effectivity and effectiveness. Yet competitive open markets with private competitors will surely make a more valuable contribution to this end than self-discipline on the part of politicians and civil servants.

Executive Management in Constitutional State

The ambivalence of public goods and the scarcity of public resources are sufficient reason to interpret continental European administration's internal modernisation at present as a primarily economic matter, for the primacy of politics and democracy as well as the constitutional system of order appear secured (Naschold, 1995, p. 89). This is what is meant by the executive management concept. The entrepreneurial management model, on the other hand, appears to be appropriate for such publicly owned companies that can compete on opened markets; however, it is not adequate for the heart of the classical administration system. The reason for this does not lie in bureaucracy's intelligence. It will be able to incorporate market mechanisms in a formalistic manner. Yet the real question is whether, beyond the transfer costs, a more favourable cost/benefit ratio can be attained for the population. In this context, it is recommendable, incidentally, to study the experiences of large private enterprises with the introduction of intercompany market mechanisms (Heckscher, 1994, p. 33).

That the classical public administration identifies itself through the regulations of a constitutional state, shows a quality which exceeds the professional and technocratic level. By its concrete stipulations, it commits public administration to human and civil rights, to the measurability of its actions, to the proportionateness of means and purposes, to the provision of legal aid, and so on. Concomitantly, the actual point is not that the civil service has found an identification formula but that endeavours to ensure justice for the citizens are guaranteed. Likewise, that constitutional state regulation does not object to the participatory democratic régime as in the civic culture administration in the Anglo-American sphere, where this has acquired historical continuity. In the German case, civil servants are sworn to the liberal democratic system laid down in the constitution and, apart from a few exceptional cases, they have identified themselves with that system of order in post-war times (Thieme, 1993). As far as the turbulences of everyday political business is concerned, the increasing party political influence in public life, interventions in favour of specific interests, the entanglement of personal relationships, and so on, the situation is different. Here, the classical public administration's self-description through the constitutional state regulation means a gain in social stability.

References

Arnim, H.H. von, and K. Lüder (eds), 1993. *Wirtschaftlichkeit in Staat und Verwaltung*, Berlin.

Banner, G., 1993. 'Konzern Stadt'. In: H. Hill and H. Klages (eds), *Qualitäts- und erfolgsorientiertes Verwaltungsmanagement. Aktuelle Tendenzen und Entwürfe. Vorträge und Diskussionsbeiträge der 61. Staatswissenschaftlichen Fortbildungstagung.* Hochschule für Verwaltungswissenschaften Speyer, Berlin, pp. 57 ff.

Benz, A., 1995. *Kooperative Verwaltung.* Baden-Baden.

Bertelsmann Stiftung (eds), 1993. 'Karl-Bertelsmann-Preis. Demokratie und Effizienz in der Kommunalverwaltung', part 1, *Dokumentationsband zur internationalen Recherche*, Gütersloh.

Böhret, C., 1993. 'The tools of public management'. In: K.A. Eliassen and J. Kooiman (eds), *Managing public organisations: lessons from contemporary European experiences.* pp. 87 ff. (2nd ed.). Sage, London.

Bozeman, B. (ed.), 1993. *Public management: the state of the art.* Jossey Bass, San Francisco.

Camp, R.C., 1992. *Benchmarking: het zoeken naar de beste werkmethoden die leiden tot superieure prestaties.* Kluwer, Deventer.

Derlien, H.-U., 1991. 'Die Staatsaffinität der Exekutivpolitiker der Bundesrepublik – Zur Bedeutung der Bürokratie als Sozialisationsfeld'. In: H.-H. Hartwich and G. Wewer (eds), *Regieren in der Bundesrepublik II*, Opladen, pp. 171 ff.

Dürr, H., 1995. 'Kann der Staat als Unternehmer erfolgreich sein?'. *Verwaltung und Management*, pp. 4 ff.

Ellwein, Th., 1981. 'Geschichte der öffentlichen Verwaltung'. In: K. König, H. Joachim von Oertzen und F. Wagener (eds), *Öffentliche Verwaltung in der Bundesrepublik Deutschland*, Baden-Baden, pp. 37 ff.

Goodsell, Ch.T., 1993. 'Reinvent government or rediscover it?'. *Public Administration Review*, pp. 85 ff. American Society for Public Administration, Washington, DC.

Gore, A., 1993. *Report of the National Performance Review, From red tape to results: creating a government that works better and costs less.* Washington.

Gray, A. and B. Jenkins, 1995. 'From public administration to public management: reassessing a revolution?' *Public Administration*, pp. 75 ff.

Heady, F., 1987. *Public administration – a comparative perspective.* New York/Basel (4th ed.).

Heckscher, Ch., 1994. 'Defining the post-bureaucratic type'. In: A. Donnellon (ed.), *The post-bureaucratic organization: new perspectives on organizational change*, pp. 14 ff., Sage Publications, Thousand Oaks, California.

Hill, H. and H. Klages (eds), 1992. *Spitzenverwaltungen im Wettbewerb. Eine Dokumentation des 1. Speyerer Qualitätswettbewerbs.* Baden-Baden.

Hood, C.C., 1991. 'Public management for all seasons?'. *Public Administration*, pp. 3 ff.

Jann, W., 1994. *Moderner Staat und effiziente Verwaltung. Zur Reform des öffentlichen Sektors in Deutschland, Gutachten erstattet für die Friedrich-Ebert-Stiftung.* Bonn.

König, K., 1970. *Erkenntnisinteressen der Verwaltungswissenschaft.* Berlin.

König, K., 1982. 'Öffentliche Verwaltung als soziales System'. In: Remer (ed.), *Verwaltungsführung*, Berlin/New York, pp. 3 ff.

König, K. (ed.), 1986. *Öffentliche Verwaltung und Entwicklungspolitik*, Baden-Baden.

König, K., 1990a. 'Zum Verwaltungssystem der DDR'. In: *Verwaltungsstrukturen der DDR*, Baden-Baden, pp. 9 ff.

König, K., 1990b. *Kritik öffentlicher Aufgaben*, Baden-Baden.

König, K., 1992. 'Zur Transformation einer real-sozialistischen Verwaltung in eine klassisch-europäische Verwaltung'. *Speyerer Forschungsberichte*, vol. 99(3).

König, K., 1993a. 'Administrative Transformation in Eastern Germany'. In: J.J. Hesse (ed.), *Public Administration*, vol. 71, pp. 135 ff.

König, K., 1993b. 'Die Transformation der öffentlichen Verwaltung: Ein neues Kapitel der Verwaltungswissenschaft'. *Verwaltungsarchiv*, pp. 311 ff.

König, K., 1993c. 'Internationalität, Transnationalität, Supranationalität – Auswirkungen auf die Regierung'. In: H.-H. Hartwich and G. Wewer (eds), *Regieren in der Bundesrepublik V*, Opladen, pp. 234 ff.

König, K., 1993d. 'Organisation und Prozeß: Zur Internationalisierung des Regierens'. In: C. Böhret and G. Wewer (eds), *Regieren im 21. Jahrhundert – zwischen Globalisierung und Regionalisierung, Festschrift für Hans-Hermann Hartwich zum 65. Geburtstag*, Opladen, pp. 144 ff.

König, K., 1993e. 'Transformation der realsozialistischen Verwaltung: deutsche Integration und europäische Kooperation'. *Deutsches Verwaltungsblatt*, pp. 1292 ff.

König, K., 1993f. 'Transformation einer realsozialistischen Verwaltung in eine klassisch-europäische Verwaltung'. In: W. Seibel, A. Benz and H. Mäding (eds), *Verwaltungsreform und Verwaltungspolitik im Prozeß der deutschen Einigung*, Baden-Baden, pp. 80 ff.

König, K., 1995a. '"Neue" Verwaltung oder Verwaltungsmodernisierung: Verwaltungspolitik in den neunziger Jahren'. *Die Öffentliche Verwaltung*, pp. 349 ff.

König, K., 1995b. 'Prozedurale Rationalität – Zur kontraktiven Aufgabenpolitik der achtziger Jahre', *Verwaltungsarchiv*, pp. 1 ff.

König, K., 1995c. 'Public sector reform – the case of Germany'. In: J.J. Hesse (ed.), *European yearbook of comparative government and public administration*.

König, K., 1995d. 'Transformation als Staatsveranstaltung'. In: H. Wollmann, H. Wiesenthal and Frank Bönker (eds), *Transformation sozialistischer Gesellschaften: Am Ende des Anfangs*, Opladen, pp. 609 ff.

König, K. and A. Benz, 1996. *Staatszentrierte Transformation*, Der Staat, pp. 109 ff.

König, K. and N. Dose, 1993. 'Referenzen staatlicher Steuerung'. In: K. König and N. Dose (eds), *Instrumente und Formen staatlichen Handelns*, Köln etc., pp. 519 ff.

König, K. and V. Meßmann, 1995. *Organisations- und Personalprobleme der Verwaltungstransformation in Deutschland.* Band 28 der Schriftenreihe Verwaltungsorganisation, Staatsaufgaben und Öffentlicher Dienst (ed. by Klaus König und Franz Kroppenstedt), Baden-Baden.

König, K., G.F. Schuppert and J. Heimann (eds), 1994. 'Zur Aufgaben- und Vermögenstransformation'. *Vermögenszuordnung – Aufgabentransformation in den neuen Bundesländern.* Band 29 der Schriftenreihe Verwaltungsorganisation, Staatsaufgaben und Öffentlicher Dienst (ed. by Klaus König und Franz Kroppenstedt), Baden-Baden.

Laux, E., 1972. 'Management für die öffentliche Verwaltung?'. *Deutsches Verwaltungsblatt,* pp. 167 ff.

Laux, E., 1994. 'Die Privatisierung des Öffentlichen: Brauchen wir eine neue Kommunalverwaltung? Visionen und Realitäten neuer Steuerungsmodelle'. *Der Gemeindehaushalt,* pp. 169 ff.

Laux, E., 1995. 'Über kommunale Organisationspolitik', In: *Archiv für Kommunalwissenschaften* 34(2), pp. 229–49.

Luhmann, N., 1985. *Soziale Systeme: Grundriss einer allgemeinen Theorie* (2nd ed.), Suhrkamp, Frankfurt am Main.

Mascarenhas, R.C., 1992. 'State intervention in the economy: why is the United States different from other mixed economies?, *Australian Journal of Public Administration,* pp. 385 ff.

Mascarenhas, R.C., 1993. 'Building an enterprise culture in the public sector: reform of the public sector in Australia, Britain and New Zealand'. *Public Administration Review,* pp. 319 ff.

Mayntz, R., 1965. 'Max Webers Idealtypus der Bürokratie und die Organisationssoziologie'. In: J. Fialkowski (ed.), *Politologie und Soziologie, Otto Stammer zum 65. Geburtstag,* Köln und Opladen, pp. 91 ff.

Moe, R.C. and R.S. Gilmore, 1995. 'Rediscovering principles of public administration: the neglected foundation of public law'. *Public Administration Review,* pp. 135 ff.

Müller, R., 1995. 'Neue finanzwirtschaftliche Steuerungsmodelle im kommunalen Bereich – Stand der Entwicklung und haushaltsrechtlicher Änderungsbedarf'. *Verwaltungsrundschau,* pp. 217 ff.

Musgrave, R., P. Musgrave and L. Kullmer, 1990. *Die öffentlichen Finanzen in Theorie und Praxis, Part 1,* Heidelberg (5th ed.).

Naschold, F., 1994. *Modernisierung des Staates. Zur Ordnungs- und Innovationspolitik des öffentlichen Sektors.* Berlin (2nd ed.).

Naschold, F., 1995. *Ergebnissteuerung, Wettbewerb, Qualitätspolitik. Entwicklungspfade des öffentlichen Sektors.* Berlin.

Naschold, F. and M. Pröhl (eds), 1994. *Produktivität öffentlicher Dienstleistungen.* Gütersloh.

Newland, C.A., 1994. 'A field of strangers in search of a discipline: separatism of public management research from public administration'. *Public Administration Review,* pp. 486 ff.

O'Toole, B.J. and J. Grant (eds), 1995. *Next steps: improving management in government?* Aldershot, Hants, England.

OECD/PUMA (eds), 1993. *Public Management Developments.* Survey, Paris.

Osborne, D. and T. Gaebler, 1992. *Reinventing government: how the entrepreneurial spirit is transforming to the public sector.* Reading.

Pitschas, R., 1994. 'Die Jugendverwaltung im marktwirtschaftlichen Wettbewerb? – Balanceprobleme zwischen Rechtmäßigkeit, Wirtschaftlichkeit und Fachlichkeit'. *Die Öffentliche Verwaltung,* pp. 973 ff.

Püttner, G., 1985. *Die öffentlichen Unternehmen. Ein Handbuch zu Verfassungs- und Rechtsfragen der öffentlichen Wirtschaft.* Stuttgart/München/Hannover (2nd ed.).

Püttner, G., 1989. *Verwaltungslehre.* Stuttgart.

Ranadé, W., 1995. 'The theory and practice of managed competition in the National Health Service'. *Public Administration,* pp. 241 ff.

Reinermann, H., 1995. 'Die Krise als Chance: Wege innovativer Verwaltung'. *Speyerer Forschungsberichte,* vol. 139, Speyer.

Ridley, F., 1993. 'Verwaltungsmodernisierung in Großbritannien'. In: H. Hill and H. Klages (eds), *Qualitäts- und erfolgsorientiertes Verwaltungsmanagement. Aktuelle Tendenzen und Entwürfe*, Berlin, pp. 251 ff.

Ridley, F., 1995. 'Die Wiedererfindung des Staates. Reinventing British Government: Das Modell einer Skelettverwaltung'. *Die Öffentliche Verwaltung*, pp. 569 ff.

Röber, M., 1995. 'Über einige Mißverständnisse in der verwaltungswissenschaftlichen Modernisierungsdebatte: Ein Zwischenruf, Manuskript'. To be published in H. Wollmann and Christoph Reichard (eds), *Kommunalverwaltung im Modernisierungsschub*.

Sommermann, K.-P., 1991. 'Die deutsche Verwaltungsgerichtsbarkeit'. *Speyerer Forschungsberichte*, vol. 106, Speyer.

Stillman, R.J., 1991. *Preface to public administration: a search for themes and direction*. New York.

Taylor, F.W., 1911 (1915). *The principles of scientific management*. New York/London.

Thieme, W., 1993. 'Wiederaufbau oder Modernisierung der deutschen Verwaltung'. *Die Verwaltung*, pp. 353 ff.

Thieme, W., 1995. *Einführung in die Verwaltungslehre*. Köln.

Werhahn, P.H., 1990. *Der Unternehmer – seine ökonomische Funktion und gesellschaftspolitische Verantwortung*. Trier.

White, L.D., 1955. *Introduction to the study of public administration*. New York (4th ed.).

Wulf-Mathies, M. and R. Scharping, 1994. *Positionspapier 10 Eckpunkte zur Innovation im öffentlichen Sektor und zur Reform des Sozialstaates vom 5.10.1994* (Manuscript).

CHAPTER FOURTEEN

Administrative Reform and Democratic Accountability

Linda deLeon
University of Colorado at Denver

Over the past decades, a new paradigm for public management has contested with the older bureaucratic model. The contest is not yet decided, although the new paradigm has won over many academics and practitioners. Reform continues to have its critics, whom its advocates should not ignore, for they raise important and difficult issues. This chapter will outline some key features of administrative reform movements in the United States and discuss the most troubling issues inherent in the new paradigm, those relating to the accountability of public organizations to citizens through their political representatives. Finally, a variety of means of resolving these accountability issues will be described.

1.   Administrative Reform in the United States

Administrative reform is an almost constant process. Several waves of change have swept US public administration in recent decades. Among the most important, Total Quality Management (TQM) and related initiatives, such as quality circles, originated in the private sector (which had copied them from Japanese management, who in turn had imported the basic principles from American consultants).

The next wave of reform again originated in the private sector, with the publication of Peters' and Waterman's highly influential book, *In Search of Excellence* (1982). Their eight principles of excellent companies included staying close to the customer, autonomy and entrepreneurship, productivity through people, simple form/lean staff, and simultaneous loose-tight properties. One would expect, of course, that a pair of business-school professors would place their faith in customer service and entrepreneurship, but unexpectedly, their ideas caught on among public managers as well. In 1992, *Reinventing Government*, by David Osborne (a professor and consultant) and Ted Gaebler (a city manager in California), took the public sector by storm. Like Peters and Waterman, they advanced a set of principles, each of which contravened the received doctrine concerning the role and operations of government. These principles included 'steering rather than rowing', empowering rather than serving, injecting competition into service delivery, reducing rules and red tape, an emphasis on results not inputs, service to the customer, and leveraging change through the market.

In the US elections of 1992, both Clinton and Bush vigorously lambasted 'government bureaucracy', always a popular tactic with American voters. Clinton had read and been intrigued by *Reinventing Government*, and when elected, he asked Vice President Gore to undertake the task of fulfilling their campaign pledge to reduce the size of the federal government as well as increase its efficiency. As leader of the so-called National Performance Review (NPR), Vice President Gore – with author Gaebler as a consultant – closely oversaw the production of *Creating a Government That Works Better and Costs Less*. This book, also known as the Gore Report, proposes reductions in paperwork and rules, empowerment of workers *and* increased discretion for managers, emphasis on results, and a focus on customers. The next year Congress passed the Government Performance and Results Act, mandating that all federal agencies develop performance measures and collect data to assess their results.

Recent reform efforts in US public management have been characterized by five key themes. The first is *a critical role for information and technology* (Pindur, Kim and Reynolds, 1993; Swiss, 1992). For the quality movement, this tenet was central. Its premise was that customers value quality – excellence and dependability – even more than low price. To achieve the level of consistent quality that satisfies customers requires reducing variations in the production process to the minimum possible (Bowman, 1994). Perfection (the 'zero defects' standard) is an impressive goal: it necessitates a very deep and thorough knowledge of the technology of production, which in turn depends upon the ongoing collection of appropriate and accurate data. The reinvention movement, too, often employs technological innovation in order to increase productivity. The most radical form of reinventing, termed 'reengineering' (see Linden, 1993 or Hall *et al.*, 1993), calls for scrapping all preconceptions and traditions about how the work is to be done, then redesigning processes from the ground up. Use of high-tech information systems is a common strategy in reengineering.

The second theme is *a passion for customer satisfaction* (Denhardt, 1993; Gore, 1993; Pindur *et al.*, 1993). The quality movement emphasized strong, continuing relationships with customers, suppliers and even with competitors (Aguayo, 1990; Cohen and Eimicke, 1994). Analysts (for example, Drucker, 1988) conceptualized this inclusiveness as a blurring of organization boundaries or as a process of bringing outsiders inside; organizations simply saw it as a good business strategy. Naturally a firm wants to retain its customers, but the willingness to include suppliers and competitors was new to the quality movement. The notion that a firm should maintain stable relations with its suppliers runs counter to the wisdom of always taking the lowest bid, but the quality movement emphasized the advantage of working with a supplier over time to work out problems and create a reliable, high-quality supply of needed materials or services. Also, the quality movement advocated the value of maintaining cooperative relations with competitors, for just as two parties never have all their interests in common, so they are very unlikely to be always at odds. Developing good relationships with competitors means that when the time comes to cooperate, channels of communication and avenues of approach are already open (Aguayo, 1990; Deming, 1986).

Importantly, too, although customer satisfaction was a key feature of quality initiatives, it was not a modernized version of the admonition that 'the customer is always right'. What distinguished the quality movement was its view of the vendor-customer relationship as, essentially, a dialogue (Cohen and Eimicke, 1994). As the two parties continued over time to interact in a two-way 'conversation', each in effect educated the other concerning tastes, preferences, and capabilities.

Third, the reform movement advocates *increased authority for public managers* (Caiden, 1994) over budgeting, purchasing and personnel matters. Since business is still viewed in the US as more efficient than government, administrative reform seeks to give public managers powers more like those of a private-sector executive. In its strong form, this doctrine even counsels the bravado of private-sector entrepreneurs, whose dictum holds that 'it is better to ask forgiveness [for a failure] than for permission [to take a risk].' Another form of this theme is the view that decision making power should be decentralized to the lowest possible level: managers close to service delivery should have more authority over work procedures, hiring, and so forth, than superiors who are more distant from the front lines.

The notion that public sector managers are hampered by rules and regulations in their attempts to be efficient was not new. In a thorough review of the literature, Rainey (1991) found that even controlling for size, government organizations are more centralized and formalized, particularly with respect to financial, procurement and personnel rules. *Reinventing Government*, then, was remarkable not in its advocacy of managerial discretion, but in the strategies it urged to achieve it – reduction in the rules and paperwork governing purchasing, greater authority to hire and fire employees (thus a reduction in the latter's civil service protections), and even financial incentives such as the right to retain savings achieved through reduced costs of operation.

The fourth theme is *flatter organizations peopled by 'empowered' workers* (Caiden, 1994; Denhardt, 1993; Pindur *et al.*, 1993). Not only should managers have more authority, but front-line workers should have the power to make authoritative decisions about work processes. Of course, there have long been those who argued that many public employees have a wide zone of discretion because they operate 'out on the street', away from the eyes of close-supervising managers (Lipsky, 1980). But the reform movement posits this as a virtue rather than a necessity, holding that only front-line workers really know what needs to be fixed, and how to do it, and that empowering them to make decisions permits much faster action than traditional bureaucratic mechanisms could ever do. Thus the quality movement implied a flattening of hierarchy and the empowerment of front-line workers (Cohen and Eimicke, 1994; Swiss, 1992). Not surprisingly, public employee unions have taken up the banner of worker empowerment, calling for greater autonomy and responsibility for front-line workers, investment in training, fewer layers of hierarchy, employment security, and accountability to all the people (IPMA, 1996).

Finally, the fifth theme is *the value of competition in improving government's services*. Like classical economics, this principle holds that competition weeds out inferior products and services: successful entrepreneurs are the fittest and therefore deserve to survive. Also, it is a tenet of faith that in the market the pursuit of individual gain yields the public good through the operation of what Adam Smith called the 'invisible hand'. Osborne and Gaebler (1992) recommend 'injecting competition into service delivery' and the Gore Report suggests both that agencies be allowed to compete with each other and, in some cases, with private firms as well.

2.   Accountability in a Democracy Polity

Critics of administrative reform have made a variety of arguments against it. Some of these have already been mentioned: 'customer' is not an appropriate concept for the people served by government (Swiss, 1992); prescriptions for reform are based on 'best practice' and anecdotal evidence rather than solid research (Overman and Boyd, 1994); some of the anecdotes are not quite accurate (Fallows, 1992; Glastris, 1992) and the innovations touted in the reform literature have not always worked in the longer run (Novotny, 1992).

All these are important issues, but the one that is mentioned in most critical discussions of reform is *accountability*. Moe, for example, asserts bluntly that 'The net result of the Gore Report when its recommendations are implemented to the maximum degree possible ... will be a government much less accountable to the citizens for its performance' (1994, p. 118). He alleges that the 'entrepreneurial paradigm,' with its emphasis on results not processes, undercuts the rule of law by encouraging managers to ignore laws and regulations that impede performance. Further, he contends that devolution of management responsibility to the lowest practicable level means that accountability will no longer be upward, to central management agencies and the President, but outward, to the customer. Increasing the authority and discretion of public managers requires placing greater faith in their abilities and motivations, not in greater control over their actions. Finally, by melting the rigid boundaries between the organizations of government and by creating interagency committees, the Gore Report disperses accountability; by making all participants responsible, it makes no single participant accountable.

Bellone and Goerl (1992) also criticize public entrepreneurship as incompatible with democracy (unless entrepreneurs are also civic-regarding). Because the goals of departments can be hard to measure, they say, giving public managers increased discretion may not result in effective accountability. Furthermore, entrepreneurs who are too eager to take risks – asking forgiveness rather than permission – violate norms of democratic stewardship, unless their ventures are preceded by public information, discussion and formal acceptance.

Accountability is a fundamental and difficult issue in American public administration. The framers of the US Constitution gave detailed attention to each of the three branches of government, but their treatment of the executive was limited to a consideration of the presidency. In fact, the word 'administration' is not used at all in the founding document (Migro and Richardson, 1992). In early days, of course, society and government were simple enough that an elaborate administrative apparatus was unnecessary. As the population and territory of the country expanded, however, various functions were allocated to government, and administrative agencies were 'chinked in' (Stillman, 1991). Since employees of administrative agencies are in almost all cases appointed, not elected, they cannot be subject to a vote of no confidence. Yet they make decisions that are ineluctably political, since they authoritatively allocate valued goods, services, and rights. By what means, then, are administrators endowed with the power to make these political decisions? By what right can public managers, not to mention public employees, act on their own initiative? Such a right must stem from the ultimate source of sovereignty, the people, but how can the people hold the administration accountable?

In the US, the traditional and prevailing view of how accountability should work was set forth by Emmette Redford in *Democracy and the Public Service* (1969). His model, which he called *overhead democracy*, asserted that 'democratic control should run through a single line from the representatives of the people to all those who exercised power in the name of the government. The line ran from the people to their representatives in the Presidency and the Congress, and from there to the President as chief executive, then to departments, then to bureaus, then to lesser units, and so on to the fingertips of administration' (pp. 70–71).

The model was based on the presumption that governmental organizations would be arranged hierarchically ('successive levels of organization, each controlling the level immediately below it') and that they would be politically responsive ('subordinate to political direction and supervision'). Of course this model is too simple – Redford's book is an exploration of the complex, convoluted webs of shared power that more realistically portray American administration – but the fundamental notion that the public sector should be tightly controlled and politically responsive remains part of our political ideology to this day.

The current wave of administrative reform challenges the orthodoxy of overhead democracy. The use of advanced technology may pose a barrier to understanding of government operations for the average citizen. Although high-tech computers may make data more readily available to the cognoscenti, they are intimidating to many Americans.

Increased authority for managers and greater empowerment for workers flies in the face of conventional wisdom that government officials cannot be trusted to act in the public interest and need to be constrained by strict rules and subject to constant scrutiny by their hierarchical superiors. A passion for customer service is problematic, of course, if the agency has mis-identified its customers (if prison administrators thought prisoners, not the general public, were their customers, for example). And interagency competition, like its counterpart in private business, can result in efficiency, but sometimes at the expense of quality, or fairness. In many arenas of government action, the fear that accountability will be diminished by reform is one of the chief obstacles to its implementation.

For those who believe that accountability requires a firm hand, bureaucracy was the apotheosis of tight control; to permit both managers and employees to have greater authority over their actions thus seems to represent a significant *reduction* in accountability, if that term is defined in the usual way. In a reinvented government, then, is accountability inevitably diminished? Or might there be other ways to give public administrators enough leeway to accomplish needed improvements (Romzek and Dubnick, 1994) while still keeping them responsive to the will of the people?

The most important early discussion of accountability in American administration was a pair of articles by Carl Friedrich (1940) and Herbert Finer (1941). Friedrich argued that in a professionalized civil service, the 'inner check' of conscience, created by personal and professional socialization, would restrain government officials from acting in anything other than the public interest. Finer replied that the inner check cannot be relied upon in all instances, and therefore external checks (for example, congressional oversight, bureaucratic rules) must be maintained as well. In subsequent years, analysis of the issue included treatment of the problems created by the large proportion of professional workers in the public service (Mosher, 1968), the discretion held by street-level bureaucrats (Lipsky, 1980), and the necessity for a code of conduct for public administrators. More recently, a more analytic approach, featuring a typology of accountability mechanisms, has been proposed by Barbara Romzek and Melvin Dubnick (1987).

Figure 14.1.   Four Types of Accountability

		Source of Control	
		Internal	*External*
Degree	*High*	Bureaucratic	Legal
of			
Control	*Low*	Professional	Political

Romzek and Dubnick begin by classifying accountability according to whether the *source of control* is (a) internal or (b) external, and whether the *degree of control* is (a) tight or (b) loose.

Bureaucratic accountability systems stress the need to follow orders, and close supervision. Legal accountability obtains when there are two relatively autonomous parties, one that can mandate expectations with the force of law, and another whose responsibility is to implement the law (a fiduciary or principal–agent relationship). *Legal accountability* depends upon monitoring, auditing and other forms of oversight. *Political accountability* allows the agency or administrator to have discretion to decide whether or not to respond to external expectations; its mechanisms involve the participation of the parties whose expectations are relevant (for example, open meetings, freedom of access to information). Finally, *professional accountability* relies upon the integrity and trustworthiness of the expert who has the special skills to get the job done. In a number of case studies analyzed using this scheme (Radin and Romzek, 1994; Romzek and Dubnick, 1987; Romzek and Dubnick, 1994), Romzek and others have concluded that American public administration should rely less upon bureaucratic accountability and more upon the professional type, since it is the administrative professional, not Congress or the average citizen, who has the necessary knowledge to make choices about how best to accomplish the goals of government. Professionals, they suggest, should have the discretion to act, but they can be required after the fact to justify their decisions to appropriate authorities.

Dubnick and Romzek's classification scheme is appropriate, but incomplete. To see why, consider again Redford's model of overhead democracy. In that model, there two links in the chain of accountability that runs from the electorate to the administrator. First, the individual worker is held accountable to his/her organizational superiors, all the way up the chain of command to the top agency executive, by the mechanisms of bureaucratic accountability. If the agency executive is elected (as is often the case in the US, particularly at the local level), then that administrator is directly accountable to the people through the mechanism of political responsiveness. If the agency executive is appointed, then she/he is responsive to the elected officials with the power of appointment, and they in turn are responsive to their electoral constituencies.

In short, Romzek and Dubnick's locus-of-control dimension actually reflects the difference between an *organizational* and an *institutional* level of analysis. Specifically, internal control refers to control mechanisms that are operative *internal to the organization* – the organizational level of analysis. That is, bureaucratic and professional control systems are ways of managing the behavior of employees within an agency (deLeon, 1976).

The external control dimension is not about managing employees, however, but about the ways in which society (or the electorate) keeps a measure of control over the institution of administration. In the legal type of accountability, for example, we might find judicial monitoring of a school district's compliance with law requiring racial integration. In such a case, one institution (the court) is controlling another (the school district); it does not control employees of the school district as individuals – the norms of the teaching profession and the bureaucratic apparatus of the district do that.

Having thus distinguished two levels of accountability, institutional and organizational, we also need to expand the varieties of accountability at each level. To do so in part reflects the difference between being held responsible for *results*, or goal attainment, versus being held responsible for *process*, or the means used to obtain a goal. In the common view, bureaucratic accountability is tight because workers must follow rules, while professional accountability is loose because these workers are responsible for results but have discretion over means. In fact, control of either dimension can be independently tight or loose. For example, when an agency is given a clearly-specified target and when failure to achieve the target will bring unfavorable consequences, it would be subject to *tight accountability for results*. A less specific target coupled with minimally unfavorable consequences (or uncertain ones) would constitute loose accountability for results.

On the other hand, an agency might be required to use particular means to achieve its mission, that is, it would face *tight accountability for process*. Under tight accountability, these means would be clearly specified and failure to comply would produce unfavorable consequences with considerable certainty. For example, a critical means by which public managers achieve organization goals is the hiring of qualified employees. Affirmative action policies in the US mandate efforts to recruit and hire minorities (blacks, Asians, Hispanics) and women. Tight accountability would occur when managers were required to hire precise quotas of these 'protected classes' of employees; loose accountability would occur if the targets were not specific or where good faith efforts at recruitment and selection were enough to satisfy judicial or legislative overseers.

Thus far, we have amended the Romzek and Dubnick scheme to suggest that control of individual employees within organizations can be tight (bureaucratic) or loose (professional), and that external (institution-level) control over the organizations themselves can be tight or loose with respect to results or means. To advance this analysis a step further, it will be helpful to use a typology that sorts organizations (or systems) according to characteristics of their task environments.

3.   Accountability and the Task Environment

Thompson and Tuden (1959) offer a simple framework for organizing some thoughts about organization structures, based on the premise that decision making is the central organizational act. They posit two important dimensions of decision situations. Firstly, are the goals to be achieved clear or ambiguous? Secondly, are the means for their achievement known and certain, or *un*known and *un*certain? Crossing these two dimensions yields the space portrayed in Figure 14.2.

Figure 14.2. Decision Characteristics and System Structure

		Preferences Regarding Outcomes:	
		Agreement	*Disagreement*
Beliefs About	*Certain*	Bureaucracy	Pluralistic competition
Cause-Effect Relation	*Uncertain*	Community	Anarchy

The top left corner of the space identifies situations where goals are clear and means certain. In this case, decisions can be made simply, by calculation, to use Thompson and Tuden's term. The organization structure appropriate to this kind of decision is a bureaucracy or, more generally, a hierarchy, with the attributes (division of labor, specialization, centralization, and so on) that Max Weber and his intellectual heirs made common knowledge.

In the top right corner of the space, decisions involve ambiguous or conflicting goals. If the conflicts could be settled or the ambiguities clarified, however, the path to their achievement would be clear, using well-understood means. In a democratic society, decisions about goals are (in theory) made in the political system, by a process of bargaining, negotiation, compromise and coalition-building. After goals are settled upon, implementation can be handled by a bureaucracy. Note that the aim of the political process is to decide upon a single, clear goal: the struggle for power ends when one or another of the contesting parties is victorious. In a pluralistic political system, the arena in which political decisions are made contains multiple contenders who compete for power, with the competition being alternately resolved by elections and then renewed. At any one time, whichever party holds power is able to make authoritative decisions for the collectivity.

Where there is consensus on goals but the means to achieve them are uncertain (that is, in the lower left corner of Figure 14.2), everyone with relevant expertise is invited to offer input, with decisions being reached by consensus. Organization structures appropriate to this kind of decision making are fairly flat, since status gradations would inhibit lower participants' willingness to contribute opinions. The traditional professions, guilds and clans are some examples of this form. These organizations or systems can be called 'communities', because they are flat, cohesive, and grounded in shared values (desired ends).

Thompson and Tuden suggest that in the lower right corner of Figure 14.2, where goals are ambiguous *and* the means to achieve them uncertain, decisions are made by 'inspiration', and the structure appropriate to such decisions is termed 'anomic'. A more recent portrayal is facetiously labeled the 'garbage can' model by its creators, Cohen, March and Olsen (1972). In the garbage can, decision situations are highly ambiguous: no single set of preferences represents the organization's intentions, and cause-effect connections are obscure. Thus problems and solutions (goals and means) roll around until, occasionally, a problem meets a solution that fits, and organizational action is possible. In this seemingly chaotic situation, there are no experts in possession of answers. Cohen *et al.* call garbage-can structures 'organized anarchies', citing three defining conditions: problematic preferences (ambiguous or conflicting goals), unclear technology, and fluid participation.[1]

The foregoing discussion may seem to suggest that the nature of the task environment in which public organizations operate may be entirely a function of objective conditions – goal clarity, good theories of cause and effect. A moment's thought, however, should remind us that the line between goals and means is slippery – one goal may be the means to another, higher, goal. Furthermore, organizations almost never deal in just one kind of decision. Therefore, although models of organization structure are affected by the contingencies of technology and environment, and although preferences among models are shaped by culture and experience, there is still a certain amount of possibility for choice: the problem-space of public organizations is, at least in part, socially constructed.

In the past few decades, the American consensus about the nature of government's problems has changed. What once seemed simple and straightforward now seems hopelessly complex. With respect to goals, we no longer find consensus but rather diversity. Where once we blithely assumed that all the heterogeneous kinds of people streaming into the country could be amalgamated in the great melting pot, we now are convinced that there are immense differences of opinion resulting from diversity, and that these differences are proving extremely resistant to old-fashioned techniques of consensus-building or, failing that, compromise.

Just as we increasingly believe that there is little consensus on public goals, we also have less faith in human ability to understand cause and effect, which is the inevitable result of the huge and obvious failure of research, conducted over decades, to solve deadly social problems such as crime, drug abuse, domestic violence, child abuse, and the rest of that terrible horde. The net result of both trends – toward thinking goal consensus is impossible and knowledge of means elusive – is to see chaos everywhere.

In summary to this point, then, the conventional wisdom concerning accountability in the US system was formed in an era characterized by great faith in know-how, or knowledge about means. Consequently, the accountability issue was thought to be one of resolving conflicting choices of ends; after resolution was achieved in the political system, government's problem was simply to create a bureaucracy to implement the agreed-upon policy. The problem-space for government organizations lay entirely along the top of Figure 14.2. Today's problems, by contrast, are thought to be much more complex, both because the political opinion is more divided and because technical expertise is inadequate. The task environment lies predominantly in the lower half of the diagram, and consequently, accountability must be handled differently.

4. Accountability in Reformed Governments

Contemporary administrative reform efforts give increased discretion to managers – and, in some cases, to empowered front-line employees as well – representing movement from internal control mechanisms that are bureaucratic to ones that are professional. In addition, at the institutional level, reform emphasizes accountability for results rather than strict rules governing process. This represents movement from external control mechanisms that are fiduciary to those that are politically responsive. But accountability for results implies agreement on goals. The foregoing argument, on the other hand, suggests that a growing set of situations are in the problem-space of anarchy. In this section, we will briefly discuss internal accountability under reform. Next, examples of accountability mechanisms that are appropriate where either goals or means can be agreed upon will be described; and finally, accountability under anarchic conditions will be explored.

As Romzek and Dubnick suggest, professional accountability is more appropriate than bureaucratic control for many, perhaps most, organizations of contemporary government. Within organizations, goal clarity is largely assumed, since the most basic definition of organization is 'a collection of people acting to achieve common goals.' But often there is uncertainty concerning how to solve the problems that are within the organization's mission. Thus, professional accountability – Carl Friedrich's notion of the 'inner check' (1940) that constrains the ideal public manager – is the most suitable form.

In the traditional professions, values and a code of conduct were inculcated during a long and arduous training process and enforced by peer pressure. The intensive socialization that creates a conscience, however, is more readily achieved in communities or hierarchies than under competitive pluralism or anarchy. As noted above, however, where cause-effect knowledge is highly imperfect, it makes no sense to punish people simply because unpleasant consequences have followed from their choices. This kind of accountability is characteristic of the traditional professions. Physicians, for example, are not liable for a patient's death merely because their diagnoses or choices of treatment were incorrect. Only if they acted with demonstrable negligence can their conduct be considered criminal.

Another method for maintaining accountability, which can be used either for control over individuals or over organizations, is performance contracting. Such a mechanism requires that there be agreement over what goals (desired results) are to be achieved. At the individual level, performance contracting is the familiar MBO, management by objectives. An analogous method for use at the organizational level had been proposed by Perry (1993). In Perry's view, a manager's professional discretion is compromised when rules are too numerous, too hard to understand, and (even when understandable) not helpful. Instead of proliferating rules, therefore, Perry recommends performance contracts between the central government and line agencies, contracts that articulate goals, identify objectives, and measure progress.

The central department would be responsible for oversight of the activities of decentralized units, for coordination of policies among them, and for integration of certain functions, such as information processing. The line agencies themselves would be responsible for creating specific policies to fit their own mission and organizational culture. The advantage of such a proposal is that it allocates a high degree of autonomy to departments and locates accountability for management where it is used, by program units and line managers. Also it shifts attention from compliance with rules to demonstration of results.

Where there is diversity of opinion concerning goals, but where an organization can foster agreements among its members on a set of basic principles of operation (means), accountability can take the form of what Davenport *et al.* (1989) have called 'design principles'. They describe a geographically dispersed conglomerate firm that wanted to decentralize its information-systems function but at the same time standardize its computing hardware and data handling. The problem was that the technical experts in the management information systems (MIS) department were not aware of the organization's overall business strategy or the details of business operations, while general managers did not have technical expertise to oversee MIS. The solution was to create a set of design principles – simple, direct statements about how the agency wanted to use information systems over the long term. The process of creating design principles involved both senior managers and a roughly equal number of technical experts acting as a 'study team'. A draft set of principles was created by the team and pilot-tested by using them to make decisions on some current issues. After the principles were revised and approved by senior management, all the MIS managers were trained in their use. Then managers were given discretion to make decisions on their own, but they could be called to account for those decisions and required to explain their actions by showing how they conformed to the design principles.

The last situation, where there is agreement on neither goals nor means, is the most difficult. If goals are ambiguous or conflicting (or results hard to measure), there is no standard by which performance can be judged. If cause-effect knowledge is absent, administrators cannot be blamed for choosing the wrong means, since no one knows the right one. In the chaos of the anarchic situation, none of the conventional accountability mechanisms would be appropriate. The only way to link organizational action to public preferences would be through direct participation in the work of the organization.

Organized anarchies (Cohen *et al.*, 1972) produce decisions when a problem (something that needs to be done) meets a choice (a program that could potentially solve the problem). If public preferences are diverse, more than one problem might attach itself to a particular solution, or more than one solution to a particular problem. Where preferences are diverse, there would be no unified public will to which a public manager could be held responsible – but there would be the particular will of the citizens who had participated in a particular decision. If means are uncertain, every citizen's expertise would be potentially valuable; that is, there would be no reason to suppose that experts exist whose opinions should carry greater weight. Participation would permit citizens to engage in those issues about which they are most concerned. Their control would be exercised *ab origine*, from their having shaped the agency's decisions as they were made.

Under the banner of the New Public Administration of the 1970s, there were some experiments with citizen participation. The programs were not often successful, but their failures may have resulted in part from their being grafted onto old-style hierarchical organizations (Emmert, Crow and Shangraw, 1991). If designed into public programs from the start – into mission statements, operating procedures, and the structure and staffing of programs – participation may prove more workable. Inclusion of constituencies in the early stages of policy formulation and design by empaneling randomly selected citizens has been proposed (deLeon, 1992) as a means of achieving a more democratic, participatory policy analysis.

Another approach has been suggested by Thomas (1990). He offers managers a sequence of seven binary choices, resulting in a decision tree with fourteen different branches. Each branch is matched with one of five types of decision making, ranging from an autonomous managerial decision (no public participation), through public consultation (with the public as a unitary group or with a segment of the public), to full public participation in the decision. Thomas' assessment of several published cases found that 'for almost every branch and decision making style, effective decisions mostly follow use of the right approach; ineffective decisions mostly follow use of a wrong approach' (p. 440).

In conclusion, there are a variety of mechanisms by which public managers and employees can be held accountable, which do not involve bureaucratic mechanisms and which are appropriate to decision arenas where goals or means, or both, are a matter of disagreement.

5. Summary

Administrative reform efforts in the United States have centered on the use of technology to improve efficiency, increased discretion for managers, empowerment of front-line workers, service to the government's 'customers', and placing government agencies in competition with other agencies or even with private firms. These initiatives, however, do not fit easily with traditional notions of accountability in a democratic system. In reformed or 'reinvented' government, internal control becomes more professional than bureaucratic, and external control becomes loose rather than tight. Yet through such mechanisms as performance contracts or design principles, individuals or agencies can be called to account for their decisions.

The most difficult problems – and government's tasks are increasingly believed to lie in this realm – are those for which there is no certain knowledge of the means to ameliorate them and no agreement concerning desired ends. In these chaotic circumstances, the only appropriate accountability must be through direct participation – by citizens, groups, other agencies and all others whose interests are at stake. The challenge is to identify correctly the varying task environments in each sphere of government action and to use mechanisms of accountability that are appropriate in that arena.

Note

1. Elsewhere (deLeon, 1994) I have used the term 'network' to describe anarchic organizations or systems. Networks are coordinative structures of various types, such as policy networks, interorganizational or intergovernmental networks, or issue networks (Heclo, 1978). They are flat and loosely structured, having neither a central authority (the appropriate image is a fishnet, not a spider web) nor rigid boundaries. Unlike communities, in which the members have many shared values and interests, networks are characterized by *overlapping* interests of members (though no one interest or value may be shared by all). Of course, actual organizations and systems fall everywhere along the spectrum from anarchy to community; particular networks may be nearer to one or the other pole.

References

Aguayo, R., 1990. *Dr. Deming: the American who taught the Japanese about quality*. Simon & Schuster, New York.

Bellone, C.J. and G.F. Goerl, 1992. 'Reconciling public entrepreneurship and democracy'. *Public Administration Review*, vol. 52(2), pp. 130–34.

Bowman, J.T., 1994. 'At last, an alternative to performance appraisal: total quality management'. *Public Administration Review*, vol. 54(2), pp. 129–36.

Caiden, G.E., 1994. 'Administrative reform – American style'. *Public Administration Review*, vol. 54(2), pp. 123–8.

Cohen, M.D., J.G. March and J.P. Olsen, 1972. 'A garbage can model of organizational choice'. *Administrative Science Quarterly*, 17, pp. 1–25.

Cohen, S. and W. Eimicke, 1994. 'Project-focused total quality management in the New York City department of parks and recreation'. *Public Administration Review*, vol. 54(5), pp. 450–56.

Davenport, T.H., M. Hammer and T.J. Metsisto, 1989. 'How executives can shape their company's information systems'. *Harvard Business Review*, vol. 89(2), pp. 130–34.

deLeon, L.W., 1976. 'Professional and bureaucratic processes of organizational control: internal discipline in the Los Angeles police department'. Unpublished Dissertation, University of California at Los Angeles.

deLeon, L., 1994. 'Embracing anarchy: network organizations and interorganizational networks'. *Administrative Theory and Praxis*, vol. 16(2), pp. 234–53.

deLeon, P., 1992. 'The democratization of the policy sciences'. *Public Administration Review*, vol. 52(2), pp. 125–9.

Deming, E.W., 1986. *Out of the crisis*. MIT Center of Advanced Engineering, Cambridge, MA.

Denhardt, R.B., 1993. *The pursuit of significance*. Wadsworth Publishing Company, Belmont, CA.

Drucker, P.F., 1988. 'Tomorrow's restless managers'. *Industry Week*, pp. 25–7.

Emmert, M.A., M.M. Crow and R.F. Shangraw Jr., 1991. *Public management in the future: post-orthodoxy and organization design.* Paper presented at the National Public Management Research Conference, Syracuse, New York.

Fallows, J., 1992. 'A case for reform'. *The Atlantic Monthly*, pp. 119–23.

Finer, H., 1941. 'Administrative responsibility in democratic government'. *American Political Science Review*, vol. 1, pp. 335–50.

Friedrich, C.J., 1940. 'Public policy and the nature of administrative responsibility'. *Public Policy*, vol. 1, pp. 3–24.

Glastris, P., 1992. 'Paradigm glossed'. *Washington Monthly*, April, pp. 39–49.

Gore, A., 1993. *Creating a government that works better and costs less.* Penguin Books USA, Inc., New York.

Hall, G., J. Rosenthal and J. Wade, 1993. 'How to make reengineering really work'. *Harvard Business Review*, vol. 71(6), pp. 119–31.

Heclo, H., 1978. 'Issue networks and the executive establishment'. In: A. King (ed.), *The new political system*, The American Enterprise Institute for Public Policy, Washington, DC, pp. 87–124.

International Personnel Managers Association, 1996. 'AFSCME examines redesigning government'. *IPMA News*, January, p. 2.

Linden, R., 1993. 'Business process reengineering: newest fad, or revolution in government'. *PM: Public Management*, vol. 75(12), pp. 8–12.

Lipsky, M. 1980. *Street-level bureaucracy.* Russell Sage Foundation, New York.

Moe, R.C., 1994. 'The "reinventing government" exercise: misinterpreting the problem, misjudging the consequences'. *Public Administration Review*, vol. 54(2), pp. 111–22.

Mosher, F.C., 1968. *Democracy and the public service.* Oxford University Press, New York.

Nigro, L.G. and W.D. Richardson, 1992. 'The "founders" unsentimental view of public service in the American regime'. In: P.W. Ingraham and D.F. Kettl (eds), *Agenda for excellence: public service in America*, Chatham House Publishers, Inc., Chatham, NJ, pp. 3–21.

Novotny, T.W., 1992. 'Government needs evolution, not revolution'. *PA Times*, 1 June, pp. 15–16.

Osborne, D. and T. Gaebler, 1992. *Reinventing government.* Addison-Wesley, Reading, MA.

Overman, E.S. and K.J. Boyd, 1994. 'Best practice research and postbureaucratic reform'. *Journal of Public Administration Research and Theory*, vol. 4(1), pp. 57–67.

Perry, J.L., 1993. 'Strategic human resource management: transforming federal civil service to meet future challenges'. *LaFollette Policy Report*, vol. 5(2), pp. 15–19.

Peters, T.J. and R.H. Waterman Jr., 1982. *In search of excellence.* Harper & Row, Publishers, Inc., New York.

Pindur, W., P.S. Kim and K.R. Reynolds, 1993. 'Reformulating organizational culture: the key to total quality management in the public sector'. Paper presented at the Annual meeting of the American Society for Public Administration, San Francisco, CA.

Radin, B. and B. Romzek, 1994. 'Accountability in an intergovernmental arena: new governance and the national rural development partnership'. Paper presented at the Annual Meeting of the American Political Science Association, New York City, NY.

Rainey, H.G., 1991. *Understanding and managing public organizations.* Jossey-Bass, San Francisco.

Redford, E.S., 1969. *Democracy in the administrative state.* Oxford University Press, NY.

Romzek, B.S. and M.J. Dubnick, 1987. 'Accountability in the public sector: lessons from the challenger tragedy'. *Public Administration Review*, vol. 47(3), pp. 227–38.

Romzek, B.S. and M.J. Dubnick, 1994. 'Issues of accountability in flexible personnel systems'.

In: P.W. Ingraham and B.S. Romzek (eds), *New paradigms for government*, Jossey-Bass Inc., Publishers, San Francisco, pp. 263–94.

Stillman, R.J., II, 1991. *Preface to public administration*. St. Martin's Press, Inc., NY.

Swiss, J.E., 1992. 'Adapting total quality management (TQM) to government'. *Public Administration Review*, vol. 52(4), pp. 356–62.

Thomas, J.C., 1990. 'Public involvement in public management: adapting and testing a borrowed theory'. *Public Administration Review*, vol. 50(4), pp. 435–45.

Thompson, J.D. and A. Tuden, 1959. 'Strategies, structures and processes of organizational decision'. In: J.D. Thompson (ed.), *Comparative studies in administration*. University of Pittsburgh Press, Pittsburgh.

Part Four

Epilogue

CHAPTER FIFTEEN

A North American Perspective on Administrative Modernization in Europe

B. Guy Peters
University of Pittsburgh

1. Introduction

Administrative change of many varieties, implemented under rubrics such as 're-form' and 'modernization', has been a preoccupation of many governments during the past ten to fifteen years. We can easily tick off a list of dozens of reform projects, large and small, in the industrialized democracies, and publications such as those of the OECD provide long lists of those changes. What is perhaps most remarkable about this reform activity in the public sector is how widely it has been dispersed. Even countries such as Japan which, at least externally, appear to be performing extremely well, have invested heavily in administrative reform (Krauss and Muramatsu, 1996). It is difficult to find any country in which there have not been some efforts to promote significant changes in the public sector. This is even true for countries of the third world who are being required to implement adminis-trative reform as a condition of receiving assistance from organizations like the World Bank.

Although there has been a great deal of managerial modernization activity around the world, that activity has been far from uniform. This is true both for the amount of reform activity being undertaken and for the types of change being attempted. There certainly has been some diffusion and some learning across countries (Olsen and Peters, 1996) but there also are distinct individual national and regional styles of administration that persist. The question that this chapter will address is whether the North Atlantic constitutes a meaningful boundary for categorization of coun-tries when we consider administrative reform. Is there a reform style that character-izes North America[1] and which, in turn, tends to make the modernization process in Europe appear somewhat peculiar to visitors from the New World? Despite their significant institutional differences are Canada and the United States more alike than they (almost certainly the Canadians) would like to admit? Or is Canada really a 'geographically challenged' European country with little in common, other than their common border, with its neighbor to the south? Luc Rouban has written about the end of French specificity (1990), but there may be a North American specificity that persists.

The null hypothesis, of course, is that the processes of change and the contents of change are more similar than dissimilar across the Atlantic and it is the general nature of government in wealthy democracies that defines the character of the reforms. More specifically, it may be that the United States and Canada share a great deal with the rest of the Anglo-American world (Savoie, 1994), so that this cultural tradition is more relevant than is simple geography in defining patterns of reform. Thus, it may be more appropriate to interpret changes in the United Kingdom as a part of an Anglo-Saxon tradition rather than as part of an emerging European pattern. While that tradition might be important for many aspects of administration, reform initiatives in North America appear to be significantly different from those in the Antipodes and the United Kingdom (Aucoin, 1996).

In addition, we should be careful in assuming that there is a single European pattern of administrative modernization. For example, the Netherlands appears to be adopting the agency model used in the United Kingdom (and borrowed from the Scandinavian countries) but this model is not being copied so directly in other European countries. Similarly, the 'quality movement' is being implemented in a number of countries across Europe (Pollitt and Bouckaert, 1995) but is not particularly evident in the Scandinavian countries, at least in that particular guise. The Scandinavian countries have, however, been very successful in implementing personnel management reforms such as pay for performance (Laegreid, 1994; Sjölund, 1994). Finally, Germany and Switzerland have been relatively uninterested in major administrative change, at least not on the level of their federal governments (Kloti, 1996; Reichard, this volume).

As with most conjectures in the social sciences there is some evidence that would support both sides of this debate. In some ways North American governments do appear a distinctive set of administrative systems, as do those in Europe appear distinctive. On the other hand, there are some important similarities. We will present some of the evidence for both sides of the argument and then attempt to reach some sort of conclusion about the North American perspective on reform.

2.   North American Exceptionalism

There are several points at which the reforms being considered in North America tend to diverge from those in Europe. Some issues which arise in Europe simply are not relevant for the North American countries and reform initiatives that are being implemented successfully west of Greenland might be anathema in Europe. Even the term 'modernization' to describe administrative change reflects some significant differences between North American and European conceptions of governing

(Olsen, 1991), as well as differences in the conceptualization of politics more generally. On the other hand, several of the issues which are provoking substantial controversy in North America are already extremely common in European adminis- tration, as well as in the Antipodes (Zifcak, 1994). The exceptionalism is perhaps especially evident for the United States, but in several instances Canada is the country where traditional patterns of governance are being dismantled more rapidly and successfully.

Participation

One distinctive pattern of thinking about the public sector in North America is the participatory, or populist (Kazin, 1995), ethos concerning the public sector. The distinguishing feature of that strand of governance is the long history of creating mechanisms for popular involvement in government decision making. Even with the existence of a number of mechanisms, there has been a drive to extend and enhance that style of decision making during the contemporary reform process. Certainly there are elements of participatory reform in the modernizations now occurring in European government, but arguably these changes are relatively meager in comparison to either the existing modes of citizen involvement and some plans for subsequent reforms, in the North American countries.

Populist thinking about government is more developed in the United States than in Canada. At the state and local level instruments such as the referendum, initiative and recall permit the public to shape legislation, or to overturn decisions by the legislature or the executive (Cronin, 1989). Further, requirements for open public hearings for a variety of decisions – ranging from zoning to budgeting – permit a great deal of mass public involvement in local government. Even at the federal level the right of the public to participate in both formal and informal rule-making (Kerwin, 1994) by the bureaucracy and additional requirements for public hearings for some policies, make the system more open than would be true in most European countries.

As noted above Canada does not have as strong a participatory ethos as does the United States, especially at the federal level, although there have been significant opportunities for participation at the provincial level. Contemporary reforms of the Canadian system are, however, stressing enhanced involvement of the public. Con- sultation is one of the more frequently heard words about reform in Canada (Varette, 1993; Aronson, 1993; Van Nijhatten and Gregoire, 1995), as is 'empowerment' of clients (Tellier, 1990; Kernaghan, 1992). Consultation has even become evident in the previously closed budgetary process (Lindquist, 1994). Given its Westminster tradition it is very unlikely that Canada will ever become as plebescitarian as subnational government in the United States can be, but there are certainly some movements in that direction.

The above having been said, however, one of the most remarkable experiments ever undertaken with the devolution of government powers and administration is now under way in Canada. This experiment is the devolution of power to the First Nations and the creation of virtually autonomous governments within the territory known as Canada. The negotiations over the exact details of this devolution are not complete, but any of the proposed models would involve creation of largely self-governing bodies (perhaps with extra-territorial jurisdiction) while maintaining a good deal of funding from the central government (Howlett, 1994; Taylor-Henry and Hudson, 1992).

For both the United States and Canada, the contemporary reform movement appears to be motivated by a negative, right-wing populism rather than the more government-oriented populism characteristic of past reforms (Stephenson, 1995; Walczak, 1995; Harrison, 1995). That is, rather than looking to government as the central mechanism for protecting the public against the excesses of big business and other powerful economic interests, the new populism tends to conceptualize government as part of the problem rather than as part of the solution. In this emerging version of populism public participation is utilized primarily to counter-act the institutional power of elected and appointed officials, especially the govern-mental elite's powers to raise taxes and increase public expenditures (Angle, 1994). The assumption driving this version of populism is that if government will simply get out of their way and out of their pockets, the people will be able to solve their own problems.

Certainly there are many elements of participatory politics and administration in Europe. Switzerland has a very clear history of governing through referenda and communal participation (Germann, 1981; Frenkel, 1994). Likewise, corporatist intermediation between state and society has some strongly participatory features, although the structured nature of interactions can at times limit participation as much as fostering it (Michiletti, 1990).[2] Further, some modernizations of European administrations now being implemented are designed to make government more open to the public. One of these reforms is the Citizen's Charter in place in Britain and now being spread to other countries. Despite its well-documented weaknesses (Connolly and McKeown, 1994), the Citizen's Charter does open British govern-ment to greater involvement by the public than has been possible in the past. In addition, the decentralization and deconcentration of government decision making in Europe (see below) also may make the public more relevant for decisions.

Reinvention and Deregulation

Although Osborne and Gaebler have been travelling the lecture circuit around the world, 'reinventing' government remains very much a North American concept. Not only is the basic text (1992) extremely American in style and substance, but the major exercises in reinvention also have been in North America, and especially in the United States. Most of the examples of reinvention have been drawn from subnational government, but some of the ideas have now spread to the federal level. The Gore Commission (National Performance Review, 1993) and the Winter Commission at the state level (Ehrenhalt, 1993), for example, were clearly guided by the ideas (sic?) of reinvention and reinvention laboratories now have been initiated in all federal departments as a result of the Gore Report. Reinvention *per se* has not been adopted at the national level in Canada (McDavid and Marson, 1991), although that has been advocated, but it has had a number of manifestations at the subnational level (Borins, 1995).

The problem with 'reinvention' is that, beyond a few now famous slogans ('Steer rather than row', 'Earn rather than spend'), it is not entirely clear what the term means. While this vagueness provides reformers a great deal of latitude to develop ways to make government more efficient, it is also vexing when attempting to understand the direction of change in the public sector. Perhaps the one defining feature of reinvention is a disregard of some of the conventions associated with traditional public administration and an associated desire to rethink government operations from the ground up. For example, many of the examples of how to reinvent government contained in the now canonical text have been argued by critics (grounded in more traditional models of government) to border on illegality. These practices certainly would not be acceptable to more legalistic administrative systems such as those found in Germany and other countries operating in the Germanic administrative tradition. These reinvention concepts have not even translated easily to the Canadian federal government with its well-institutionalized public service ethos.

As well as reinvention, some of the reform activity in the North American world has been in the direction of 'deregulating' the public sector (Barzelay, 1992; DiIulio and Nathan, 1994; Wilson, 1994). The fundamental concept is that a principal cause of inefficiencies identified in the public sector is the number of internal rules and regulations that have been developed to impose *ex ante* controls on managers and management. These controls include personnel rules (Horner, 1994), rigid pay schedules, budgeting rules, restrictive purchasing laws (Kelman, 1994) and a host of other regulations. The assumption is that if the public sector can eliminate these restraints then it can become more businesslike and more efficient.

Again, especially in the United States, these internal rules have been developed in response to a pervasive distrust of the public sector, and public bureaucracy in particular and often reflect the desire of Congress to micro-manage the public sector as a way of gaining easy political points with their constituents (Gilmour and Halley, 1994; Fisher, 1991). As well as any government-wide controls over personnel and budgeting, Congressional committees will impose particular regulations and controls on agencies to ensure that those agencies do not exercise discretion in a way that will damage the political fortunes of the committee members.

The deregulatory movement differs from the widespread use of market models in Europe in part by not having any clear substitute for the rules and hierarchy that are being abolished by reform.[3] In many of the European reforms instruments such as internal markets are being implemented to substitute for the control that had been provided through hierarchy (Jerome-Forget, White and Wiener, 1995). In addition, there is perhaps less need for deregulation in most European countries, given the relative absence of the detailed rules and regulations that have been used to control bureaucracy in the United States and, to a somewhat lesser degree, in Canada. As we will point out below, some of the deregulatory goals for administration in the United States (decentralized personnel administration for example) have been common for years in many European countries.

The adoption of ideas like 'reinvention' and 'deregulation' represents another feature of reform and modernization in North America – the ready adoption of gimmicks as an attempt to solve real problems in the public sector. This has resulted in a 'Baskin-Robbins' approach to governance, with a flavor of the month for reform (White and Wolf, 1995). This to some extent reflects the close connection between the public and private sectors in the United States, and the borrowing of many techniques from business. It further reflects the absence of a real theory about governing and the state, and the consequent attraction of quick fixes for complex problems.

3.   Why Are We Not Surprised and Amazed?

With so much reform activity going on on both sides of the Atlantic and all around the world, some reforms appear extremely innovative and startling and others excite little more than a yawn among outsiders. When we look at contemporary administrative modernization in Europe from the perspective of North American traditions and contemporary reforms, there are changes occurring in several European countries that appear extremely familiar. Indeed, for North Americans these changes may be little more than institutionalizing components of an appropriate system of public management. The same changes are, however, the source of substantial discussion within those European administrative systems.

Similarly, there are some institutionalized components of administration in Europe that have represented major challenges to the status quo in North America when they have been proposed and administratively we sometimes see ourselves as laggards. Looking at these events and non-events (at least when seen from the opposite sides of the Atlantic) can help illuminate the nature of administration, and administrative reform, in the two continents. Further, this discussion will emphasize the role of context and comparison in understanding almost all political phenomena, not least of which is public administration.

European Changes in the North American Style

This chapter is intended primarily as a North American perspective on the modernization of European public administration and therefore we will begin with a discussion of European changes that appear familiar to us North Americans. We can identify more similarities in these changes to public administration and management already existing in the United States, but some of the emerging features in Europe also would appear familiar to Canadians. Also, we will attempt to be careful in nuancing the discussion, given that Europe is substantially less homogenous even than North America and consequently there are several different administrative traditions producing and implementing contemporary reforms.

Agency structure

One of the more important structural changes in European reforms is the creation of 'agencies' or semi-autonomous organizations responsible for the implementation of public programs. Large, integrated departmental structures headed by a minister are being disaggregated into a large number of executive agencies responsible for implementing services, with each agency responsible for one or a limited number of services. A much smaller policy, planning and coordination staff remains lodged in the department. This style of reform has been most visible and perhaps most contentious, in the United Kingdom in the form of the 'Next Steps' program (Greer, 1994), but analogous programs are also being implemented in the Netherlands and Denmark (Kickert, 1995). Of course, for Northern European countries the agency structure (Petersson and Söderlind, 1992) has been in place for a number of years and the administrative system of Sweden to some extent functioned as the basis for the Next Steps program in the United Kingdom (Kemp, 1990).

Implementing these structural reforms in Britain has created some consternation and a massive outpouring of academic writing, but for Americans the changes do not appear at all revolutionary. Many administrative agencies within American cabinet departments have operated autonomously for years (Crenson and Rourke, 1987). The formal separation between agencies located within a cabinet department and the central departmental structure itself is perhaps not so great as in the United Kingdom (or in the Swedish template for the Next Steps reform) but in practice it often is. Also, many of the agencies themselves are multi-purpose, rather than the more narrowly circumscribed organizations implied in the British reforms. For example, the United States Coast Guard is responsible for the safety of recreational boaters, enforcing a variety of standards in the shipping industry, traffic control in harbors and on navigable rivers and has some responsibility in interdicting smuggling. It must also be prepared to become part of the US Navy in times of war.

The cabinet departments in the US federal government have been described as 'holding companies' (Seidman and Gilmour, 1986), with their constituent agencies, offices, and bureaus being the important operating elements of the federal bureaucracy. These agencies have closer contacts with client groups, tend also to have closer contacts with Congressional committees than do the departments themselves and generally constitute the principle focus of government action. In addition to the numerous agencies comprising the cabinet departments there are a number (approximately 40) of independent executive agencies that report directly to the President. Some of these independent agencies are major policy organizations, for example, the Environmental Protection Agency or the Veterans Administration prior to 1988, although most are relatively small and mono-functional, for example, the National Aeronautics and Space Administration or the National Labor Relations Authority. Two central agencies – the Office of Personnel Management and the General Services Administration – also fall into this category of organizations.

The Canadian federal government still retains most of its traditional governmental structure, with large cabinet departments performing most functions. If anything, the recent reforms and consolidations of departments have tended to move Canada away from an agency structure and towards 'mega-departments', each performing a number of different functions (Aucoin and Bakvis, 1993; Seidle, 1993). There are, however, several experiments with agencies in Canada. First, the Crown Corporation is a long-established structural element of government that has some features of executive agencies in other settings (Laux and Molot, 1988). The Canadian government more recently has been experimenting in a limited way with 'Special Operating Agencies', very similar to the executive agencies in Britain, as a means of delivering some services (Wex, 1990; Clark, 1991; Wright, 1995). Thus, even if not yet as fully institutionalized as in the United States, the idea of the agency is not antithetical to Canadian government (Pullen, 1994).

Even for countries that are not engaged in a major exercise in agency creation, there is some movement towards more autonomous organizations and quasi-governmental organizations (Modeen and Rosas, 1988). For example, in France, the traditional unitary ministerial structure is being modified by the creation of autonomous organizations in education (Trosa, 1995). The model of core cabinet departments planning policy with implementation being conducted through relatively autonomous organizations is now on its way to becoming the norm rather than the exception in government (Kickert and Jørgensen, 1995).

Decentralization

Another common aspect of administration in both Canada and the United States which appears antithetical to administrative traditions in many European states is geographical decentralization. Both North American countries are considering even greater devolution of activities and responsibilities to sub-national governments, for example, converting many existing categorical programs into block grants, but the established tradition in both countries already is to utilize the provinces, states and local governments to implement federal programs. Further, the constitutional rules of federalism in both countries allocate a number of functions to the regional level that in many European countries would be delivered directly by central government. These subnational governments have been the 'laboratories of democracy' in which policy innovations can be tried without having to be implemented in the entire country at once.

Given the long history of decentralization and deconcentration of administration in North America, the furor created in some countries over much limited forms of decentralization appears startling. Of course, there are several federal European states, for example, Germany, in which the same type of decentralization is also in effect. Even in those countries, however, the degree of internal variation in policies found in North America would probably not be acceptable. Thus, the decentralization in France (Loughlin and Mazey, 1995) and the regionalization of Spain and Italy do not appear to be path-breaking innovations. To some extent, the average North American student of government finds it more difficult to understand the *status quo ante* than the reforms currently being implemented in those countries.

Managerialism
Another form of change creating a good deal of excitement in Europe but which appears relatively normal in the North American context is 'managerialism' (Pollitt, 1990). Like reinvention, this term can have a variety of meanings but one dominant component is generic management, or the belief that public and private management are essentially alike (Perry and Rainey, 1988). We can argue that despite a strong public administration tradition in the North American countries, managerialist thinking has been just beneath the surface of government. The absence of a state tradition (at least in the United States – a 'stateless society' (Stillman, 1991)) has meant that the public sector was more amenable to importing ideas and techniques from the private sector. Further, given the dominance of business thinking in the US, the use of free market ideas when possible was probably a virtue for the public sector.

It also appears clear that the North American countries have not yet faced quite the onslaught from advocates of the New Public Management that many European countries have, so that the above statements may be premature. That having been said, some of the earlier experiments with pay for performance and other managerialist ideas were in the United States, with most of the controversy about these programs being that they were inadequately funded to provide a real test of their efficacy (Perry, 1992). In addition, many of the canons of the New Public Management have been in place for any number of years in state, provincial and local governments, seemingly without creating much controversy. Quite the contrary, managerialism appears to have been welcomed at these levels of government. It appears that North Americans continue to be more willing to think in managerial, as opposed to more strictly public administration, terms about running the public sector.

Managerialism is a very broad concept, with a number of different dimensions (Hood, 1991). Different countries in Europe have been more or less involved in implementing those different dimensions. For example, in addition to their structural reforms the British government has adopted a number of financial and budgetary reforms, such as the Financial Management Initiative and resource accounting (HMSO, 1994). Similar budgetary reforms oriented towards outputs have been put in place in Denmark. Another dimension of managerialist reform has been changes in personnel management including pay for performance mentioned above. Still another dimension is the development of specific performance standards for public services, as has now been adopted in almost all European systems. Thus, although there are different interpretations of managerialism there are also some common factors among the European countries.

Non-career public managers

Implementing the ideas of managerialism is one of several ways to think about developing closer links between the public and private sectors. One aspect of the creation of executive agencies in Britain and the general spread of managerialism throughout the public sectors of Europe, is that there are plans for an increased interchange between public and private sector managers. Many senior executive positions in the public sector (especially in the quasi-autonomous agencies) would be opened to competition from private sector managers. Although the early evidence is that public sector careerists do reasonably well in these competitions, the end of exclusivity of the public sector career has created substantial consternation among long-term members of government.

A number of European countries also have a tradition of substantial interchange between public and private sector management. In France this movement has tended to move in a way opposite to that creating concerns in Britain, with many managers trained by ENA parachuting into lucrative positions in the private sector. Also, the Scandinavian countries have had relatively open competition for public sector positions, provided that the basic legal qualifications for public jobs are met by all applicants. In the United States the interchange between public and private management is well-established and is one of the distinguishing features of American public administration. Although its efficacy has been questioned in a number of places (Heclo, 1977; MacKenzie, 1987), the use of political appointees in approximately 3000 senior positions in the executive branch continues. If anything, there has been an increase in the number of positions available for political appointment (Light, 1995), as well as an increasing use of political appointments in the Senior Executive Service (Levine, 1988; Ingraham, 1995, pp. 104–5).

To Americans the current debate over open competition for managerial posts in Britain and elsewhere does not appear particularly exciting, although it almost certainly does for Canadians.[4] Indeed, the more open, competitive mechanisms being utilized in those recruitments appear preferable to the highly personalized, politicized, and largely non-competitive forms of appointment used in the United States. The caliber of political appointees in federal positions has increased from earlier days, in part because of the development of issue networks (Heclo, 1978) surrounding all major policy concerns, but there are still more political 'hacks' appointed to office than anything aspiring to be a modern, efficient government can bear. For the US then the question is less that these appointments are from the private sector than whether they have the capacity to perform the job once in office.

Rights

Last, but certainly not least, many of the reforms being imposed in Europe have the effect of creating a stronger conception of the rights of citizens in the process of governing. As with all the differences we have been discussing it would be easy to push this contrast too far, for in any democratic system there are certainly some ideas about the rights of citizens to gain redress against the administrative system. It might be argued, in fact, that the systems of administrative law in many European countries provides a better option for recourse by citizens than do the mechanisms in place in North America (Rohr, 1995). That having been said, however, individual rights – whether those contained in the American Bill of Rights or those in the Canadian Charter of Rights and Freedoms – sometimes appears to be a particularly North American conception of how best to deal with government.

It is important to note that to some extent the rights debate *vis-à-vis* the public sector in Europe is qualitatively different from the usual discussion of rights in North America. The rights advanced through instruments such as the Citizen's Charter in the United Kingdom (Pollitt, 1990) and other European countries are primarily the rights of consumers, rather than the rights of citizens; rights-based arguments in North America tend to be defined more in terms of citizenship and even the obligations of government. The consumerization of the public sector in Europe is an important development, albeit one still not conceptualized or understood well (Hood, Peters and Wollmann, 1996; Barnes and Prior, 1995). This movement provides citizens redress against some inefficiencies of government, although it does much less to protect citizens against excesses by bureaucracy, or to provide citizens with *ex ante* controls over policies. Of course, once citizens (consumers) become accustomed to making rights-based arguments *vis-à-vis* the public sector they may find themselves extending the domain of these protections (Lewis and Birkinshaw, 1993).

As implied above, the move towards greater exercise of rights by citizens in European administration is not uniform and also means different things in different countries. One of the more common approaches to enhanced participation is the Citizen's Charter, although even that instrument means different things in different European countries. Rights also now imply the right of choice among different ways of consuming public services. For example, education is becoming less of a public monopoly and more of a market with the parameters of competition established by the public sector. The rights of citizens are exercised in part through vouchers and other market mechanisms and in part through expanded opportunities for political participation (Leonard, 1988).

4. Summary

The contemporary modernization process in the public sector is an interesting study in comparative politics. It demonstrates the different reactions of a number of different political systems to a set of relatively common stimuli for change. The ideas that have guided modernization or reform – the market, participation, internal deregulation, and so on – are almost the same around the world (Peters, 1996).

What is different is how political systems have interpreted the ideas and responded to the demands and/or opportunities for inducing administrative change. These ideas have been interpreted through the lenses of national administrative traditions (Peters, 1994). This has meant that some ideas have been rejected almost entirely in some settings, while being very welcome in others.

The question here has been whether there is a meaningful North American administrative tradition that has spawned some reforms and provided an interpretative frame for other ideas about administrative change. There is some evidence to support such a position, but there is also some evidence that would bring that argument into severe question. The political and administrative system of the United States is the more distinctive of the two North American systems, with the separation of powers principle producing Congressional micro-management of administration and helping to produce autonomous agencies. Canadian government shares some features found in American government, including the impact of federalism and populism on administration, but in some ways appears to function more like a European system (Smith, 1994). More than anything else, this discussion points to the importance of understanding administrative traditions and their role in shaping responses to the ideas of modernization. Just as there is no singular and clearly definable North American administrative tradition, there is no single European approach to modernization. There are a number of common elements identified above, but there are also important differences in the European modernization programs. Even when there are apparently common elements in modernization, they may be interpreted differently depending upon national administrative history and concepts. This simple fact is true whether the nations are separated by the North Atlantic or only by a line on a map.

Notes

1. We will be writing about Canada and the United States here. Mexico is a North American country sharing some features in common with the other two members of NAFTA, for example, federalism, but having both an Iberian heritage and a distinctive political history that separate it from the other two systems.
2. The argument is that corporatism selects certain groups for participation and excludes others, as well as excluding the mass public from most opportunities at involvement in public decisions. The design of consultation exercises in Canada is intended to correct some of those defects.
3. The public sector in the United Kingdom may have had some of the same rule-bound character as the North American ones, but the reforms during and after the Thatcher government have replaced many of those.
4. In Canada the Mulroney government appointed in essence a second cast of deputy secretaries responsible more for policy advice than management of the departments. At the time this created a great deal of concern in Ottawa. These are, however, in marked contrast to the current British developments in which the outsiders are appointed for managerial rather than policy reasons.

References

Angle, M., 1994. 'Initiatives; vox populi or professional ploy?'. *Congressional Quarterly Weekly Report*, vol. 52, pp. 29–82.

Aronson, J., 1993. 'Giving consumers a say in policy development'. *Canadian Public Policy*, vol. 19, pp. 367–78.

Aucoin, P., 1996. *The new public management: Canada in comparative perspective*. Institute for Research on Public Policy, Montreal.

Aucoin, P. and H. Bakvis, 1993. 'Consolidating cabinet portfolios: Australian lessons for Canada'. *Canadian Public Administration*, vol. 36, pp. 392–420.

Barnes, M. and D. Prior, 1995. 'Spoilt for choice?: consumerism can disempower public service users'. *Public Money and Management*, vol. 15(3), pp. 53–8.

Barzelay, M., 1992. *Breaking through bureaucracy*. University of California Press, Berkeley.

Borins, S., 1995. 'Public sector innovation: the implications of new forms of organization and work'. In: B.G. Peters and D.J. Savoie (eds), *Governance in a changing society*, McGill/Queens University Press, Montreal.

Clark, I., 1991. 'Special operating agencies'. *Optimum*, vol. 22(2), pp. 13–8.

Connolly, M. and P. McKeown, 1994. 'Making the public sector more user friendly? A critical analysis of the citizen's charter'. *Parliamentary Affairs*, vol. 47, pp. 23–36.

Crenson, M.A. and F.E. Rourke, 1987. 'By way of conclusion: American bureaucracy since World War II'. In: L. Galambos (ed.), *The new American state: bureaucracies and policies since World War II*, Johns Hopkins University Press, Baltimore.

Cronin, T.E., 1989. *Direct democracy: the politics of initiative, referendum and recall*. Harvard University Press, Cambridge MA.

DiIulio, J.J. and R.R. Nathan (eds), 1994. *Making health reform work: the view from the states*. Brookings Institution, Washington, DC.

Ehrenhalt, A., 1993. 'The value of blue-ribbon advice'. *Governing*, vol. 7 (August), pp. 47–56.

Fisher, L.C., 1991. 'Congress as micromanager of the executive branch'. In: J.P. Pfiffner (ed.), *The managerial presidency*, Brooks/Cole, Pacific Grove, CA.

Frenkel, M., 1994. 'The communal basis of Swiss liberty'. *Publius*, vol. 23, pp. 61–70.

Germann, R., 1981. *Ausserparlamentarische Kommissionen: die Milizverwaltung des Bundes*. Haupt, Bern.

Gilmour, R.S. and A.A. Halley, 1994. *Who makes public policy?* Chatham House, Chatham, NJ.

Greer, P., 1994. *Transforming central government: the next steps initiative*. Open University Press, Buckingham.

Harrison, T., 1995. *Of passionate intensity: right-wing populism and the reform party of Canada*. University of Toronto Press, Toronto.

Heclo, H., 1977. *A government of strangers: executive politics in Washington*. The Brookings Institution, Washington, DC.

Heclo, H., 1978. 'Issue networks and the executive establishment'. In A. King (ed.), *The new American political system*, American Enterprise Institute, Washington, DC.

HMSO, 1994. *Better accounting for the taxpayer's money: resource accounting and budgeting in government*. HMSO, London (Cmnd. 2626).

Hood, C.C., 1991. 'Exploring variations in 1980s public management reform: towards a contingency framework?'. Paper presented at conference on comparative civil service systems, Leiden/Rotterdam, October 17–19.

Hood, C.C., B.G. Peters and H. Wollmann (1996). 'Public management reform: putting consumers in the driver's seat?'. *Public Money and Management*, vol. 13(2), pp. 56–64.

Horner, C., 1994. 'Deregulating the federal service: is the time right'. In: J.J. DiIulio (ed.), *Deregulating the public service*, The Brookings Institution, Washington, DC.

Howlett, M., 1994. 'Policy paradigms and policy change: lessons from the old and new Canadian policies toward aboriginal peoples'. *Policy Studies Journal*, vol. 22, pp. 631–49.

Ingraham, P.W., 1995. *The foundation of merit: public service in American democracy*. Johns Hopkins University Press, Baltimore.

Jerome-Forget, M., J. White and J.M. Wiener, 1995. *Health care reform through internal markets*. Institute for Research on Public Policy, Montreal.

Kazin, M., 1995. *The populist persuasion: an American history*. Basic Books, New York.

Kelman, S., 1994. 'Deregulating federal procurement: nothing to fear but discretion itself?'. In: J.J. DiIulio (ed.), *Deregulating the public service: can government be improved?*, The Brookings Institution, Washington, DC.

Kemp. P., 1990. 'Next steps for the British civil service'. *Governance*, vol. 3, pp. 186–96.

Kernaghan, K., 1992. 'Empowerment and public administration: revolutionary advance or passing fancy?', *Canadian Public Administration*, vol. 35, pp. 194–214.

Kerwin, C.M., 1994. *Rulemaking: how government agencies write law and make policy*. CQ Press, Washington, DC.

Kickert, W.J.M., 1995. 'Public governance in the Netherlands: an alternative to Anglo-American managerialism'. *Administration and Society* (forthcoming).

Kickert, W.J.M. and T.B. Jorgensen, 1995. 'Management reform, executive agencies and core departments'. Special Issue of *International Review of Administrative Sciences*, vol. 61.

Klöti, U., 1996. 'Adapting a working system: changes and reforms in the Swiss public sector, 1965–1992'. In: J.P. Olsen and B.G. Peters, (eds.), *Learning from administrative reform*. Scandinavian University Press, Oslo.

Krauss, E. and M. Muramatsu, 1996. 'Japan's administrative reform: the paradox of success'. In: J.P. Olsen and B.G. Peters (eds), *Learning from administrative reform*, Scandinavian University Press, Oslo.

Laegreid, P., 1994. 'Norway'. In: C.C. Hood and B.G. Peters, *Rewards at the Top*, Sage, London.

Laux, J.A. and M.A. Molot, 1988. *State capitalism: public enterprise in Canada*. Cornell University Press, Ithaca, NY.

Leonard, M., 1988. *The Education Act of 1988: a guide for schools*. Blackwells, Oxford.

Levine, C.H., 1988. 'Human resource erosion and the uncertain future of the US civil service: from policy gridlock to structural fragmentation'. *Governance*, vol. 1, pp. 115–43.

Lewis, N. and P. Birkinshaw, 1993. *When citizens complain: reforming justice and administration*. Open University Press, Buckingham.

Light, P.C., 1995. *Thickening government: federal hierarchy and the diffusion of accountability*. The Brookings Institution, Washington, DC.

Lindquist, E., 1994. 'Citizens, experts and budgets: evaluating Ottawa's emerging budget process'. In: S.D. Phillips (ed.), *How Ottawa spends 1994–95*, Carleton University Press, Ottawa.

Loughlin, S. and S. Mazey, 1995. 'The end of the French unitary state?: ten years of regionalization in France (1982–1992)'. *Regional Politics and Policy*, vol. 4(3) (special issue).

McDavid, J.C. and D.B. Marson, 1991. *The well-performing government organization*. Institute of Public Administration of Canada, Victoria, BC.

Mackenzie, G.C., 1987. *The in-and outers: presidential appointees and transient government in Washington*. Johns Hopkins University Press, Baltimore.

Michiletti, M., 1990. 'Toward interest inarticulation: a major consequence of corporatism for interest organizations'. *Scandinavian Political Studies*, vol. 13, pp. 255–76.

Modeen, T. and A. Rosas, 1988. *Indirect public administration in fourteen countries*. Åbo Academy, Åbo.

National Performance Review, 1993. *Creating a government that works better and costs less – The Gore report.* Government Printing Office, March, Washington, DC.

Olsen, J.P., 1991. 'Modernization programs in perspective: institutional analysis of organizational change'. *Governance*, vol. 4, pp. 125–49.

Olsen, J.P. and B.G. Peters, 1996. *Learning from administrative reform.* Scandinavian University Press, Oslo.

Osborne, D. and T. Gaebler, 1992. *Reinventing government.* Addison-Wesley, Reading, MA.

Perry, J., 1992. 'Merit pay in the federal government'. In: P.W. Ingraham and D. Rosenbloom (eds), *The promise and paradox of bureaucratic reform.* University of Pittsburgh Press, Pittsburgh.

Perry, J. and H.G. Rainey, 1988. 'The public private distinction in organization theory: a critique and a research strategy'. *Academy of Management Review*, vol. 13, pp. 240–58.

Peters, B.G., 1994. *Administrative traditions and administrative reform.* Unpublished Paper, Department of Political Science, University of Pittsburgh.

Peters, B.G., 1996. *The future of governance: four emerging models.* University of Kansas Press, Lawrence, KS.

Petersson, O. and D. Söderlind, 1992. *Forvaltningspolitik* (2nd edn). Carlsson, Stockholm.

Pollitt, C., 1990. *Managerialism and the public services.* Basil Blackwell, Oxford.

Pollitt, C. and G. Bouckaert, 1995. *Quality improvements in European public services.* Sage, London.

Pullen, W., 1994. 'Eyes on the prize'. *International Journal of Public Sector Management*, vol. 7, pp. 5–14.

Rohr, J.A., 1995. *Founding republics in France and America: a study in constitutional governance.* University of Kansas Press, Lawrence.

Rouban, L., 1990. 'La modernisation de l'Etat et la fin de la specificité française'. *Revue francaise de science politique*, vol. 40, pp. 521–45.

Savoie, D.J., 1994. *Reagan, Thatcher, Mulroney: in search of a new bureaucracy.* University of Pittsburgh Press, Pittsburgh.

Seidle, F.L., 1993. 'Reshaping the federal government: charting the course'. *Policy Options*, July–August, pp. 24–9.

Seidman, H. and R.S. Gilmour, 1986. *Politics, power and position: from the positive to the regulatory state.* Oxford University Press, New York.

Sjölund, M., 1994. 'Sweden'. In: C.C. Hood and B.G. Peters (eds), *Rewards at the top*, Sage, London.

Smith, A., 1994. *Canada – an American nation?* McGill/Queens University Press, Montreal.

Stephenson, M., 1995. 'Right in the heartland'. *Saturday Night*, vol. 110(4), pp. 19–25.

Stillman, R.J., 1991. *Preface to public administration: a search for themes and directions.* St. Martins, New York.

Taylor-Henry, S. and P. Hudson, 1992. 'Aboriginal self-government and social services'. *Canadian Public Policy*, vol. 18, pp. 13–26.

Tellier, P.M., 1990. 'Public service 2000: the renewal of the public service'. *Canadian Public Administration*, vol. 33, pp. 123–32.

Trosa, S., 1995. 'Quality in the French public service'. In: C. Pollitt and G. Bouckaert (eds), *Quality improvements in European public services.* Sage, London.

Van Nijhatten, D.L. and S.W. Gregoire, 1995. 'Bureaucracy and consultation: the correctional service of Canada and the requirements of being democratic'. *Canadian Public Administration*, vol. 38, pp. 204–21.

Varette, S., 1993. 'Consultation in the public service', *Optimum*, vol. 23 (Spring), pp. 28–39.

Walczak, L., 1995. 'The new populism'. *Business Week*, vol. 3415, pp. 72–8.

Wex, S., 1990. 'Leadership and change in the 1990s'. *Optimum*, vol. 21, pp. 25–30.

White, O.F. and J.F. Wolf, 1995. 'Deming's total quality management movement and the Baskin-Robbins problem: part I, Is it time to go back to vanilla?'. *Administration and Society*, vol. 27, pp. 203–25.

Wilson, J.Q., 1994. 'Can bureaucracy be deregulated?: lessons from government agencies'. In: J.J. DiIulio (ed.), *Deregulating the public service*, The Brookings Institution, Washington, DC.

Wright, J.D., 1995. *Special operating agencies: autonomy, accountability and performance measurement*. Canadian Centre for Management Development, Ottawa.

Zifcak, 1994. *New managerialism: administrative reform in Canberra and Whitehall*. Open University Press, Buckingham.

Index